The Accidental Martyr

How and Why Sakine Cansiz Survived Torture, Led Women in Combat and Was Murdered for Kurdish Freedom

By Hamma Mirwaisi

Edited by Douglas Brown

Published by Caltrop Press

Copyright © 2017 by Hamma Mirwaisi.
All Rights Reserved.

No part of this publication may be reproduced, distributed, or transmitted in any form or by any means, including photocopying, recording, or other electronic or mechanical methods, or by any information storage and retrieval system without the prior written permission of the publisher, except in the case of very brief quotations embodied in critical reviews and certain other noncommercial uses permitted by copyright law.

Cover Photo Credit

PKK guerrilla women on the march in the Qandil mountains,
By Thomas Koch via ShutterStock.com

Production

This book was edited and published by Caltrop Press

http://www.Caltrop-Press.co.business

ISBN: 1976050146

ISBN-13: 978-1976050145

What They're Saying

Kurdish-American writer Hamma Mirwaisi uses the 2013 execution-style murder of Kurdish activist Sakine Cansiz in Paris as a launching point to explain Kurdish history, Kurdish aspirations, and the Kurdistan Workers Party (PKK) which has waged a decades-long insurgency against Turkey. He seeks to explain why the Kurds picked up arms against Turkey and why women like Cansiz flocked to the PKK.

With attention to detail and an easy flow, he takes readers from mountain skirmishes to Diyarbakir's tortuous prison onto the streets of Syria and then back to Paris, explaining PKK philosophy, evolution, and ambition. In a region where perception can trump reality, The Accidental Martyr is an excellent resource to understand why so many Kurds have come to embrace the PKK and its offshoots.

While Turkey and many Western governments label the PKK as a terrorist group, its supporters describe it as an intellectual and political liberation movement. Whatever one's perspective, one thing is clear: Neither the Kurds nor the PKK can be ignored any longer, and neither are going away. While The Accidental Martyr may infuriate Turkish nationalists and frustrate historians and diplomats, it is a must-read to understand where the PKK has been and where Turkey and Syria's Kurds may be going.

--Michael Rubin, Resident Scholar, American Enterprise Institute

"I became a part of my grandmother's stories."

The female guerrilla Viyan, after being engaged in combat against ISIS

Sakine Cansiz wasn't planning to be a martyr for her cause. She wasn't even expecting to die, at least not on the day she did.

Many martyrs actively seek out their end. They believe their cause will gain more credibility or support as a result of their death. They push the envelope to provoke someone into killing them.

From the age of 20, Sakine Cansiz was prepared to die a heroine's death for Kurdish freedom, if that was how things turned out, but she didn't want to, and she never sought it out. She never wanted to die at all, except perhaps during some of the worst moments of the years she spent undergoing brutal torture. On the contrary, she was a fighter and a survivor. For over a decade, she absorbed unspeakable abuses by jailers who were so sadistic that even their own repressive regime eventually executed them. Somehow, she survived that.

She became a famous guerrilla leader, actively fighting for the cause of Kurdish rights and expecting to die at any moment. Several times, she came all too close to having that opportunity. After a decade of battling with one of the most advanced military forces in the region, she survived that too, becoming a legend as a brave, powerful (and yes, female) fighter.

Eventually, she became too valuable for the Kurds to lose her in some insignificant firefight in the remote mountains. They sent her to the civilized cities of Western Europe to become a diplomat and fund-raiser for the Kurdish cause. She had to give up combat patrols in order to print pamphlets and meet with heads of government. She excelled in that too, so much so that some government agencies got nervous. Eventually, one of them caught up with her.

In Paris, she hadn't sought death out, and she wasn't expecting it. Instead, it came to her, the heroine, in a most unheroic way. Yet the very mundane nature of her death made her into an icon, not just to Kurds seeking liberation but also to women across the Islamic world.

She didn't intend become a martyr. It happened anyway. This is her story.

Table of Contents

Publisher's Foreword 1

CHAPTER 1. ASSASSINATION IN PARIS 5
    The Investigation 7
    Grander Implications 8
    The Victims 11

CHAPTER 2. THE SHOOTER 14
    The Unknown Favorite 15
    A Bigger Picture 21

CHAPTER 3. THE USUAL SUSPECTS 24
    The Long List of Suspects 25
    Could It Be An Inside Job? 27
    It Must Be the Turks 28
    Why Not the Turks? 29

CHAPTER 4. A VERY ANCIENT PEOPLE 32
    Beyond Western Timelines 32
    Pre-History 32
    Not Those Aryans 37
    The Medes 38
    Living With The Persians 40
    Detour to Egypt 41
    More on the Persians 43
    Islam Arrives 45
    Are the Kurds Medes? 47

CHAPTER 5. UNDER TURKISH RULE 49
    Working Within the System 49
    Saladin 50
    The Ottomans 52
    Ataturk 53

CHAPTER 6. FROM RHETORIC TO REVOLUTION 59

 Revolutionary Roots 59

 Organizing Dissent 61

 Enter Öcalan 63

CHAPTER 7. SAKINE MEETS APO 68

 Zazas and Alawites 70

 Sakine Awakens 71

 Urban Revolutionists 74

 Birth of the PKK 76

 Politics By Other Means 79

CHAPTER 8. THE PAINFUL PRICE OF BECOMING A LEGEND 82

 The High Price of Loyalty 83

 The Women's Program 85

CHAPTER 9. GUERRILLA LEADER 92

 An Equal Role for Women 92

 The First Unit of Women 95

 What Women Won 98

 Heroines and Martyrs 104

  Beritan *104*

  Zilan *105*

  Ronahi (Andrea Wolf) *106*

  Vian Jaff (also known as Vian Soran) *108*

CHAPTER 10. CRUSADER FOR WOMEN'S EQUALITY 109

 Roadblock to Understanding 109

 Moving Forward On the Women's Liberation Ideology 111

  The Basic Principles of the PKK Women's Liberation Ideology *117*

 Jineology 118

 Continuing Abuses of Women 119

CHAPTER 11. SAKINE THE DIPLOMAT 122

 The Capture of Öcalan 122

 Division in the PKK 124

 Diplomatic Mission 130

    Return to Normalcy: Turks vs. Kurds 138

CHAPTER 12. OPPORTUNITY IN SYRIA **143**

    The Fickle Americans 143

    Why Were the Kurds in Syria? 149

    Enter the Assads 151

    An Identity for Kurds in Syria 153

    Sinjar and Beyond 158

    Walking the Talk: Life in a PKK Territory 160

    Turkey Takes Stock of the Situation 164

CHAPTER 13. AFTER THE MURDERS: KURDS ASCENDANT **166**

    The AKP-Gülen Rift 167

    Intervention in Syria 170

    Faceoff in Sinjar 172

    The Police Case In Paris 175

CHAPTER 14. THE SAKINE LEGACY **178**

APPENDIX A: THE CABLE **186**

    SUBJECT: Blocking money flow to the PKK 186

    Background 187

    Legwork is Already Underway 187

    Three-Part Strategy 188

        Working with Europe *188*

        Working with Iraq *188*

        Working with Turkey *189*

APPENDIX B: REFERENCES **190**

    About the Author 192

Publisher's Foreword

For some years now, Kurds have received occasional but increasing mentions in the mainstream media. Articles may touch on their constant pursuit of ethnic autonomy, but only as an incidental detail in the more dramatic accounts of their support in the USA's various misadventures in the Middle East. Their full story is seldom explored; they just get passing mentions in dispatches from a place that most Americans are tired of hearing about, and much of the rest of the world would prefer not to hear about.

Quite simply, even for those who follow the news more than most, we don't know much about these Kurds, whoever and whatever they are. Considering everything they are doing for us, they deserve better.

Hamma Mirwaisi's book goes a long way towards answering it in a way that may be both comprehensible and interesting to the mainstream English-speaking reader.

Most books on the geopolitical and theological differences that beset the Middle East are either histrionic or insufferably dense. Instead, Mr. Mirwaisi conveys how Kurds see themselves and the conditions to which they are subjected by illustrating the "Kurdish question" with a story, in this case the near-mythology surrounding a Kurdish national heroine, Sakine Cansiz. She was a Kurdish activist, an atrocity victim, a soldier, a diplomat, and finally a martyr. In each of these roles, she comes to epitomize the key aspects that make the Kurds who they are.

We should tell you up front that this book will be distressing for:

• Turkish nationalists who are completely and unquestioningly in favor of anything that current and previous governments may have said or done

• Members of law enforcement or military security organizations who might get in trouble for reading anything to do with the PKK, or

• Those who believe (as many do) that any mention of an organization that someone considers a terrorist entity simply glorifies and encourages its activities.

If that's you, stop now before you upset yourself (or get yourself in trouble). Give it to a library or university. Your side of the story can be told in the next book.

Why would such concerns arise, and are they legitimate?

It would be impossible, or certainly meaningless, to write a book about George Washington and how he became "first in war, first in peace, first in the hearts of his countrymen" without mentioning that he had been a delegate to the Revolutionary Congress or the leader of the American Revolutionary army.

In the same manner, one cannot explain the phenomenon that Sakine Cansiz was (and posthumously remains) without extensive mention of the organization she helped found, made her famous, and eventually got her killed. That organization was the Kurdistan Workers' Party (in Kurdish, the Partiya Karkeren Kurdistan or PKK).

The publication of this book does not endorse the objectives or actions of the PKK or any other entity engaged in violent non-military conflict anywhere. It just tries to explain - to some small degree - what is going on.

Like it or not, this conflict is happening; we must understand it if we want to do anything about it. Mr. Mirwaisi, as a Kurdish nationalist, uses sources that are inevitably biased towards that point of view. Since most means of expressing opinions are illegal in Turkey, the PKK is often the only source of Kurdish opinion.

The PKK is struggling to obtain greater Kurdish autonomy, if not outright independence, from governments, primarily Turkey, that, like most governments, does not wish to entertain such notions. In attempting to explain why the Kurds do what they do, the book must bring up Kurdish grievances against those governments and against oppressive societies in general. Whether they are valid complaints or unsupported rumors and myths is, of course, very much open to question, especially as seen by those governments and other cultures.

Why not just print the truth? Would that we knew it. It is not always found in official records; the Kurds contend that those records are the least truthful of all. Alternative sources might include:

- Contemporary unofficial records such as journals that cast light on what might actually have happened
- Oral histories that pass down from generation to generation the truth that officialdom does not permit to be told, or
- What your gut tells you makes sense after hearing several completely conflicting versions of the same events.

In the case of the Kurds, on this as in many other matters, you'll have to accept "most of all the above" as a possibility.

Throughout the Middle East, the "mainstream media" repeats only government-sanctioned stories, under the very real threat of arrest or execution. Such history texts as do exist are pre-approved by government entities. The works of pro-Kurdish authors have been suppressed and continue to be so, as indeed the authors themselves have been, for the past 2500 years. Sometimes the truth, or at least an alternative viewpoint, comes to us only in whispers, or is brought to light only after being stolen and handed over to online "publishers" such as Wikileaks.

As a result, much of the information in the book came to Mr. Mirwaisi directly from non-traditional sources within the Kurdish community such as oral histories, personal records and alternative media entities. Some comes from PKK publications that are openly biased. Much more comes person-to-person; nobody knows whether the providers are affiliated with the PKK or not. We can be sure that those sources too are distorted, perhaps intentionally, perhaps through emotional response, or perhaps just through the natural embellishment that occurs over decades and centuries.

As the publishers of this book, we've tried to make sure that Hamma Mirwaisi's knowledge and perspectives are backed up wherever feasible by other documentation, and to add to a naturally one-sided narrative by noting the potential concerns and motivations of other actors in the story. It's made the book a lot broader (and a lot longer) than the author intended originally. We think the additional perspectives will make the book that much more interesting for the many readers who aren't already deeply steeped in the Kurdish narratives and/or emotionally biased in the Kurdish direction.

Before agreeing to help Mr. Mirwaisi publish the book, we sought to validate much of the factual content in the book against other sources. We used source-validation software to identify where much of the material may have come from. It turned out that most of the text in commonly-accepted references is cross-posted from one source to another and most obviously originates with Kurdish nationalist activists ... because nobody else cared enough or knew enough to contribute.

Since this isn't an academic thesis or an indisputable reference source, we decided to forgo using hundreds of footnotes of somewhat dubious value. Instead, you can read the story as a story, and look up for yourself any historical event you want to know more about.

It just isn't possible to form an entirely indisputable record. That's what happens when you destroy all the reputable sources, and when key players keep dying before their times. To understand the Kurds, you have to see them as they see themselves, even when they are wrong. Most readers will be able to get past that bias when it is openly declared.

The point isn't who provided the material, nor to resolve conclusively what the truth is. The point is to find out what the Kurds **believe** to be true, because those beliefs drive their actions.

When every normally legal avenue is made illegal, the average Kurd seeking only to retain some vestige of ethnic identity has no choice but to look to the illegal but commonly condoned PKK as a voice.

But let's not just fall back on "one man's freedom fighter is another man's terrorist." Let's not kid ourselves. The PKK has done many violent things in past years. The US, the UK, and the EU have listed it as a terrorist organization, with plenty of justification.

In consideration of its focus on military targets rather than civilian deaths, and the extreme provocations and lack of alternatives offered by the Turkish government (among others), the EU initially chose not to list the PKK. More recently, the EU reversed itself after the PKK abandoned its ceasefire with the Turkish government, claiming that the government itself had already violated it on a regular basis. More recently again (by 2017) the EU has started to question the Turkish government's true commitment to human rights and perhaps its true agenda, and to take a more favorable view of the PKK.

One can also question whether the TAK group that emerged in late 2016 to commit a number of horrific terrorist actions is or is not affiliated with the PKK. It claims to be. The PKK says it is not.

On the other hand, despite being on the terror list, the PKK is a formal part of the US-led anti-terrorist coalition in Syria, receiving US air support in operations against ISIS and/or the Syrian government.

For the reasons noted above, the publisher cannot take any responsibility for the accuracy of the claims made by the author, nor place much weight on any counterpoint offered by official sources. We'd encourage you to question the validity of information received from any official source as much as from any individual, in all aspects of your life just as much as in this book. Your best bet is to read more, investigate more, and speak with more people on the matter of the Kurds. That's really what the author had hoped for, and it is all the Kurds are asking for.

Chapter 1. Assassination in Paris

Thursday, 10 January 2013, 01:10.

A cell phone dials 112. In Paris, as in the rest of Europe, this connects to the police emergency line. A man's voice comes on the line to report that three women have been found, shot to death, in an office at 147 Rue La Fayette. The three women are Fidan Doğan, Leyla Saylemez, and Sakine Cansız.

The gears of the investigative process begin to turn.

The location is in the 10th Arrondissement. While it's not exactly in the Montmartre district, at least not the trendy part, the street does have a Starbucks coffee shop. By French standards, the preference for a chain store, and an American one at that, makes it quirky already. This area, immediately behind the Gare du Nord, is even more highly differentiated from the average Paris neighborhood to the point that it has its own nickname: Little Kurdistan. Unlike so many of the other majority-Muslim districts that have sprung up in Europe, it's not a ghetto. It is neither wealthy nor poor. It just has a lot of Kurds in it.

Close to the corner of Rue de Saint Quentin and Rue La Fayette, the building itself is a 19th-century classic, with a chiseled stone arch above a battered wooden door. On the 2nd story (the third by US counting) is a wrought-iron balcony. On one side is an electronics supply store; on the other, a small grocery.

Beneath the balcony is a row of windows belonging to a first-floor residential apartment (again, second floor by the US count). A flight of stairs leads up to this apartment from the entrance hall. The apartment, which is being used as an office space by an entity styling itself the Kurdistan Information Office (KIO), has three rooms; two of the rooms have windows that look out below the balcony to provide a view of the busy street and the pedestrians below. A third room is at the back of the building, and this is where the shooting has occurred.

This particular ethnic community is close-knit and word travels fast, if not always accurately. The leading Kurdish outlet is Ajansa Nûçeyan a Firatê (ANF), a Kurdish news agency located in Germany where it goes by the more comprehensible name of Firatnews.com. The French police investigators would later cite the challenge of finding people who have something to say. ANF has not had any such difficulty.

Chapter 1. Assassination in Paris

147 Rue la Fayette, 75010 Paris, France

This willingness to speak up is quite remarkable. Among Middle Eastern expatriates, making any public statement that offends or, worse, contradicts anyone in a position of power is considered unwise. It is likely to result in a violent visitation by the government of your country of origin to your spouse, children, aunts, third cousins, or people who live in the village you came from 40 years ago. Overcoming that concern is a powerful testament to the importance of the victims in the life of this community; even so, coming up with sources is one thing and getting names is another.

One of ANF's early witnesses was a close friend of victim Fidan Doğan, who had been known in the community as Rojbin. She told ANF that they had spoken the previous evening but on the day of the actual murder, Wednesday, January 9th, her phone calls went unreturned, which was very unusual given their many years of friendship. Eventually, calls to other friends revealed that nobody had heard from Rojbin that day; late in the evening, a small group went to the apartment-office to see whether she was there. They arrive just after midnight and noticed a light still on in the office.

Chapter 1. Assassination in Paris

Although the source had a key to the office and the entry code for the office building main door, the inner lobby door required yet another key which they did not have.

"We rang and rang the office buzzer; no one answered. So we started to ring all the doorbells for everyone in all the apartments. Finally, one man answered. We asked him to open the door because we wanted to check on our friend. He told us to go away, or he would call the police to arrest us."

A male friend, the one who would eventually call the police, had joined the party by then. He shouldered open the door and they went up to the office.

"It was nightmare and savagery, mass murder. It's hard to describe what I felt."

ANF's second witness said: " *We went to the third room and turned on the light; that's when I saw the feet. That was Sakine. She was dead, leaning back on the cupboard and her knee and one of her eyes was swollen. Then I moved forward and saw the face of Rojbin who was lying on her back, with a trail of blood from her mouth and her eyes closed. Her face seemed frozen. Between both bodies was a suitcase, and several things still lay outside the suitcase. At that moment my friend screamed. I went over to where she was, and I saw Leyla lying face down on the floor in blood."*

An official from the Kurdish association in Les Mureaux confirmed that Fidan and Sakine had travel tickets for a 1:30 p.m. train, so they must have been planning to leave the office around noon or before. In fact, Leyla had departed their office at 9:50 a.m. to take the tickets to the KIO, and from there she had called back at 11:30 to report meeting up with Fidan Doğan. Fidan and Sakine were to have gone to the station together, so another volunteer went to the KIO to give Leyla a ride back to Les Mureaux; but when the volunteer arrived there at 1:30, nobody answered the door.

The Investigation

There doesn't seem to be much dispute about what happened. The larger mysteries were *when* it happened ... and, of course, who did it.

Investigators quickly determine a rough time of death: some 8 hours before the discovery time of 1 a.m., which places the event at around 6 to 7 p.m on Wednesday, the 9th of January. We get the sense from the first witnesses that the victims seemed to have dropped off the scene by noon of that day.

Chapter 1. Assassination in Paris

The timeline means that the gunmen held the women for over 6 hours before shooting them. If they were hoping to wait until the regular street activity died down, they had miscalculated; the early evening is one of the busiest times for both the neighboring stores, as their customers pick up items on the way home from work. Still, nobody heard anything. This isn't a thieves' alley type of neighborhood, where anybody who did hear anything is making sure they can't be found. The police have no shortage of people to interview; apparently, the locals, who idolize this Sakine Cansiz, are desperately anxious to help in any way they can, but they are unanimous in saying that nobody heard anything.

Paris public prosecutor François Molins said, *"There were no signs of a struggle. Indeed, four glasses of water were found in the room; one was presumably offered to the assassin. Two of the women were killed with three bullets to the head, and the third one had four bullets to the head, the impact so close and powerful that their eyes came out of their sockets. Ten shots, apparently no misses, and it seems no one heard a sound, leading to the presumption that the killer or killers used a silencer"*.

The idea of a burglar with a silencer complicates the story. Burglars are after money, not confrontations. Their business is stealth and speed. If they carry a gun, it's only for dire emergencies. They don't want to use it, and most of them don't even know how. If they do need one, then they don't want the added complication of a silencer getting caught in their clothing at the worst possible moment.

Held at gunpoint for 6 hours, then shot with a silencer. That's not a viable scenario for a routine street burglary gone wrong. If not a burglar, then a professional gunman. Now things are getting even more complicated.

The police are collecting evidence, but they're professionals: they keep it confidential. The story doesn't make a big splash in the mainstream media. Not at first, anyway. The crime, while suitably gory, is about ethnic foreigners, not actual Parisians. The crime starts out with the appropriate public statements from the investigating police. As its political implications emerge, the official updates will become fewer and less informative until soon they dry up altogether.

Grander Implications

The political implications are not the usual type dealt with by most police forces: cleaning up after a drunk and disorderly nephew of a city council

Chapter 1. Assassination in Paris

member, or, more exotically, keeping a publicity lid on a misdemeanor that a politician or their immediate family members may have committed. This little case that has emerged from an obscure, ethnic enclave of limited interest to the average Parisian may be geopolitical in scope.

The tenant of the office in question goes by the name of the Kurdistan Information Office. There is no country of Kurdistan. To the degree that such a non-country is represented at all in the rest of the world, the entity doing so is the Partiya Karkeren Kurdistan (PKK), the Kurdistan Workers' Party, which NATO has listed as a terrorist organization. There is a Kurdistan Cultural Center, located a few blocks away, that caters to the Kurdish community in general, while the KIO is more ... selective.

Everybody who cares knows that the KIO is really the de facto headquarters of the PKK in Paris. Now three persons affiliated with that organization have been murdered, and very clearly not in a random event.

Obscure as it may be to the average citizen around the world, those in the intelligence business know about the PKK, although perhaps they don't really know very much about it. Respectable government entities including NATO and the EU, of which France is a member, have branded it as a terrorist organization. By many objective standards, so it is.

But in the murky world of intelligence and counter-terrorism, things aren't quite that simple.

In the ongoing Global War on Terror, it's not very clear as to which side many of the other Middle Eastern players actually do line up on for any given day. By contrast, the Kurds are clearly and consistently the good guys. Their issues are not issues in Paris or Berlin, so their presence is not only tolerated but somewhat acknowledged as a convenience, but neither the people nor the governments have any interest in attracting attention that might bring the conflicts of Mosul and Damascus to the streets of Paris. The French government has turned a blind eye to the PKK as long as it doesn't set off any bombs in Paris.

Today, the violence has arrived here anyway. Now the blind eye has been poked with a sharp stick. Somebody has made it impossible for French government officials to ignore that there are Kurds in their midst.

For the next three years, after the initial sensation passes, the case will remain shrouded in official secrecy, partly because of its political implications but more so because it never moves beyond the grand jury stage.

Chapter 1. Assassination in Paris

Nonetheless, we know quite a bit about it thanks to the community grapevine.

French Interior Minister Manuel Valls visited the scene of the crime and officially pronounced the killings as "assassinations." That isn't a word high-level officials use casually. It's a word reserved for the deaths of prominent people for political purposes.

How can a few obscure expatriate pamphlet-pushers be important enough to be "assassinated" in the first place, and why would it be worth anyone's trouble and risk to decide to do so?

The Kurdistan Information Office has to exist outside of an embassy or a formal tourist bureau because there is no embassy. That's because there is no country of Kurdistan; that, in turn, is because there are a number of powerful entities who want to make sure that it stays that way.

Those power players have stifled any discussion of an independent Kurdistan, and they endorse and practice repression of the Kurdish communities within their borders to prevent them from banding together to create a Kurdistan. Nonetheless, the Kurds have some friends in high places because, despite all these official efforts by states that are despotic and rather unreliable themselves, the Kurds have shown themselves to be one of the few capable, self-reliant, reliable allies the West has in that region.

The official players cannot offend each other by mentioning this, so they minimize any mention of the Kurds' achievements and deeds to the mainstream media, despite its constant demands for news of the often-announced but rarely seen progress in the disaster area that is the Middle East. The Kurds have to find other ways of getting media attention to their issues. They must bring themselves to the fore through a more grass-roots effort to get the word out to the average Western person and arouse sympathy so that the public can start exerting upward pressure to respect and someday recognize the Kurds.

That's where the Kurdistan Information Office comes in. It is intended to remind world government, or western ones anyway, which is what counts, of the contributions the Kurds are making, and of the commonalities between western and Kurdish heritage and values, which differ so sharply from those held in the bulk of the Islamic world

That dissonance of philosophies is the reason that the governments of Iraq, Syria and Turkey cannot tolerate having a distinct Kurdish community that numbers in the millions within their borders, and most especially fear having

Chapter 1. Assassination in Paris

one just across their border. Kurds have an instinct for openness and equality, and they know no cause other than the distinctness of the Kurdish community. As we shall see in the following chapters, they have waited a very long time to reassemble that community.

Some Kurds, especially the families that control the regional sub-government in Iraq, have elected a policy of accommodation and waiting for the right opportunity. Most activist Kurds are well aware that such opportunities have seldom arisen in the past 2500 years. For them, the preferred voice is the PKK, which operates on a wider scale and with a clearer agenda: freedom to be Kurdish now, internal autonomy soon, nationhood someday.

Limited in funding by its official non-existence, the Information Office does what it can. Mostly, it distributes leaflets on the Kurdish situation. As funding permits, it organizes events at which Kurdish people can assemble and maintain their identities, and it arranges Kurdish speakers and leaders for such events. There are similar offices in other European countries and, taking advantage of the open borders and short distances within Europe, they coordinate their activities to build the audience from multiple countries. That increases crowd sizes while minimizing the number of occasions on which key Kurdish leaders need to expose themselves to the authorities through these events. You never know when a government is going to stop overlooking the Kurds.

Now the office has been hit, and hit hard.

The Victims

The murderers have had much more impact than a random assault on this office would usually yield. Leyla Saylemez is a member of the Kurdish youth movement, 24 years old, born in Mersin, Turkey, where she had been arrested briefly for membership in an organization that itself was associated with the PKK. She was a regular employee of the Information Office and might well have been found there on a regular basis.

The other two victims are more significant.

Fidan Doğan is a well-known personality in the Kurdish community in France. Born in 1982 in Elbistan, in southern Turkey, she had moved with her family to France when she was young, growing up in Strasbourg, where she completed her university education. She is the French representative at the Brussels-based Kurdish National Congress. She doesn't operate from this

Chapter 1. Assassination in Paris

office; she is more likely to be found at the Kurdish Cultural Center. She happens to be at the Kurdistan Information Office because she is picking up materials and travel tickets for herself and the third woman, Sakine Cansiz, with whom she was to travel to Berlin.

Sakine Cansiz is more than a personality. She is a cult figure across the entire Kurdish diaspora, well-known in Turkey, Iraq and Syria. She is a founding member of the PKK. She's known personally to French President Hollande. She is the essential gun-toting revolutionary with unmistakable looks, thanks to her flaming hair, that Hollywood would cheerfully have invented had it been even remotely interested in the Kurds.

Hollywood is not remotely interested. It is only interested in stories of heroic mavericks who must battle the incompetence of the US military and the evil George W. Bush. The Kurds are US allies who, if the facts are told truthfully, helped Bush win the war in the Middle East by 2007. Hollywood will never make that movie, nor the one about how Barack Obama squandered that victory and left the Kurds to hang on somehow. Bottom line: the Kurds are not on the studios' agendas. Nor are they on the list for other media outlets, which are controlled either by foreign governments or, in the US, by the same anti-Bush cabal. The Kurds must handle their own publicity, and that is what Sakine does ... until the 10th of January, 2013.

Of late, Sakine has seldom been seen at the KIO or anywhere else, because she's been warned to stand down. This is partly because the French want to be seen as complying with NATO ally Turkey's request to crack down on the PKK. The less obvious Sakine makes herself, the easier it is for them to say that they haven't seen her lately. It's also partly because the PKK is undertaking peace discussions with that same Turkish government and doesn't want any incidents derailing the process; besides, Sakine is a key member of those negotiations.

The interviews in the subsequent days will reveal that Fidan Doğan and Sakine Cansiz are at the office together because the quantity of materials that they must carry to Berlin is too much for one person and too much for the two of them to carry via public transport. One of the regular volunteers will pick up Fidan, Sabine and the materials, and take them to the station. Perhaps he will provide a measure of additional security for two women traveling heavily laden; in any big city, even one as safe as Paris usually is, undesirables can show up.

The volunteer, Ömer Güney, is a fixture at the Kurdistan Cultural Center. He has even met Sakine Cansiz, at the PKK's Eiffel tower protest the previous

Chapter 1. Assassination in Paris

year. Doubtless, he will be thrilled to see his reclusive idol again. But the short ride to the station will never happen.

This event occurs on the only day in months when Sakine's movements pin her down to being in a certain building at a certain time. It happens on the only day in years when Ömer Güney knows that she will appear. How much coincidence can we stand?

And now she is dead, in a way that intends to send a message to both Kurds and Western governments alike. But until we know who sent it, we can't know what the message is.

Chapter 2. The Shooter

There's no dispute that these deaths came at the hand of an assassin who was acting on someone else's orders. To this day, we are left with the question: who owned the hand?

The assassin is now also dead too, so even if he might have been inclined to name his handlers rather than face life incarceration, that is off the table now.

His death doesn't come in any particularly sinister way (as far as we know). It's one of those things that happen if you're incarcerated for four years, even under the reasonably benign watch of a Western European government, when you're afflicted with a pre-existing condition that can be hazardous if not treated skilfully. Such was the situation of Ömer Güney.

Let's start from there: beyond being just a name, who was this assassin? What do we know about him? Perhaps that will help us to see who might have sent him.

About the only likely suspects we can rule out would be other operatives of the PKK (although the Turkish government will claim that this is exactly who did it). It's not that they wouldn't have done something like this; the PKK has been quite open about its policy of eliminating traitors and defectors, and quite successful at achieving those goals. In this instance, their involvement is pretty improbable, given the identities of the victim and the shooter.

Then again, the shooter himself is a somewhat improbable story too.

****

The news of the murders in the Kurdistan Information Office comes as a shock to the entire Kurdish nation, and especially those who live in Europe. The next day, 13 hours after the discovery of the bodies, nearly 24 hours after the actual time of the murders, a large number of Parisian Kurds and many of their non-Kurdish friends have gathered on the Rue de Lafayette.

In the corners of several video clips, a man stands just outside the doors of number 147, watching the activity around the crime scene as investigators go in and out. He looks very much like the 30-year-old driver, translator, and comrade of two of the victims. He will also become the only suspect.

Rusen Werdi is the head of the human rights office at the Kurdish Institute of Paris. Located at 106 Rue la Fayette, only a few doors down from the Information Office, the Institute is one of the principal Kurdish organizations

Chapter 2. The Shooter

in Paris. Werdi's press interview serves as a prime example of a curious paradox surrounding this case, telling reporters on the one hand that the murderers were very unskillful and, on the other hand, that the criminals acted so professionally that they left no evidence for investigators to find.

The reader may find those views incongruous. Get used to it. The pattern seems to be common in Kurdish speech, perhaps in the Levant in general. In a world of extreme ideas that tolerate no middle ground, the only way to express less than complete certainty is to make statements that contain inherently incompatible views almost within the same sentence.

The Unknown Favorite

A few days after the murders, Ömer Güney, a known friend and helper of Fidan Doğan, one of the murdered women, visits the police voluntarily and tells them that he saw the victims the day they were murdered. Apparently, it has not occurred to him that the office might have had closed circuit cameras. It did, and they recorded him. The recordings tell a very different story from the one he has come to tell.

He was indeed going in and out of the building on the day of the murders, but not at the times that he related to the police. On film, he leaves the apartment with a heavy bag, which the police later find and examine. It shows traces of gunpowder. Güney walks into the interview presumably hoping to walk out with his 15 minutes of fame as a crucial witness. He does indeed become a crucial figure, but he does not walk out at all; in fact, he will never do so. Now the police have a prime suspect in the murder of three Kurdish women in Paris.

The suspect's identity creates another shock for the Parisian Kurdish community. In hopes of building bridges across communities, many of them have gone out of their way to befriend, and to accept gestures of friendship from, people they view as occupiers: Turks, Iranians, Iraqis and Syrians. Güney is a Turk. He's fairly well known in the community. Members know that Güney took part in protests against the killings. That very weekend he had been to a memorial service for the dead women.

There's no suggestion that he is a crazy person. People are confused by the arrest of a suspect who has worked with them closely for years. Why would he suddenly have wanted to kill these women? Did someone order it?

Chapter 2. The Shooter

The assumption that some other force was behind Güney leads to a long list of potential co-conspirators. Numerous state or quasi-state actors might have had a hand in this crime.

Omer Guney (photo: GazeteDuvar.com.tr)

The members of the Kurdish people organizations begin to turn the questioning inward, asking how they could have accepted such a person without knowing him. Who brought him in to be trusted with an important leader like Sakine Cansız?

Some suggest that there was never any "bringing in" to it. Güney and his friend Fidan Doğan had the same experiences as children of the Turkish emigrants who grew up in France. Güney was a charming man, enough so anyway as to win the confidence of Fidan Doğan, who eventually introduced him to Sakine Cansiz.

Ömer Güney's family are ethnic Turks from the city of Sarkisla, a town in the Sivas Province of Turkey, in the region called Anatolia. It is in the very center of the country, some 300 miles east of Ankara and 200 miles either way to the Black Sea and the Mediterranean, where the rugged terrain begins to turn into formidable mountains. Ömer, the only son, was born in Sarkisla, as were his four sisters.

Chapter 2. The Shooter

According to Anne-Sophie Laguens, the government-appointed lawyer, the Güney family emigrated to France in 1988, when Ömer was only five years old. They settled in Georges-Les-Gonesse, an outer suburb of Paris. By 2005, the Güney parents were making a living in their newly-opened kebab restaurant in the nearby town of St. Denis.

A local barber who knew Ömer's father described the father and his family as friendly people who seemed to have no particular opinions about politics and religion. That's a wise policy for any immigrant. It is possible that the family members were really Turkish activists and had been coached to hide their religious and political beliefs, but there is no evidence that this is the case.

There is not much other information about Güney's early life or school experiences, at least none that the public can get to even today. He finished high school with a diploma. That is a much more significant achievement in France than it would be in the USA; the French diploma is challenging, and many graduates do not receive it. He then took mechanic training from a vocational-professional lycée.

After his arrest as a suspect, more information about him becomes public. He had met a Turkish woman and married her in 2003. Later they moved to the outskirts of Munich, Germany, where he found a job related to his education at Kinshofer, a medium-sized firm that makes cranes and forklifts.

He held that job for several years, moving on in 2009 to a job as a tea seller at Türkspor, a Turkish sports association. It's hard to imagine this as a move for upward mobility from his job as a skilled worker in an industrial company, but it did keep him in closer contact with people who were more interested in being Turkish than in joining the German middle class.

More likely, Güney had already been in contact with such activists from the beginning. One of Güney's Kinshofer colleagues recalls that nobody came to work at that plant without the endorsement of the Turkish association, and it was not easy to get. One has to wonder how an unknown young man arriving from outside the country managed to acquire such sponsorship.

That co-worker described Güney as a quite ordinary fellow, well dressed, but with an unusual interest in weapons. He had an extensive collection of knives and an air pistol that he took to work. The co-worker said another co-worker, an Albanian, *"told me once to be careful associating with Güney, it could lead to terrible things for you, because he is always armed."* In a country

Chapter 2. The Shooter

that frowns on private weapon ownership, an immigrant making a name for himself as armed and possibly dangerous has to raise some red flags.

Co-workers also describe him as a passionate adherent of the Nationalist Movement Party (MHP), an ultra-nationalist party in Turkey. Making friends with Kurds is completely counter to the norms of the MHP. Many Turkish nationalist extremists worked at Kinshofer, and many would routinely harass the few Kurdish employees in the company.

Güney did not join in. On the contrary, he had taken an interest in meeting Kurds and expressed an interest in Kurdish issues, claiming to his Turkish co-workers that he had a Kurdish grandmother. He would later take that claim to a new level after his return to France, insisting that he is and has always been a proud Kurd.

It seems improbable that a pro-Kurdish double-émigré (from France as well as Turkey) who is actively proselytizing for fairer treatment of the Kurdish minority will find favor with the highly-nationalistic Turkish association. Yet to get and keep his job, Güney must have had that support.

One route out of this conundrum is to speculate that his increasing involvement in the Turkish associations led him to handlers from the MHP or MIT. Possibly they saw an opportunity of turning this young man back into the French community, where he was known before his involvement with the MHP, with letters of introductions from such Kurds as he might befriend in Germany. Once re-integrated, he could become a useful source of information.

A Kurdish co-worker Güney befriended in Germany related: "*Güney asked me who I meet and who my contact is. He asked me to take him to meetings and said 'Trust me, I have good friends, be assured nothing is going to happen to you.' I did not know him well enough to do that*".

In 2010, Güney informed Türkspor that he had a tumor in his head and took several months off work. When he returned, he told his colleagues that he was fine, but that his marriage was deteriorating.

Ömer Güney divorced his wife in 2011; according to his lawyer, he then began to make frequent trips to France. During one of these trips, he joined a Kurdish association in Villiers-le-Bel, a town very close to his parents' home. Mehmet Subasi, the director of the Kurdish Cultural House, remembered him signing a membership application form, but observed that there was nothing very remarkable about that. The association door was open to anyone who

Chapter 2. The Shooter

wanted to join. He said: "Our group is open to anyone without checking their background, and we are always welcoming people, including Turks."

Director Subasi said: "There was no reason for me or any other members to be suspicious of Ömer Güney. At that level of the organization, screening is not required." Local activists agree it is not unusual for left-wing Turks to join the movement out of sympathy and concern for human rights. Such Turks were marginalized in their own Turkish communities, and of course were clearly not accepted as full-fledged Germans or French; the Kurdish groups offered a haven that was not only non-judgmental but open and welcoming.

Güney actively began to spend more time working for the association than any other members. He always volunteered and offered to help with errands.

In hindsight, the association's members would discover that he gave many different versions of his background. He told some people his father was Kurdish. He told others that he was assuming a Kurdish identity to obtain political asylum in France. Until the murders, it had never occurred to those who knew him to compare notes and find out that he was always lying about so many things.

In August 2012, Ömer Güney moved out of his rented room in Germany, according to his former landlady. Neighbors friendly with his parents said this move happened after the death of his grandmother. His lawyer stated that Güney also traveled to Ankara several times during his time in Germany. He used tickets on one of the European super-no-frills low-cost airlines, which suggests that the Turkish intelligence agencies had not funded the trips.

As with most of Güney's activities, this was almost, but not quite, normal. Güney's lawyer says, "The trips were to find a perfect wife." A leader of the Kurdish BDP Party in Turkey tells investigators that it was very strange that Güney would have traveled to Ankara instead of his family hometown. It may be true that his intent was exactly as stated, but it doesn't conform to the Middle Eastern tradition of marrying relatives or people they know from their hometown. The town of Sarkisla and the elder Güneys are pretty traditional; wife-hunting in Ankara doesn't seem to add up.

In 2012, Ömer Güney returned to Paris, claimed that he had a mental health problem, and moved back in with his parents. He worked briefly as a maintenance officer at the Charles de Gaulle airport, but he lost that job when he suffered a seizure while at work. He was taken to Saint-Anne Hospital in Paris for treatment, and then he was examined by the specialist

Chapter 2. The Shooter

center for neurology and psychiatry. After his release from the hospital, Güney received over 700 euros per month in French disability payments.

His lawyer, Anne-Sophie Laguens, said that Güney had been diagnosed with a brain tumor, which caused frequent bouts of amnesia and provoked seizures. Güney's uncle from Sivas claimed in an interview with Turkey's CNN affiliate that he was not acting normally, saying that he was "unable to remember what he ate an hour ago."

Laguens summarized her case: "He suffers from severe neurological difficulties."

Ömer Güney's unemployment in early 2012 gave him time to work as a volunteer helping Kurdish people in Paris. Many Kurds, activists and non-activists alike, recalled that this was when he started appearing at the Kurdish Cultural Centre in central Paris.

Nobody seems to remember knowing or even meeting Ömer Güney before he turned up in the Kurdish facilities. What people do remember is that he certainly was helpful. In a short time, he was a local favorite. Only much later on would people come to realize that they didn't know much about him. He never gave up much information about himself or his family; in retrospect, no one really knew him at all. He just hung out around those centers, smiled, and talked with people in Turkish.

Ömer Güney had been five years old when his parents moved to France. He grew up and went to school there. His fluent French language and knowledge of Turkish gave him the chance to translate for Kurdish men and women who spoke only Turkish and wanted to communicate with their French doctors, or with government officials for immigration cases.

He helped people by driving them, free of charge. Berivan Akyol, one of the Kurdish translators in the community said that Ömer Güney did not exhibit any neurological problems. He was there on time for every appointment. He was able to drive, and he never complained of headaches or lost his balance while driving or translating for people.

The Kurdish Cultural Centre where all this volunteer effort was happening is a large facility that houses several Kurdish associations. It is a short walk from the Kurdish Information Office on the Rue de Lafayette.

People looking back at the photographs from the past found out that Güney had already connected with the PKK activists by March of 2012. In a photograph from that time, Ömer Güney is seen on the Eiffel Tower's first floor, holding a banner supporting the jailed Kurdish leader Abdullah Öcalan

Chapter 2. The Shooter

and the PKK struggle for peace and freedom of Kurd in Kurdistan. Also present at that event was Sakine Cansiz.

Is Guney a sympathetic volunteer, or a planted sociopath?

A Bigger Picture

This crime is obviously intentional, obviously politically-motivated. For those waiting for closure, the investigation proceeds slowly. The French government has arrested Güney for the murder of the three Kurdish women, but they also are also insisting that he acted alone. Technically, at that moment in that room, it might be accurate to say that he was alone, but everyone can see that this picture needs to be painted on a larger canvas.

One of the more remarkable findings in the years of investigation that followed the arrest is that Güney, having recently returned from another of the mysterious Ankara trips in December, went three weeks later to his "home" Kurdish center in Villiers-le-Bel, where he photographed the membership roster. Once discovered, that puts the final strokes on the picture: Güney is certainly working for somebody. But it has not yet been discovered when, two weeks later, he's asked to drive a Kurdish representative to meet Sakine Cansiz for what is just a simple errand, but is also an unusual and brief moment when it is known where she will be and when. During that short window of opportunity ... she dies.

As the facts make their slow emergence, the Kurdish people in France are able to connect the dots with little difficulty. Probably the French investigators have made those connections also, and much earlier, but prosecutors must prove the case, not just feel it. They are limited by politics, both in what they can say and in their dependence on cooperation by a foreign government for some of the essential facts needed.

To establish any link to any other entity, the French must investigate whether Güney has any contacts in Turkey and who those contacts are. To do so, they must necessarily work with the Turkish government, which is not famous for responsiveness in the best of times. To ask for that help in deciphering the actions of a lone madman is one thing; to request the government to look into larger forces that may be at work is quite another. It would require the French to accuse the Turks either of sponsoring the murders directly or of housing a rogue group that is actively undermining the government's public positions. Only if that accusation takes hold is there any

Chapter 2. The Shooter

reason for the Turkish government to start any form of self-examination, and to what end will it do so?

The investigators have already pushed the limits of diplomatic propriety by stating publicly that this cooperation has not been forthcoming. There will be no cooperation whatever by the Turkish government.

Besides, the Kurdish people suspect that the French are not entirely on the level in this matter either. They see a cover-up by the French government to protect its interests in Turkey. So does the French press (in the few instances when they consider this case at all). Most of the European countries have engaged in cover-ups to avoid exposing or aggravating the Turks, the Iranians or various Arab governments unnecessarily. Those countries have oil or defense treaties to sell. The Kurdish people have no independent country, and much of their oil in Iraq is pledged to the national government. They are, once again, on their own. After 2000 years of that, they are at least used to it.

Gültan Kisanak was one of the group of women who were imprisoned and tortured along with Sakine Cansız in the 1980s. DIYARBAKIR (a publication of the Kurdish agency DIHA) reported in its usual hyperbolic style:

"Tens of thousands of people joined in the massive march held in memory of three Kurdish women politicians in Diyarbakir. Pointing at Ankara as being behind the massacre, the BDP Co-chair and Diyarbakir Metropolitan Mayoral candidate Gültan Kisanak said, "The killers planned the massacre in Ankara. This massacre is an international murder and received collaboration from countries like Germany and France. Both of our hands will be on the throats of those who carried out the massacre. Erdoğan knows those who triggered the massacre, those who are behind the massacre, and which parallel groups supported it. They are not delivering these to the court."

The prosecutors conclude in 2015 that it will not be possible to win a guilty verdict without more specific information to build a convincing motive. They need to know more about Güney's actions when he traveled to Turkey, and what they really need to know is what, if any, relationship had existed between him and various Turkish intelligence organizations. The Turks had made it clear that such information would not be forthcoming. Although the case is not closed, the prosecutors cease any active effort to move the case forward. Nobody arises to demand that the police must either charge him or release him, so apparently it suits everybody to have him remain in custody. On 18 December 2016, the investigation sputters to an official halt when Ömer Güney dies in prison. Assuming that Güney died without having revealed who his handlers were, there is nobody left to prosecute.

Chapter 2. The Shooter

Under pressure from the families of the victims, as well as an apparent shift in the electoral mood towards law-and-order in Europe, the police announce in 2017 that the case will be re-opened. At this point, it would be foolish to expect that justice will eventually reach the perpetrators of the murder of Sakine Cansiz. The best and most likely suspect is dead, so he will never confess. Even if he did, hardly anyone cares about him. What everyone, even the families of the victims, wants to know is: who sent him?

Only a change of government in Turkey would bring any relevant documents to light, and that assumes that any such documents (or even any connection) exist in the first place.

Our time, then, is better spent in seeking to understand:

- Why the Kurds are so sure that the Turks must be behind this crime;
- Why the Turks (some Turks, whoever they were) would have found it so important to kill Sakine Cansiz;
- Why the Kurdish people view this death as an atrocity, much more so than any of the thousands of other Kurds whom the Turks have indisputably killed in the past decades; and
- Why this particular woman might have been seen as an especially desirable target, why she was such an iconic figure to all the Kurdish people, and why the community takes her loss so hard.

Let's start with the first question: Why are all these people so sure that the Turkish government must in some way have been behind this?

Chapter 3. The Usual Suspects

Nobody seems to dispute that Ömer Güney killed Sakine Cansiz and her colleagues, nor that someone else recruited him to do the deed. Although he is a Turk, that does not mean that the recruiters are Turks, nor that they have done this at the behest of the Turkish government. This drama has many other candidates for the role of suspect; the hard part is trimming the list down to a manageable number.

The Iranians (Persians), Turks, Israelis (Jews) and Kurds have been engaged in co-dependent and usually destructive relationships for over 4000 years. The Arabs introduced themselves to cauldron over 1000 years ago. The next chapters will explore some of that convoluted history to give a better understanding of the causes and character of these enmities, so that you can form your own opinions as to whether that long-standing feud plays some part in this particular murder.

While reading this history, try to keep in mind that the Kurds, and most other Middle Eastern societies, do not appear to draw any distinction between 6:30 p.m. and 630 BC.

The previous sentence sounded much better written that way but, out of respect for non-Christian readers, the rest of the book uses the generic date form of "Before Current Era" (BCE), rather than just BC, and CE (Current Era) instead of AD.

The Western world's concept of history seldom stretches back beyond about 1100 CE, which saw the end of the Dark Ages and the rise of reliable written records. The Greeks (300 BCE) and the remarkably self-documenting Romans (100 BCE to 400 CE) are considered "Ancient History." Their languages are dead, their history is no longer taught in schools, and the entire subject area is considered arcane, even though almost all Western societies are founded on their precepts. In other words, those events are far beyond what Westerners consider a "reasonably current" timeframe.

What is a Western timeframe? Consider that from 1939 to 1945 the US, UK, Soviet Union, Germany and Japan fought the most destructive war this planet has ever seen. Within a half-century, after the reunification of the partitioned Germany, they were all steadfast allies and the best of friends at almost every level of society. All, that is, except the USSR which, after killing many more millions of its own citizens to sustain its regime than the country

Chapter 3. The Usual Suspects

suffered as casualties during the actual war, had died anyway, unlamented, at the tender age of 73 years. Today, only the shadow of that empire remains. Oddly enough, one of the few peoples actively impacted by that shadow today is ... the Kurds, caught up in Vladimir Putin's efforts to re-establish Syria as a Soviet satellite state on the Mediterranean.

The Long List of Suspects

In a region where centuries-long blood feuds erupt over perceived slights of honor, over interpretations of religious texts, or over rounds of tit-for-tat killings, it's usually a lot quicker to make up a list of your friends than your enemies.

Setting aside the Turks and potential traitors within the PKK, viable suspects include:

- Israel, because ... well, because it is Israel. Kurds are not immune from the general Islamic hatred of Judaism. Like many Muslims, they spend boundless energy concocting fantastic schemes that they believe the Israelis are concocting about them. Most Kurds suspect Israeli complicity in the capture of Öcalan, because nobody else in the region has armed forces competent enough to pull off that snatch. Why not attack Cansiz too? In reality, Israel is in favor of anything that keeps its many enemies too busy to attack it; it will not stand in the way of Kurdish guerrillas in Syria, Iraq or Iran.

- Iran: Kurds and Iranians have been in conflict in Iraq for decades via Iran's Shiite surrogates, and they have thousands of years of bad history between them. The Iranians have no interest in the success of the PKK, which undermines the Iraqi and Syrian governments that Iran aims to control. In 2013, Iran was under stringent international sanctions over its nuclear activities. It should not have wanted to waste its limited political capital in countries that were helping it evade those sanctions, as France traditionally does. But their regime has proven itself fully capable of choices that seem irrational to others.

- Syria: Assad has repressed the Kurds for decades, and they are actively in rebellion in 2013. Perhaps the Syrians wanted to stop the flow of European funds to the PKK. However, as we'll explore further in a later chapter, the Syrians appear to see the Kurds as the least of its problems in its civil war.

Chapter 3. The Usual Suspects

- Saudi Arabia and other conservative Arab states find the PKK's religious and social beliefs intolerable. Would that generic disapproval translate into international hit-squad operations? Or is the PKK only a very small fish in their pond?
- Various elements of the Turkish political structure in 2013 (allegedly) do not conform to the policies of the central government.
  - The Nationalist Movement Party (MHP) is an extremist ultra-nationalist political party. Not only do they oppose any rights for Kurds, but they also want to exterminate (no, not "deport") anyone who isn't a Turk who is found in Turkey.
  - The Gray Wolves, an even more violent offshoot of the MHP, may or may not be actually under the MHP's control. They have been behind other attacks on Kurds. Why not this one?
  - Turkish Hezbollah, also known as the Kurdish Hezbollah or Hezbollah in Turkey, is a Sunni Islamist militant organization whose members are mainly Turkish and many are Kurds. It is active against the Kurdistan Workers' Party (PKK) and the Kurdish people in general. On the other hand, it has so far confined itself to Turkey.
- French agents may have been acting to rid the capital of a terrorist entity, or perhaps doing a favor for some other intelligence service that doesn't have a lot of operatives on the ground, such as ... well, such as Turkey, as it happens. Even if they weren't actively participating, they could have agreed to look the other way at the right time.
- Other intelligence agencies: It is common knowledge that Paris is crawling with secret agents. This job is well within their capabilities, and their agendas are complex enough that it is impossible to rule out the existence of some inscrutable motive.

On top of all these, we have everybody's favorite candidate, the Turks themselves, a term that goes well beyond the official government agencies.

Means, opportunity and motive form the classic trinity of the detective novel. We've established that the Kurds have amassed a long list of enemies. Every one of the members of this list have all three components working for them.

Chapter 3. The Usual Suspects

Could It Be An Inside Job?

Through much of their very long history, the Kurds have been their own worst enemies. The Turkish government is quick to claim that the murders reflect internal struggles among the violent extremists within the PKK.

The PKK underwent a serious split in 2001 after Öcalan was arrested, and again in 2005 when it chose to return to combat. Sakine was deployed to Europe by the fighting side of the PKK, which remained loyal to Öcalan. It's possible that the former leaders who had chosen to seek a political solution seek to remove the fighting PKK's chief revenue source. If they see peaceful negotiation as the better way, why now resort to murder in the case of Cansiz?

Perhaps the fighters who remained in the PKK might be seeking to get Sakine out of the picture because they disapprove of having a woman in the leadership ranks, and clearly Öcalan will not return to protect her. In addition, Hurriyet, a Turkish daily newspaper, had reported that Sakine was at odds with Ferman Hussein, the alleged head of the PKK's armed wing. That isn't a recipe for long life and good health. But at this moment the PKK is standing down pending the outcome of the peace negotiations. Such an attack might have been plausible at almost any other moment, but why now, and why attack one of the lead peace negotiators?

The Turks claim that this is all just a PKK internal feud. That assertion is diluted by the fact that this is what they always say whenever Kurds are killed, even when it is obviously done in military operations by the Turkish army. Turkey has been making the same claim for decades about the Armenians. More than 40,000 Kurds have died since 1984, the vast majority being Kurdish civilians killed in attacks by the Turkish armed forces. The Turks claim that all of this is the result of inter-factional fighting within the PKK.

Another group of Kurds makes a more plausible candidate.

Massoud Barzani and Jalal Talabani and their *peshmerga* (militia armies) control the Kurdistan Regional Government (KRG) in Iraq. Turkish Kurds say the KRG has sold out to the Iranians and Turks in a deal that will maintain their families in power, surrendering their people's dream of Kurdish independence in return for a non-aggression pact. The PKK alleges that these two wish to establish their families' rule in northern Iraq as a de facto fiefdom of the Erdoğan government, much as was done to the Kurds in the days of the Ottoman Empire and, as we shall see, for thousands of years before that.

Chapter 3. The Usual Suspects

For a couple of years, the Turks will adhere to the deal with the KRG, while maintaining a free hand to deal with the Kurds within Turkish borders. In 2013, both the Iraqi and Syrian Kurds are fully engaged in gaining control over the land that ISIS has captured, and there is enough to do there that they have not yet come into direct conflict. Soon, as the battles die down, they will begin fighting each other for control of the area, but that is in the future. In any case, Sakine Cansiz seems to be a very improbable target; her activities to motivate the PKK-affiliated Kurds in Europe are also yielding additional support and revenue for the KRG, whose fight in Iraq is better known.

The Kurds are a small group that can hardly threaten the sovereignty of most Middle Eastern states beyond the immediate area of Iraq and Syria. Likewise, the catalog above didn't mention religion much. If the issue is not pragmatic politics and not religious dogma, who is it that can hate the Kurds even more than that?

It Must Be the Turks

Despite the lengthy list of other potential culprits, the Kurdish community is nearly unanimous in believing that some Turkish element is to blame. For them, the only question is: which one? There are several plausible candidates.

Muzaffer Ayata, another of the founding members of the PKK, has been living in Germany since 2002. He says that they have heard rumors of rogue elements within the Islamist Turkish state anxious to stop the peace process.

Many Kurdish people, not confined by an official position or political considerations, suspect that the killer or killers were part of a plot, but not one cooked up by shadowy "rogue elements." They believe that the mainstream part of the Turkish Government is executing a plot to infiltrate the PKK organization and assassinate the activists who are hurting their interests the most. Perhaps the killers didn't get the message that, with the peace process in play, the operation was no longer needed. Perhaps they did, and chose to ignore it. Perhaps there was no such message.

Compounding that suspicion is the fact that in the immediate present, i.e. the time of the Rue de Lafayette murders, the Kurds are beginning one of their very rare up-cycles. They are gaining worldwide legitimacy and are starting to set up local governments that are fully autonomous from the

Chapter 3. The Usual Suspects

national governments within whose arbitrary boundaries they happen to reside.

Turkey has made no secret of the fact that it is unalterably opposed to the creation of an integrated Kurdistan. It sees autonomous regions as an inevitable gateway to independence, and that is probably correct.

The PKK is, after all, designated by the international community at Turkey's insistence to be a terrorist organization because of its continuing attacks on Turkey. Combining these two facts provides a perfectly valid reason to try and terminate a key PKK leader, even if she isn't actively on the field of combat. In fact, the statement may be more dramatic: it sends the message that there are no "desk jobs" exempt from consequences in this game.

It is obvious even to the most casual observer that the Turkish government must be considered a leading suspect in this affair. The French police quickly came to this conclusion, and they still hold that view to this day.

Why Not the Turks?

Unfortunately, it's not as simple as it might seem. For instance, it may depend on whom exactly we mean by "the Turkish government."

At this particular moment in 2013, the Turkish government is negotiating with Öcalan; they are close to declaring a ceasefire and will shortly do just that. It would not seem to serve their interests to kill a key Kurdish leader during the actual negotiation process.

President Recep Tayyip Erdoğan has not yet revealed his apparent intention of becoming President for Life. An objective that is clear already is dismantling the secular state and replacing it with Islamic law.

In that ambition, the AKP's primary ally is the Islamist Fethullah Gülen Movement. Its leader is a self-exiled cleric, Fethullah Gülen, who lives in the US. Gülen believes in a state that is homogenous. The culture should be Turkish and only Turkish; the religion should be Islamic and under the control of Turkish clerics. No Kurdish language, culture, or deviant forms of Islam can be tolerated.

On these points, the AKP and Gülenists are in total agreement.

In 1999, Gülen had exiled himself in the US to escape the secular government's charges that his religious group is a front for a subversive

Chapter 3. The Usual Suspects

political organization. In 1999, that was just an allegation. By 2013 it is an openly acknowledged fact that his role in the alliance with the AKP has for several years been to run a shadow government inside the various Turkish security-related agencies.

In 2013, such a concept might have seemed bizarre in the US, until not more than three years later we would observe exactly the same phenomenon. In 2017, legions of supposedly non-partisan bureaucrats, including those in the intelligence community, would do everything they could, legally and otherwise, even at the expense of US security concerns, to thwart an incoming administration that threatens their bureaucratic world-view.

So it is in Turkey in 2013, at least this early in the year. Gülen's followers have burrowed into the upper ranks throughout the police, the judiciary and the military - the very groups that the AKP will need to co-opt or sideline if it is to turn the state upside down.

Gülen himself has quietly joined with the AKP to endorse a clandestine initiative by the head of the National Intelligence Organization (MIT), the Turkish secret service, to conduct peace negotiations with Kurdish leader Abdullah Öcalan. Perhaps the Movement has become broader than the man. With Gülenists entrenched in the security agencies who have been battling the PKK for decades, it's quite plausible that one of them saw a target of opportunity and felt it irresponsible not to take it, despite the government's temporary position to the contrary.

Besides that, the alliance with the AKP, although in place for a decade, is a marriage of convenience between two totalitarian groups. Only one can emerge supreme. It wouldn't be at all surprising if the Gülen group had decided to undermine the AKP's process by making use of its international connections to strike at the PKK when the opportunity presented itself. Many Kurds in France believe that this is exactly what happened.

The third party in the negotiations is Abdullah Öcalan, the founder and leader of the PKK. This too is a little odd, since the Turks already have him in jail. As a duly-proclaimed international terrorist, he is only alive because the Turks are trying to get into the EU and have had to abolish the death penalty. Mehmet Ulker is the head of the Kurdish Associations Federation, a Kurdish umbrella organization that in many different countries coordinates the activities of groups like the Kurdistan Information Office in Paris. He believes that the Turkish government did indeed carry out these murders in this critical time, in order to intimidate the Kurdish leader while the talks over a

Chapter 3. The Usual Suspects

possible ceasefire continued. Perhaps it worked: the deal was signed very quickly after the murders, and the PKK didn't get much out of it.

The majority of Western media reporters (The Guardian, Spiegel, CNN, and BBC) follow the opposite trail, speculating that these three women were killed as a provocation that would put an end to the peace process between Abdullah Öcalan and Turkish Government.

Why do the Turks and Kurds mistrust each other so much? Perhaps they know each other too well. They've been at odds for over 2500 years.

Chapter 4. A Very Ancient People

The Kurds have not forgotten the Persian overthrow of their empire 2500 years ago (around 500 BCE), nor the Turkish destruction of their religion in 650 CE. On the other side of the coin, the Turks and Persians have not forgotten the near-constant rebellions and betrayals by the Kurds ever since then.

Beyond Western Timelines

The preceding chapter noted that "ancient' by European standards, meaning the beginnings of Rome's power in about 100 BCE or perhaps Alexander the Great in 300 BCE, only takes you back to about the halfway point from the start of documented Kurdish history.

When Alexander arrived, the Kurds had already descended from their pinnacle and were already under the rule of the Persians. Since then, they have been subjects of the Greeks, Romans, Mongols, Ottomans, British and French Empires. All of them are gone. The Kurds, Persians, Arabs and Turks remain. So does their struggle.

The Kurds trace themselves back to the early chapters of the Bible, Torah or Koran, to times well before even Nebuchadnezzar (650 BCE). Hundreds of years earlier, the Assyrians, Hittites, Medes and Persians were the powers of the day. Israel and Judah were just primitive tribes, an occasional source of slave labor for several empires of massive wealth and power.

The march of the Roman Empire east from Constantinople did not stop because there was nowhere left to go. It started abutting equally strong civilizations that would not permit any further conquests. Those eastern empires claimed lineages that dated back thousands of documented years and, based on oral traditions, tens of thousands more before that.

Pre-History

It might seem a little extreme to take the story of a thoroughly modern woman back to the dawn of civilization, but to this is an essential element of Kurdish society. Professors of antiquity will argue that the history is cloudy and, in any case, people did not envision any identity beyond their tribe or some petty king until nearer the time of the Medes, so the very concept of

Chapter 4. A Very Ancient People

who their ancestors might have been is specious. The Kurds will argue that since the written history is cloudy, their oral tradition is just as valid.

Besides, it doesn't matter who they really are; it matters who they think they are. You don't have to believe in the doctrine, of which we will say as little as possible, but you do have to understand that their entire political, cultural and religious existence is wrapped around and dictated by their beliefs.

In the ancient Sanskrit (i.e. Hindu-based) texts, "humanity" consisted of everyone who lived in the northern part of the Indian sub-continent out as far as the rugged mountains that surround it. This society was organized into four social groups, known as Brahmin, Kshatriya, Vaishya and Shudra. Over the centuries, this four-group society developed rifts.

Zoroastrians believe that a great flood occurred in about 6000 BCE. Whether this belief drove the Torah account or the other way around, or whether the event really did happen, remains unknown, but it's one of many examples of the common roots of the Aryan and Jewish religions. One of the consequences of this flood was that the societies got separated.

One part of the society followed Prophet Mahabad (Mahabhara) into the monotheistic worship of a supreme deity known as HU. That early religion was known as Mithraism, which was later adopted as the Aryan religion in 5600 BCE. Its most widely-known prophet was Zarathustra, whose name the Greeks corrupted to "Zoroaster". He added the concept of a Holy Spirit that enhanced the human's ability to communicate with their God HU.

Over five thousand years later, the statements of the concept of the Trinity by Jesus of Nazareth were identical to the Trinity found in Prophet Zoroaster's Aryan religion. That was neither coincidental nor outlandish: Zoroastrianism was alive and well in all of the lands around Judea in 25 CE.

The remaining part of humanity (meaning northern Indians) abandoned HU and began to worship another variant of the lead god, Dêw or Devas or Arimanus. The Deva religion also evolved to recognize a Trinity (Trimurti) of gods, but it was of a very different nature. Those gods are Brahma the creator, Vishnu the preserver, and Shiva the destroyer and transformer. Some of those names persist until this very day in Hinduism, Buddhism, Jainism and other Indian-based religions.

Because of that religious difference, the followers of the God HU and followers of Arimanus have been in conflict for several thousand years. The Kurds are the descendants of the Medes, who descended from the Kshatriya,

Chapter 4. A Very Ancient People

those who worshipped God HU as members of the Aryan and later Zoroastrian religion.

Greek and Jewish scholars would start referring incorrectly to Aryanism as Zoroastrianism, which in a modern context would be much like referring to Christianity as John-Paulism. In this case, Zoroaster was the chief prophet, but the much, much older religion was actually Aryanism, which also governed the system of governing the society itself.

Spreading out from India, the Kshatriya came to rule all of the lands from India to the European borders, and from Egypt to parts of modern Russia. This empire is known in the Torah and Christian Bible as the empire of the Medes.

Modern scholars have a different, although reconcilable, interpretation. Today's Indo-European languages appear to have originated in a melding between an Aryan civilization that spread from the steppe lands around the Caspian Sea and northern India's Tamil civilization (which, to confuse matters further, is the ancestor of, but not the same as, today's Tamil religion). Good fences make good neighbors: it's fairly easy to see how a loose association of people on either side of the massive barrier of the Hindu Kush could form, and likewise how a rupture of that amity (or, for that matter, a great flood) could have been interpreted as a "separation" into the Devas and Aryan sides.

The conflict may have been truly religious, or it may have been based on territorial impulses masked by claims of religious motives. Most likely it was both. The conflict between the followers of HU and the followers of Arimanus (i.e. the Aryans and the Indians) continued for thousands of years. According to the Rigveda (Book 7, hymns 18, 33 and 83.4-8), the climactic event was the Battle of Ten Kings, in the year 2400 BCE. King Sudas, the forefather of the Medes, defeated the nine Devas kings who ruled over the worshippers of Arimanus.

Among the defeated Devas group were the Persians, who became vassals of the Medes and provided military units as their feudal duty.

Here we should note that in this book "Persians" is not the same as the modern "Iranian". It means a specific ethnic and political grouping of tribes that derived from the geographic area in and around Persia (Iran) where they migrated from India. Depending on their political fortunes, they might dominate large swathes of the Middle East, or they might revert to tribalism behind their mountain walls.

Chapter 4. A Very Ancient People

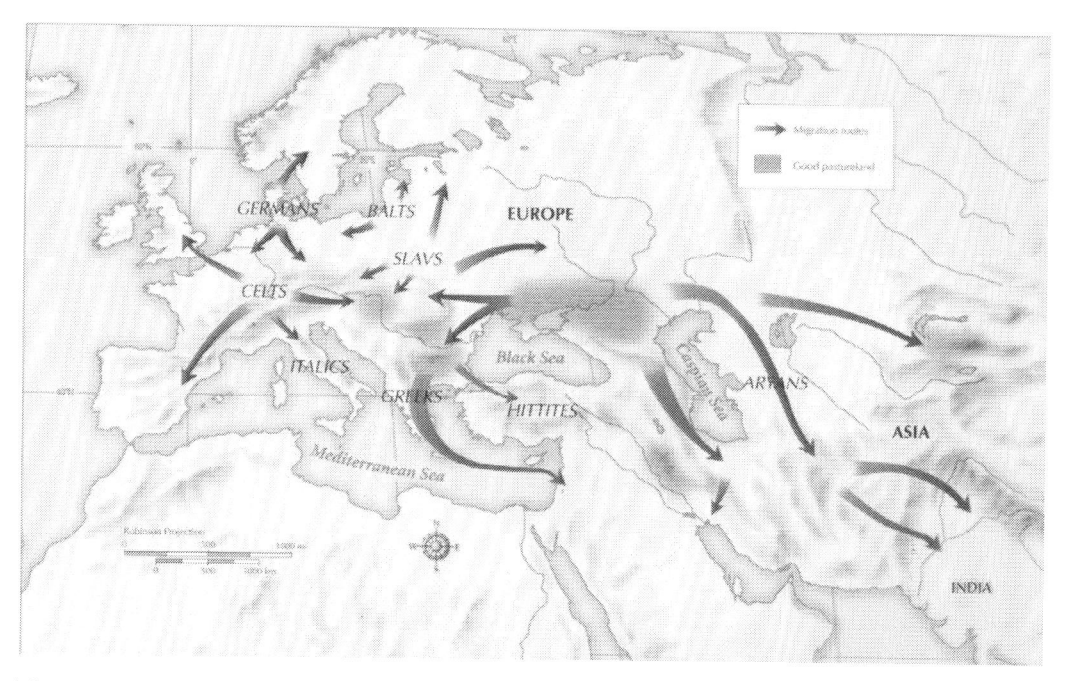

The Medes, while sharing in the joint pre-history, were not from lower India. Even in the ancient four societies, they had been the mountain people. By the time of the Battle of Ten Kings, which approaches the edge of recorded history, ethnographers speculate that the Aryans had worked their way around the Caspian Sea. Pockets of their culture, in the form of ancient Lak communities that persist until today in mountainous strongholds in the Russian state of Dagestan, in Azerbaijan, and in parts of the Ukraine. Eventually the Aryans re-entered Anatolia (Turkey) from the west in the form of the Hittites in around 3000 BCE. From there they proceeded back to the east to the mountainous frontiers of modern Iran, where in essence they met themselves again, but in a form that they no longer recognized.

The people living in the Middle East at that time, and even a great empire such as the Hittites, didn't have records or even oral traditions that were more than perhaps a thousand years old. If their historical records only go back to about 2500-3000 BCE, then the "start point" of the recorded histories is actually only picking the story up in the middle of the migratory circle. The Hittites, and by extension the Aryans, probably did seem to have appeared out of the Caucasus.

[35]

Chapter 4. A Very Ancient People

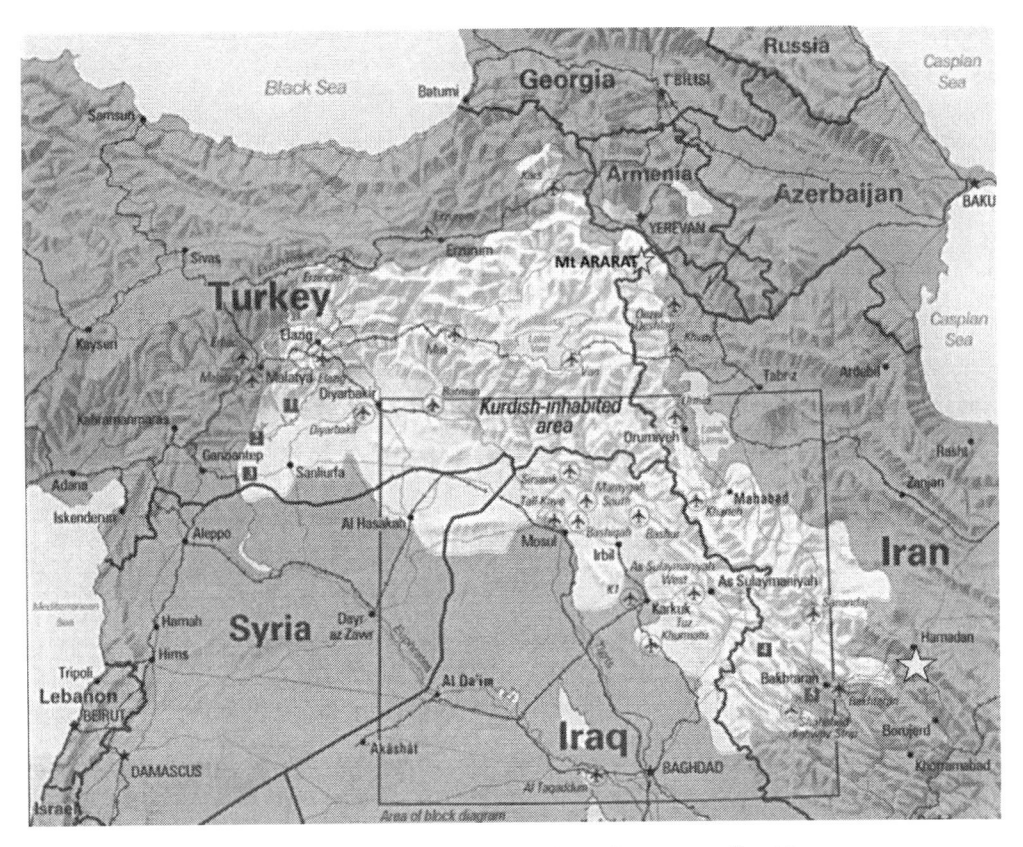

Map courtesy of University of Texas collection:
http://www.lib.utexas.edu/maps/middle_east_and_asia/kurdish_lands_92.jpg

The Zagros Mountains, comprising almost the entire western part of Iran, are part of a geological fold that includes the Lesser Caucasus, (today's Armenia) which in turn is just a lesser fold of the main Caucasus chain. Joining the Zagros mountains in northwestern Iran are the Elburz Mountains that form Iran's northern slope to the Caspian Sea, and it is essentially at that junction that the Medes would decide to place their capital city, Ecbatana (today's Hamadan). That is the location of the grave of King Astyages of the Medes and his Jewish queen, Esther, who is celebrated in the Torah and Bible. Later, these forbidding mountains would protect the Medes and the Kurds for thousands of years, permitting them to survive wave upon wave of marauding hordes.

It's also not very far from Hamadan to the spot where many believe that history restarted itself after the Great Flood: Mount Ararat. It lies atop a notch in the borders where Iran, Turkey and Iraq come together. This happens to be within the territories inhabited by the Kurds. For a culture and

Chapter 4. A Very Ancient People

religion that claims to be the ancestor of every modern people, having the site of Noah's Ark as one's base is a powerful starting point.

Not Those Aryans

There's another aspect of this early history that we must address. The term "Aryan" has entered, completely incorrectly, into common usage in modern language to reflect the ravings of the megalomaniac Adolf Hitler. Ironically, the person who brought the term to our consciousness appears to have been thoroughly misinformed about the Aryans.

Some Kurds believe themselves to be the ancestors of all European civilization. The linguistics of the Finnish language tells us that they did arrive at the Baltic coast to create pockets of Aryan communities. However, the Norse languages are very different from the Sanskrit-based languages, and yet it's easier to adopt a new language than to change the physical characteristics of an entire culture.

Aryans, while referred to as "white" by their contemporaries, and even today being markedly paler than southern Indians and those from the Asian heartland, were and still are universally dark-haired and certainly offer little comparison with Scandinavians.

No surviving society (Semitic, Indian, the various ethnicities of east Asia, and even the Aryans themselves) has experienced more than minor changes in their own physical attributes in the entire periods during which they have kept records. It seems improbable that, during their great trek across northern Europe, during a time of fewer than 2000 years, the dark-haired dark-eyed Aryans somehow transformed themselves so that a vast proportion of their entire society possessed blue eyes and light hair.

The tall blue-eyed blondes over whom Hitler and Goebbels slobbered as the epitome of "Aryan perfection" were nothing of the sort. They were classic Nordics, descendants of the Vikings; in most ethnographic studies, that population is considered quite distinct. They certainly didn't evolve from a very different-looking Aryan people in the short span of a few hundred years.

Who else could have been considered dark-haired, somewhat shorter, and of a more sallow complexion than most Nordics? Why, yes: Adolf Hitler himself! Quite possibly he was the true Aryan while his Master Race was not. How ironic!

Chapter 4. A Very Ancient People

The Medes

The mighty Semitic Assyrian empire had dominated this area since about 1300 BCE. Its neighbor was the equally powerful Hittite empire, an Aryan civilization that ruled northern Turkey and parts of the Balkans. The language of the Hittites persists in the Kurdish language today. Despite the longevity and stability of these empires, they became casualties of a phenomenon known as the Bronze Age Collapse that took place between 1000-900 BCE. Empires across Europe and Asia seem to have simply disintegrated, returning to small village-based societies. The cause remains an object of academic speculation today.

In building back from that fractured situation, an Aryan group, the Medes. emerged as one of the kingdoms in the mountains of northern Iran. They would be incorporated into the resurgent Assyrian Empire as a vassal kingdom, beginning a cycle that will become very familiar.

The capture of Jerusalem by the Assyrian emperor Sennacherib is described in 2 Kings 18-19 and occurred about 751 BCE. This third edition of the Assyrian empire was based in Nineveh and stretched from Egypt to Iraq (but not Iran) and up into modern Turkey.

By 626 BCE the Assyrian empire was in a constant struggle to maintain control over its many unruly vassals. In 614 the Medes "emerged", although they had been in the area for thousands of years, to lead a coalition of the vassal states to victory over the Assyrians. The Medes occupied Nineveh and established their own empire over Persia, Iraq, the Caucasus region and eastern Turkey. (In 2016, the terrorist regime of ISIS has just destroyed the buildings that remained from that same Nineveh). Originating as it did in a confederation of allies, it is not surprising that the Medes would also allow the constituent kingdoms to retain their identities.

The Medean Empire must have been quite a spectacle in its time. In these early days of recorded history, and even over the ensuing millennium, it was the only one that would be large, powerful and cultured enough to have yielded any surviving documents and artifacts. Their distinctive arts and crafts clearly translate back to a Sanskrit heritage. Over time, their empire would spread to the Aegean Sea, integrating many of the peoples found in those lands, and the capital would move eastward into Iran, but they continued to regard themselves as people of the Caucasus region, separating slowly from Asia, yet not European.

Chapter 4. A Very Ancient People

During that period, the Bible refers to the Elamites, considered by researchers to be one part of the larger society of the Aryan Medes of which the Hebrews had become aware by that time.

The Medean Empire was truly powerful in its heyday. Unlike Hitler's would-be Aryan empire, the kingdoms of the Aryans (including the Hittites and the Medes) did last about a thousand years, or many more if you count from 2400 BCE, the year the Kurds claim that they established a stable kingdom. In the end, it fell prey to the multi-culturalism that an empire must necessarily rely on to sustain itself as its territory grows beyond its original cultural base.

For instance, by the 7th century BCE the growing Medean Empire had incorporated Judea. Again it proved impossible to enslave all of the conquered people, so the Hebrews were allowed to maintain a vassal kingdom. However, the Medes had decided that the Hebrews' main forefather Abraham was one of the minor deities of the Arimanus (Hindu) religion, so the Jews had to renounce Abraham and their god and convert to Aryanism if they were to be recognized at all in the Median society. Many did so, some sincerely and many for public purposes. Armed with this dispensation, Jews were free to move within the empire to make their fortunes, or at least to escape the desolate landscape of Canaan.

The invocation of Abraham is not as odd as it might seem at first glance. Recall that Abraham did not live in modern Israel; he lived in Ur, in today's Iraq, and later moved to Haran (in today's Kurdistan). His son Ishmael would migrate south to Arabia while the other sons moved to the west, wandering as nomads around the Levant, eventually to be enslaved in Egypt, from whence Moses would bring them to permanent residence in Canaan.

The tolerant multi-cultural politics of the Medes created an environment in which a story that belongs in the Thousand and One Nights could flourish in real life. The seed of the ultimate undoing of the Medean empire was an improbable love match between the powerful prince and a less-aristocratic but intelligent and talented girl.

Somewhere in the 6th century BCE (between 599-500 BCE), a Hebrew princess, Esther, married the Medean prince Ahasuerus for political reasons that turned into a love match. During the course of his reign, Esther revealed to her husband that she and her advisors had never renounced Judaism. Based on her wise counsel and devotion, he went against his current advisors and started bringing in more Jews to his inner circle.

Chapter 4. A Very Ancient People

No good deed goes unpunished. Those same Jewish advisors recruited a cabal of Persian generals who deposed Ahasuerus and turned the Medean empire over to the Achaemenid Empire, which itself was a major component of the Persian Empire. The Persian emperor (who was Ahasuerus' grandson) allowed the Medes themselves to retain positions of honor at court. For the next 200 years the Medes had no kingdom or formal existence, but they were a clearly identifiable ethnic group and retained their communities.

The date itself and the actual protagonists are uncertain, and not just because of the transliteration of the names from one language to another. This same set of events recurred repeatedly over a 200-year span. At least for mythological purposes, Kurds use these frequent betrayals of the Medean and Persian emperors, rather than the religious issue, as the reason that they despise Jews. Appropriately, the Turks keep in mind a similar set of insider betrayals by the Kurds.

Living With The Persians

It often happens that conquerors take on some of the better aspects of the societies they have conquered. When they had been subjects of the Medean Empire, the Persians had eventually abandoned their Devas religion and adopted the Aryan religion, which today we know as Zoroastrianism. This was done not by force but by pragmatism. As with the Jews, the Persians had to renounce the Abrahamic connection to operate openly in the Empire. Later, both the Persians and the Medes would be forced to convert again, this time to Islam, which also claimed its descent from Abraham.

After the Persians gained the ascendancy, the Medes were not systematically removed from the Persian Empire. They simply fell prey to the land sharks. The second sons of the nobility and the middle classes used the increasing power of the empire for their own advancement, by becoming landowners in the provinces, the nearest of which happened in this case to be the territory of the Medes. Then as now, politically-connected families found ways to scam or force long-term inhabitants off their own land. Most of the Medes were not rich nobles or merchants; peasants tied to the land could not afford to leave. They had to accept greatly reduced circumstances, but they retained a community pride in their glorious past.

The Achaemenid Empire lasted only 192 years. In the third century BCE, Alexander the Great stormed out of Macedon and swept across the East. First in his path lay the former Medean Empire. This provided a measure of relief for at least one segment of the population: the Hebrews, who would manage

Chapter 4. A Very Ancient People

to latch on in the service of the Greeks, and then of the Romans, while secretly maintaining centuries-old ties to Persian aristocrats. The reservoir of mistrust that the Jews had already created with the Medes due to the Esther business swelled further.

During the Greek occupation, known as the Seleucid Empire, the Medes became known as Kurds, and the prophet Zarathustra became known as Zoroaster. The Seleucids were in their turn overthrown by the Parthians, an ascendant tribe of the Kurds, who reconquered Mesopotamia and the region occupied by the former Medean empire. The Parthians then spent the next 400 years, from 247 BCE to 220 CE, in near perpetual conflict to protect their Kurdish Empire from the Greeks and then from the Romans.

They also faced a new threat. On their northern flanks, the Parthians faced the vanguard of an unending stream of migrating Turkmen retreating from central Asia before the Mongol hordes. The Turkmen had started out as Asian steppe nomads, departing northwest China in 177–176 BCE and arriving in the Caspian Sea area in waves beginning around the year 1 and continuing for centuries. The lands of the Kurds, in the northwestern part of the Parthian empire, lay in the path of the oncoming Turks. That was how, 2200 years ago, the conflict between the Turks and the Kurds began.

Just as the Persians had done to the Medes, the Parthians were constantly under pressure from the Romans, whose system of political advancement required a steady cycle of conquest. Roman governors with an eye on their political futures came out to the East to conquer and re-conquer it, bringing home fabulous wealth with which they could usually buy enough power to set themselves up as the new rulers of Rome. Those familiar to European readers would include the members of the First Triumvirate set up between Crassus, Pompey and Julius Caesar in 60 BCE. The Parthians entered this part of the story by defeating Crassus in 53 BCE and thereby opening the door to Caesar's autocratic rule. By 49 BCE they had re-established control over the entire Levant except for Anatolia (i.e. modern Turkey), which remained under Roman rule.

Detour to Egypt

After the assassination of Caesar, the Parthians decided to support the faction of Brutus, Cassius and Pompey. The defeat of that faction led to the Second Triumvirate under Octavian, Lepidus and Mark Anthony. The Eastern region became the domain of Mark Anthony, who would have to re-conquer it from the Parthians to bring home any of the riches. In 42 BCE, the powerful state of Egypt agreed to ally with the Romans to gain a significant share of the spoils, and Mark Anthony set up a logistical base there for a retaliatory strike against the Parthians. But he became involved with Cleopatra and forgot about the larger mission, and instead it was the Parthians who invaded Rome's remaining territories in 40 BCE.

Despite having a handy and prepared base, Anthony was unable to respond because he had to return to Italy to deal with Octavian, who had in turn been obliged to put down a rebellion sponsored by Anthony's family. On this occasion, the legions refused to fight one another, the triumvirs patched up their quarrel, and Anthony was sent back to the East to deal with the Parthians. Enmeshed again with Cleopatra, Anthony delayed again, but his able lieutenant Ventidius defeated the Parthians, restoring the Roman borders in 39 BCE. In 38 BCE, Ventidius inflicted a total defeat on the Parthians in which their emperor was killed. Anthony freed himself from Egypt long enough to put the affairs of Judea in order, clearing out the opposition to a puppet king by the name of Herod, self-styled "the Great", who would soon play out his role in creating a major new world religion.

In 36 BCE, Cleopatra came through again for Anthony, furnishing a massive army with accompanying ships and supplies. He was able to recover Armenia from the Parthians, but his subsequent attempts to defeat the Parthian Empire itself in open battle failed as the Parthians refused to engage directly. They were, however, able to disrupt his logistics base, and eventually Anthony withdrew with the remaining 40 percent of Cleopatra's troops to secure his base in Syria. This may sound eerily familiar in considering the Russians' experience in Afghanistan and the Americans' miscalculations in Iraq. In this part of the world, things don't change much!

With his territories reduced but now stable, Anthony withdrew himself to Egypt and once again failed to focus on the business of governing. The Roman Empire effectively split into two non-communicating halves until Octavian defeated Anthony and Cleopatra in 30 BCE. Octavian reunited the Empire, renamed himself Augustus Caesar, and deified himself.

The activities of Mark Anthony get more space here than much longer-lasting and perhaps more significant events because he is a character familiar to the English-speaking reader. Introducing the Parthian angle helps to dispel the illusion created by typical Western "classical education" that the Greek and Roman empires were monolithic masters of the known world. In fact they were by no means the only ones on the scene, nor were they all-powerful even at the peak of Rome's power. The known world was considerably larger than

Chapter 4. A Very Ancient People

Rome's "known world" and Rome was just one of many more or less equivalent powers.

It also serves to reinforce the idea that the Kurds are not nearly as obscure as we might have thought. They have been part of the Judeo-Christian, European and near-Asian environment for millennia. It's just that since the demise of the Medean Empire 3500 years ago, they've been living in the shadow of other conquerors.

The Augustinian period saw yet another significant event involving Kurds, or certainly Aryan people. A Magus is the term for a priest of the Zoroastrian religion, which was founded by the Aryans (Medes) and adopted by the Persians. Around 4 BCE, three Magi visited an obscure hamlet in Judea to witness a prophesied birth. The child, of course, would wind up becoming the founder of Christianity. And it was the son of Mark Anthony's Herod who would end up sentencing that child to the crucifixion that would make him into the inspiration for that global religion.

Sometimes a dead martyr is at least as valuable as a live leader. In a much smaller way, this has happened to Sakine Cansiz. She is today an inspiration to the Kurdish people, even those who would never have considered joining the insurgency of the PKK.

More on the Persians

The Parthian Kurdish Empire continued for another two centuries until it was, as usual, brought down from within by a rebellion, being supplanted in 227 CE by the Sassanid Empire. One should note that, after defeating the Parthians, the Sassenids had to conduct an additional campaign to suppress the Kurds at the local level, overcoming an initial significant defeat before finally bringing them under control.

The Sassanids inherited their predecessors' problems: the Roman Empire to the south, now clustered along the Mediterranean shore but anxious to recover its riches throughout the Levant, and the continuing threat of the Turkic nomads, pressing out as always from the Caspian Sea, but now also from Bactria.

By 300 CE, the Romans had recovered Armenia and Georgia, and the Sassenids had to withdraw to the Tigris River (in modern Iraq). Not long afterwards, with the Sassenids apparently weakening and a young boy on the throne, Arabs began raiding northwards. Fighting off these incursions seems to have provided an effective training ground for the boy emperor Shapur II,

Chapter 4. A Very Ancient People

who eventually took control of Transoxania (modern Afghanistan), and then defeated the Romans in 359 CE to recover all the lands that had been ceded in 300 CE. During that campaign, Shapur recorded that he had found Kurdish units serving as mercenaries for the Romans; rather than taking reprisals, he recruited their units.

With the borders secured, Shapur was able to turn his attention to religion, enforcing Zoroastrianism and suppressing the Christianity that the Romans were spreading across the Byzantine Empire. In a now familiar story, his descendant married the daughter of the exiled Jewish king, and allowed her advisers to come to court. Once again, he was then deposed through an insider deal between the Jewish advisors and his wife's nephew, who then permitted the Persian Jews to survive the transition in regimes yet again. Christianity, meanwhile, endured several centuries of on-again off-again tolerance and repression.

The Sassenids conquered modern Uzbekistan, continued to fight off the traditional attackers of the frontiers and dealt with new threats: African raiders (actually Arabs from Egypt and the Arabian peninsula, which Kurds consider to be part of Africa) and an even more persistent lot: the Hephthalites (White Huns), who arrived in 400 CE. Initially defeated by Bahram V and his son, the Huns continued their assaults for over 100 years, finding more success against weaker rulers from whom they exacted tribute. In 484, they nearly overthrew the Sassenid Empire altogether.

The Sassenids decided that loosening up on religious matters had caused a lot of this ill fortune. Kavadh I was initially deposed for excessive liberalism and military inaction, but was restored to power in 498 CE under the promise of a return to what had been working. It took three years of bumbling to get the hang of the new job requirements, but by 532 CE he had administered several defeats to the Romans, who agreed to an "eternal peace" that included massive tribute to be paid to the Sassenids.

Apparently, "eternity" is not such a long time span after all: seven years later, Kavadh's forces captured Petra (modern Jordan) in 541 CE, and his son Kosrau sacked Syria in 573 CE and established vassal kingdoms and military bases in Aden and southern Arabia. After the Kosrau's death in 576 CE, the empire teetered for the rest of the century due to internal strife, rebellions and coups. Fortunately for the Sassenids, the Byzantine Empire was not in any position to capitalize on this. Revitalized in 602 CE by Kosrau II, the Sassenids began assaults on the Romans' outpost cities in Armenia and by

Chapter 4. A Very Ancient People

621 CE had captured the entire Levant as far as Egypt. Constantinople had become an Imperial seat with no empire.

The Sassenids, however, had become an empire with no treasury. Despite all their conquests, the endless warfare had drained their wealth, and they were in no position to capitalize on Byzantine weakness. While most of the Sassenid forces were enmeshed in a protracted siege of Constantinople, the Byzantine Emperor Heraclius was able to mount a major counter-offensive with the assistance of the Turkic people who lived around the Caspian Sea and the Black Sea. He recaptured the entire Levant and much of Mesopotamia (modern Iraq) by 627 CE, and peace was restored when the Sassenids agreed to remain within a much smaller territory not far beyond the borders of modern Iran. Peace came too late; a century of under-resourced the war had left them too weakened to fight off another old foe, now rejuvenated.

Islam Arrives

The Arabs returned to the Levant, bringing Islam with them.

Perhaps it was far-seeing prophecy, or perhaps it has just been made self-fulfilling, but when the Hebrews wrote down their oral traditions some 2000 years before Muhammad (or Mahomet) came on the scene, they recorded the fate of the nation that Ishmael would raise. Although it would be a people separated from their kin by hundreds of miles of impassable desert, it would transpire that "*his hand will be against everyone and everyone's hand against him, and he will live in hostility toward all his brothers*". It has unquestionably been so since the 7th Century CE, with no sign of abatement.

Until he started seeing visions, Mahomet must have followed some other faith. Judaism's texts were incorporated into Islam wholesale and its offshoot, the Christian faith, had been the official creed of the entire Roman Empire for over 200 years. As a merchant, he must have been aware of the Zoroastrian faith, since it was the faith that had been practiced everywhere in the Levant under Medean and Persian control for the previous 4000 years.

Other beliefs were to be found: some Indian scholars insist that the black rock of Mecca had been a temple to Shiva before it became an Islamic cornerstone. They also suggest that Mahomet's family had actually been the official guardians of Shiva's shrine. It may not be such an outlandish claim: one cannot help but note that the recruiting pitch for Shiva's followers was that people who didn't join in with them would be exterminated. The Koran is

Chapter 4. A Very Ancient People

essentially a layering of precisely such dystopian rants on top of a direct transcription of the Torah.

In 632 CE, armed with this murderous fervor, the Muslims arrived on the Sassenid frontier. Defeated in early encounters, their armies continued in waves that eventually eroded the Sassenids' ability to resist. The Empire collapsed, with the nobility fleeing to mountain strongholds in Bactria (Afghanistan and the surrounding areas). Before then, however, the Muslims had captured the outer territories of the empire, including the lands where the Kurds resided. By 650 CE, the Kurds had acquired yet another overlord wanting to suppress their language, culture and religion.

The fall of the Sassanids to Islam was hastened by the fact that they were still continuing to defend their northern frontiers from the ceaseless assaults by the Turkmen. The White Huns had not gone away either; they just took a detour along a northerly route. Many remained in today's "Stans", others proceeded into Russia; and yet more dropped down to the Caucasus and towards the home of the Kurdish people from yet another direction.

The Turkmen were at this point being instigated and funded by the Romans who, unaware of how serious the threat would soon become, were also instigating the Arabs against the more immediate threat from the Persians. As often happens, diplomatic double-dealing and expediency led to dire consequences.

In proper evangelistic fashion, as soon as the Sassenids were out of the way, the Islamic armies continued to march. The next available targets were their erstwhile allies: the Turkic populations in Bactria and the Caspian area. Given the choice of conversion or death, the Turks converted en masse and joined the Islamist armies, which gave an additional boost to their nomadic migration. Some headed to the east to bring the blessings of forced conversion to the Indian sub-continent. Many more joined the Arabs in a great arc leading to the Mediterranean and Egypt. Still others moved off to a mass colonization of Anatolia (modern Turkey) as a prelude to seizing Constantinople, the first gate in the European frontier.

Now both the Arabs and the Turks were attacking their former benefactors in Byzantium. The Turks were not yet residents of the country we know today as Turkey, but by 676 CE they were headed that way.

On their way towards what is now a Turkish heartland, they encountered the Kurds, a people that may have resented their Persian overlords but shared the same ethnic and philosophical backgrounds. Despite centuries of

Chapter 4. A Very Ancient People

forced removals, they remain the substantial majority among those living in the large stretches of land between the mountains of Iran and the Caucasus. This people had learned to kowtow to the Persians and would do so to the Turks and their newly-adopted religion of Islam, convinced after thousands of years of such experience that setbacks measured in decades and centuries are to be expected. With a little wheeling, dealing and foul play, there's always the possibility that the tables can be turned.

Are the Kurds Medes?

In 650 CE, the mighty Medean Empire was not the product of mere myths, but it was certainly a memory that had been dead and buried for 1000 years, except in the hearts and minds of the Kurdish people. Their lands have been taken, they have no independent political existence, their religion is under threat, and religious and civil authorities are suppressing their language. Yet they maintain their separate identity, and they manage to survive in that manner even though (or perhaps because) they spend a great deal of time tweaking their masters' noses. Today, in 2016, all of these things have been going on for over 2000 years. Most of us don't realize it is happening at all. The Kurds never forget it. Nor do those who have had to control them.

This isn't just an exercise in ancient history. Today's Kurds still see themselves as the descendants of those Aryans and Medes, even if their Empire is to the rest of the world just an obscure reference in ancient texts. Despite having no land of their own, they have maintained their sense of cultural identity, even in the face of centuries of constant and active repression and forced assimilation. They remember their glorious past, and they maintain awareness that they are not Arabs, not Turks, not part of any of the would-be regional powers. They are Kurds.

Some modern researchers, relying on linguistics, question the Kurds' view of their lineage. They suggest that the Kurdish language has more in common with societies that evolved from the Iranian rootstock than any Indo-based Aryan culture, indicating that Kurdish is younger, not older, than Persian.

The history of the Medes themselves speaks of millennia of intermixing the components of mighty empires of disparate ethnicity as they swirled around this relatively small portion of the world, first as rulers, then as slaves and outcasts, and in some cases making the cycle again and again. Somewhere in those cycles, we have the chickens and we have the eggs. Despite the Medes leaving far more artifacts than any other culture of the time, there is no way to know which was the creator and which was the copy.

Chapter 4. A Very Ancient People

Even the physical evidence of writings found on Kurdish artifacts dating from the early centuries CE can't prove much either way; the Medean Empire had dissolved 500 years earlier, and the ways and values of the Persian empire had been grafted onto 12 or 20 generations of artisans before these artifacts were made. The grafting didn't just go one way; we know that the Persians adopted the Medes' Aryan religion, for instance. A lot of overlap was to be expected. It's very doubtful that a deductive science such as linguistics, or even a physical science such as DNA testing, could resolve the matter.

It is of no great consequence whether this mystery can be resolved by science or not. The Kurds have a rich oral tradition that permeates their culture. They believe themselves to be descended from the Medes, and since nobody else claims that distinction, perhaps it is true. At least it gives the Kurds a substantial measure of self-respect in a world that has for the past 2000 years variously ignored them, denied that they even exist, or persecuted them. For the past thousand years, the overlords exercising those choices have been the Turks.

Chapter 5. Under Turkish Rule

When the Turks overran the entire Middle East apart from the areas controlled by Arabs, their forces proved to be brutally efficient for victory but not well organized for conquest. When the Sassenids collapsed under the initial onslaught, the Turkish wave passed on, leaving a power vacuum that allowed many small principalities to emerge, including several that were Kurdish.

Working Within the System

In the east, the Kurds re-asserted themselves in the Mosul area in 838 CE. With the Turks occupied in their drive to the Mediterranean, it fell to the Caliph's Arab troops to suppress the uprising. This they did with extreme vigor and mass executions, followed by the conversion of the Kurds who remained alive.

The conversions provided the eastern Kurds with a bit more freedom of action. In the next century, the Caliphs needed ever more troops to fill their armies and made extensive use of Daylamite Kurds, even in the highly trusted ranks of the Personal Guard. Eventually, the Daylamites were given most of modern Iraq and Iran to rule, which they did for the next 200 years. Other Kurdish principalities existed for much of this period in Azerbaijan and eastern Anatolia.

The mass of Turkic nomads hovering around the Caspian Sea coalesced in the 900s into the Seljuk Turks, who around 1000 CE embarked on the capture of the former Sassenid Empire from its Arab overlords. Upon the capture of Baghdad in 1055 CE, the new Caliph of Baghdad (also an Arab) conferred on Tugrul Bey the grandiose title of "King of the East and West" and sent him on his way.

Tugrul's first target was the eastern part of the former Roman colony of Anatolia, the very land currently claimed as a homeland by today's Kurds. It was a collection of war-lord dominions that as early as the 7th century had found themselves out of range of the steadily weakening control of Constantinople. Some were Kurds, others were Roman, and others led pockets of various ethnic groups left over from centuries as a crossroads of migration patterns. These barons played Tugrul against the remnants of the Byzantines to maintain a balance of power until 1071, when the Roman

Chapter 5. Under Turkish Rule

Emperor Diogenes overplayed his hand and was defeated and captured at the battle of Lake Van.

The Seljuks moved forward into central Anatolia, at which point the Turks had finally arrived in the actual country that would become known as Turkey. The Seljuks were fighters, not administrators. They delegated that burden by incorporating the existing independent principalities as-is, including the Kurdish enclaves, which also provided substantial forces.

[*From this point forward, unless it's a confusing situation, we'll be using dates without the BCE and CE markers, since the 4-digit dates will be quite familiar*].

The Seljuk reign lasted only a century. They never found peace with Byzantium in the northwest, Crusaders launched themselves at the Holy Land in the southwest, and the Arabs continued to press from the southeast. Worst of all, the Mongols, who had first driven the Turks to start migrating centuries before, thousands of miles away, continued their implacable advance from the northeast and began to arrive on the scene.

Once again, the most important factor that brought down the Seljuks was someone they had considered to be one of their own. Once again, the betrayer of the Turks would be a Kurd.

Saladin

The most notable (at least in the Western tradition) of all the characters who emerged from this turbulent period was yet another Kurd: Saladin. He is known in romantic history novels as the chivalrous opponent of Richard the Lionheart of England. To the Turks, he was yet another Kurdish turncoat.

As a youth, Saladin had joined his uncle, also a Kurd, who was to lead an expeditionary Seljuk army that was itself composed largely of Kurds. The army left from Aleppo in Syria to put down a rebellion in Egypt, won their battle, and reinstated the Seljuk governor. The grateful governor then named as his vizier the inexperienced Saladin. At that point, Saladin abandoned his playboy ways, became something of an ascetic, wrested control of military forces in the region, and by 1170 began taking on the Crusaders.

Saladin's overlord was Nur-al-Din of the Zengid dynasty, which was in turn a subordinate part of the overall Seljuk empire. Nur-al-Din died in 1174, leaving a young boy to become the Zengid emperor. Saladin decided that his feudal homage to Nur-al-Din did not transfer to the child and marched north

Chapter 5. Under Turkish Rule

to confront not the Crusaders but the Zengids, who declined an offer to split the land at Damascus. Saladin then defeated them at the battle of the Horns of Hama and attained lordship over Syria. Over the next few years, Saladin won and lost some small battles with the Crusaders, but devoted his main effort to securing Mesopotamia (Iraq). He had founded the Ayyubid kingdom, eventually an empire comprising Egypt, Jordan, Iraq, Lebanon and Syria. He had won it fair and square through open combat, but he did not take it from the Crusaders. He took it from the Seljuk Turks. This fact still plays into the animosity between the Turks and the Kurds.

However, in 1187, in a campaign that was more of a comedy of errors initially intended only to make Raymond de Chatillon desist from his new hobby of piracy, Saladin did end up defeating the Crusaders at the battle of the Horns of Hattin (a different place from the Horns of Hama), and went on to recapture Jerusalem.

Western readers may be more familiar with the stories of courtly chivalry exchanged between Saladin and Richard I (nicknamed "Lionheart") of England. Richard defeated Saladin decisively in 1191, and could have moved on to retake Jerusalem, but Richard judged that the Crusaders did not have the logistical strength needed to hold it. Instead, he concluded a 3-year truce that provided the Christians with access to Jerusalem. Richard returned home with a major victory to his credit, obscuring the fact that he had not actually restored control of the Holy City. Meanwhile, Saladin, who had lost the war, still retained control of his empire.

It didn't last long. In 1243 the Seljuk Turks were defeated at Kose Dagh by a new entrant, the Mongols, who then turned the multiple vassal states into vassals of their own. The Kurdish Ayyubids lasted a bit longer, until 1341, when their domains also fell to the Mongols.

Then, from a Levantine perspective, the Mongols simply disappeared. They just wandered off, leaving their new empire behind.

Their departure was not as whimsical as it seemed to the Levantines. It arose from a combination of causes, including natural disasters that led to dynastic strife back in the homeland and a plague that spread by sea. The plague first decimated the Mongol forces then trying to subdue the Black Sea ports, from which it spread quickly to the Mongols' inland armies as well. In 1405, the last remaining Mongol ruler, a particularly vicious character known as Timur the Lame, took his armies back to China in a bid to take over the entire tottering Mongol empire, allowing his own domain in Turkey to evaporate almost overnight and leaving nothing in its place.

Chapter 5. Under Turkish Rule

The Ottomans

The small principality of Oghuz in western Turkey survived under the hands-off administrations of the Turks and Mongols, and produced in the late 1300s a warlord named Osman. He began defeating and absorbing the neighboring small principalities into an ever-expanding domain that became the Ottoman Empire. By 1400 the Ottomans had established control of most of Anatolia and even formed beachheads on European territories of the crumbled Byzantine Empire. Constantinople stood alone, and it continued to do so for over 50 years, falling at last in 1453.

Meanwhile, the disappearance of the Mongols allowed Persian and Kurdish princes to reinstall themselves in the east. It was during this period that the Kurds introduced to conventional Islam the sects known as Zaza, Qizilbash or Alawism, which survive to the modern day. Chapter 7 provides additional detail on how the Kurds were able to slide their Zoroastrian heritage back into the Islamic religion that they had been forced to adopt.

By 1501, a succession of Persian mini-dynasties attempted to consolidate their own rule while stretching to the west before running into the emergent Ottomans. They carried on this conflict for nearly 300 years with varying degrees of success. The Kurds lived in the domains of both the new Persian emirs in the east and the Ottomans in the west and, as usual, staged a number of local rebellions against their overlords.

Some were successful, although, as so often happened with the Kurds, they couldn't win even when they were winning. The family of Shah Abbas I of the Safavid dynasty had originally been Yazidi Kurds, but his grandfather had converted to Shi'a Islam. Abbas undertook a repression of his Sunni subjects, including the Kurds and numerous other ethnic groups, all of whom then sided with the Sunni Ottomans against Abbas. By 1600, Abbas returned the favor: he developed the idea of wholesale deportations of troublemakers, not just Kurds but also Circassians, Armenians and Georgians. He relocated many Kurds to Khorasan on the Turkmenistan border, where many ended up as slaves, and their descendants still speak medieval Kurdish today.

The conflict continued through a peak in the all-out Persian-Ottoman War in 1775. By then the Zands, who were Shi'a Lak Kurds, had succeeded the Safavids. They defeated the Ottomans and moved into Iraq and the Caucasus, but not for long. In 1794 the Zands were in turn supplanted by the Qajars,

Chapter 5. Under Turkish Rule

Shi'a Azeri Turks, who retained their rule over Persia into what we might consider modern history.

Meanwhile, in the western part of the Ottoman Empire things were going much better for the Kurds. As the Ottomans consolidated their reign beginning in 1501, Selim I appointed Idris Bitlisi the Historian, a Kurd, to organize the Empire. Bitlisi arranged for Kurds to occupy lands vacated in the decades of warfare, and across Anatolia Kurdish principalities resumed. It was a mixed blessing; the intent of awarding these territories was to have them serve as a border protection force, and they would certainly earn their keep. For the next 200 years, Kurds who lived in eastern Anatolia and northern Iraq found their lands to be the target of every spat between the Ottomans and the Persians.

Eventually, the two kingdoms achieved equilibrium and the Ottomans began to consolidate their rule within their domains. Beginning around 1800, they started suppressing the independent principalities and cities, eliminating the last of them in 1847. The indomitable Kurds were back at it again in 1880 when Sheik Ubeydullah staged an uprising against both the Ottomans *and* the Persian Qajars, demanding an autonomous Kurdistan. Taking on the two regional powers at the same time was bound to end poorly, and so it did.

While that effort was repressed, the Ottomans elected to defuse the situation by appointing Kurds to prominent government positions, and this seemed to suffice for the next 40 years. Large numbers of Kurdish troops served faithfully in the Ottoman army during World War I. On the other hand, a fair number of Kurds also assisted the British in their campaign in the Levant. Both sides promised the Kurds an autonomous homeland after the war.

When an independent Kurdistan appeared on the maps of the Sevres Treaty, their goal appeared to be in sight.

Ataturk

The man known as Kemal Ataturk was not born with that name. That accolade, which translates in effect to "Father of the Turkish Country", would not be awarded until 1934. Although it was Kurdish troops who had put him in power, he rewarded them only with use and murder. The Kurds would never recognize him as a father-figure, other than perhaps as an example of a violent abuser.

Chapter 5. Under Turkish Rule

At the end of the World War, Mustafa Kemal, one of the most successful of the Turkish generals, had wound up in command of the Palestine front. Even the accounts of his British opponents record that he performed very successfully. When the Armistice was signed, he oversaw the evacuation of all Turkish troops south of Turkey back to the home country. The remnants of the Empire continued to operate from its base in Constantinople, as did the occupying Allied forces

The British had seen a need for a somewhat functioning Turkey to contains the Russians. They left the Ottoman Empire in place to rule over its very diminished territories, with fairly substantial armed forces for self-defense.

Concerned at the prospect of turning over the control of the military to a man with a public image as one of the country's few war heroes who was also showing an unhealthy interest in politics, the Ottomans decided not to install Kemal as the head of this army as he had anticipated. Instead, he received an assignment that was a transparent snub. He found himself commanding an Army Corps based in the middle of nowhere and composed of seven divisions of non-Turkic troops (in other words, largely formed of Kurds and other Caucasian ethnicities) who were assumed to have little interest in the machinations of Turkish politics. Clearly, they knew little about the Kurds.

Upon arriving at his Corps' base near present-day Ankara, Kemal declared that the national sovereignty was under threat, which was inarguably true, given that the country was already under Allied occupation under the terms of the Armistice. However, that observation ran counter to the Emperor's current policy; the Ottomans declared him an outlaw and ordered him arrested which, since he controlled one-third of the army, was impractical.

In response, he convened a meeting of those who were active in opposing the British occupation. The attendees appointed Kemal as the head of the executive committee of the group that would become known as the Sivas Congress, and they created the "National Pact" to resist the occupation. That, in turn, formed the basis for a nationwide group that swept to victory in the next and last elections under the Ottoman Empire in December 1919. In March 1920, that Parliament enacted the National Pact, prompting the British to dissolve it. Kemal then organized new elections across Turkey and set up another body, the Grand National Assembly, which in turn elected him as Speaker.

The Armistice to end the war had been signed and was being implemented, but the details remained to be resolved via the Treaty of Sevres. That treaty

Chapter 5. Under Turkish Rule

featured the partition not only of former Ottoman possessions, which was expected. The uncertain factor was the outline of the country of Turkey itself. That was not simply a matter of putting it back the way it was before the war; historically there was no country of Turkey, nor had there ever been one. There were regions that the Turks considered their homeland, and the Kurds made the same argument about Kurdistan, and both territories appeared on the Sevres map.

Kemal lobbied hard for a unitary Turkey, but the Emperor's Vizier signed the Treaty anyway.

The GNA authorized the formation of a standing army. Over the next few months, the GNA forces held the combined forces of the Allies and the troops that had remained loyal to the Ottomans in check in Constantinople.

Meanwhile, Kemal defeated the Armenians (who were under French leadership) on the eastern border in 1921. Kemal also directed the elimination of the entire Armenian population in the region, which had already been reduced from millions to an estimated 20,000 people by the Ottomans' systematic exterminations since 1915. Note that Kemal's massacre was technically carried out while Turkey was still under the rule of the Ottoman Empire; he is remembered as replacing that government and is seldom linked to his own phase of this massacre. The Western world continues to press this issue with Turkey, which has shown no remorse and does not even admit that it happened. The Kurds believe that, given the opportunity, it might happen again ... only to them.

Far less well-known was the 1921 Kochgiri Rebellion. The Kurds had hoped for national recognition at the end of the World War; in 1918 their leaders met in Constantinople to form the Society for the Rise of Kurdistan to negotiate that outcome. As the post-war diplomacy dragged on, British Army major Edward Noel used the increasing Turkish seizures of lands held by Kurds as the focal point and succeeded in bringing the situation to a boiling point among the Kochgiri tribe, which resided in the area of Dersim, the hub of the Kurdish community.

Ironically, the Turks had used largely Kurdish troops to form the bulk of the army that had been sent out to crush the Armenians. Now the non-Kurdish troops returned to do the same to the Kurds. One of the Turkish Army leaders (the records are hazy as to which one) who set out to crush the Armenians, is reported to have announced the Kochgiri campaign in the following terms: "In Turkey, we cleaned up people who speak "zo" [Armenian], I'm going to clean up people who speak "lo" [Kurdish] by their roots". Among

Chapter 5. Under Turkish Rule

the thousands of casualties were most of the troops who had accompanied the Turks into Armenia. With very few survivors to tell the tale, it's not entirely clear what exactly did happen during this rebellion. What is certain is that it was so brutal even by Turkish standards that its leader, Nurettin Pasha, was hauled back to Ankara for trial by the Grand National Assembly and was saved only by the direct intervention of Kemal.

By the time that the western diplomats finished their cocktail parties and settled into the business of actually producing a final treaty, the Turks had already made themselves a de facto state by crushing and annexing the various ethnic areas that might have had an equally valid claim to self-representation, most particularly the Kurds. Eventually, in 1923 the League of Nations acceded to replacing the Treaty of Sevres with the Treaty of Lausanne that removed the partition provisions, confirmed Turkish control of the Dardanelles and the Bosporus, and recognized the GNA as the government of Turkey within the borders that the GNA itself had defined. Once again, Kurdistan literally disappeared off the table.

Kemal, who had been exposed to European countries during his military service, was determined to make Turkey into a modern secular state. Neither "secular" nor "state" appealed to the Kurds. They'd already experienced the rise of the Young Turks who had taken over the Ottoman government during the war and decided to deport the Kurds from the provinces near the Russian frontier, ostensibly because they might be security risks but in reality to disperse them and weaken their political cohesiveness.

By 1924, Sheik Said from eastern Anatolia, who was reputed to be a Kurd, led a group that opposed much of what Kemal sought to accomplish because it contradicted Islamic law. On a grander scale, they also insisted that the Caliphate should not have been overthrown because, despite its dismal record in ruling, the Caliphate was an essential component of the Sunni version of Islamic doctrine. Although Said launched local militias, Kemal refrained from mobilizing a military response to purely political opposition; he was able to confront and defeat Said's adherents in the Congress through parliamentary and legal means over the next 3 years.

However, Kemal did have to suppress a number of other Kurdish revolts over the next decades, including the Beytushshebap rebellion in 1925, the Mukti rebellion in 1927, and the attempt sponsored by the British in 1927 to create a Republic of Ararat. As revolts continued into the 1930s, with uprisings at Savur, Seyidan, Berazan and Dersim, the Turks placed Kurdistan under martial law. In 1934 the GNA passed the Law On

Chapter 5. Under Turkish Rule

Resettlement, which required the Kurds to become Turkish in their manners, dress and speech, or face resettlement elsewhere.

Having only recently seen what Turkification had looked like for the Armenians, to the Kurds it seemed that there wasn't much difference being killed in place or being deported in order to be killed somewhere else. Under the leadership of Seyid Riza, they resisted this law. That choice ended up creating the very outcome they had feared in the first place: the 1937 Dersim Massacre. Over 40,000 Kurds are known to have been killed and many more are simply unknown due to inadequate records. Even so, the Turkish government realized that it would be impractical to resettle all of the Kurds.

Fortunately for the Kurds, it was too early by only a few years for the Turks to observe the demonstration by Hitler as to how to solve such a problem on a mass scale. Instead, the Turks started to solve the problem through the reverse process: importing Albanians and Assyrians to dilute the population. It was also as a result of the Dersim Massacre that the Turks changed the town's name from the Kurdish Dersim (motherland) to the Turkish Tunceli (bronze mine).

More recently, on November 23, 2011 then-Prime Minister Erdoğan, who was seeking rapprochement with the Kurds while he was working on subduing the Gülen movement, gave an apology for the Dersim operation, describing it as "one of the most tragic events of our recent history".

After Ataturk's death in 1938, more open-minded Turkish administrations would move towards offering more Kurdish participation in the government, peaking in the 1950s. That ended with the 1960 coup.

Further east, in Iraqi Kurdistan, the Kurds did manage to establish a Kurdish Kingdom from 1924-25, and thereafter maintained a level of autonomy until conflict flared up again in the 1960s and 1970s, when substantial oil reserves were discovered in the Kirkuk region.

We've made the journey from 2500 BCE to a time within living memory for some readers. Throughout that time, the Kurds have been oppressed by someone, and for the past 1500 years, those people were the Turks.

Readers from countries such as the UK, France, Germany and Japan, which slaughtered millions of each other's citizens within the past 100 years and yet are fast friends today, may find absurd that these ancient histories are somehow relevant as a *casus belli* today. To American readers, with attention spans measured in minutes and very little education about even

Chapter 5. Under Turkish Rule

their own limited 400-year history, it's impossible to imagine that these stories are much more than fairy tales like the Arabian Nights.

Those who had the opportunity to serve in Iraq and Afghanistan will attest that past histories are very relevant in this part of the world. Its inhabitants make very little distinction between 635 BCE and 6:35 p.m.

Chapter 6. From Rhetoric to Revolution

We have reached the part of history where we have written records on both sides and we can support or refute those records with personal memory rather than handed-down tales. Even so, meeting the Turks and the Kurds of today requires an acknowledgement that a large part of who they are is enmeshed with who they have been, or, more particularly, who they think they have been.

Their mutual perceptions are unflattering, and their long history provides many objective reasons for the Turks and the Kurds to distrust one another. As it happens, all that history is just an aggravating factor. They've done plenty enough to each other in just the past 50 years to fuel the continuation of that mistrust for many generations to come.

Revolutionary Roots

The Apoist revolutionary movement began with the worldwide protests that built up through the decade but came to a peak in 1968. Americans think of the youth unrest in the late 1960s as an American phenomenon. It was much wider.

It was, however, the American connection that turned the mixture of university-age idealism and hooliganism into global hysteria. There was no high moral cause; the Americans had brought on the age of television and had inadvertently discovered its striking power to elicit a strong emotional reaction to whatever messages the networks chose to disseminate. The media brought down the US President, Lyndon Johnson, through its disingenuous coverage of the Vietnam War and the domestic protests, and it appeared that, given supportive media coverage, mass protests and street violence could undermine a government to the point of surrender. The protests in the US were matched by marches and movements in London, Paris, Berlin and Rome.

The problem was that then, just as now, getting traction required getting media coverage. In a congested field getting media coverage meant doing something even more news-worthy (i.e. outrageous) than anyone else. Strikes and protests spread worldwide, especially in 1968. That year's events included the French season of wildcat strikes in May; the open emergence of the Troubles in Northern Ireland; the Tlatelolco massacre in Mexico City in

Chapter 6. From Rhetoric to Revolution

October; and the eruption of a hot-war guerilla campaign against the military dictatorship in Brazil.

Turkey, too, saw the emergence of a young socialist movement that caused its share of trouble. The Revolutionary Youth Federation, while speaking the language of human rights, was more often to be found urging the violent overthrow of the Turkish Government.

This anti-government fervor was odd occurring in Turkey, which had only emerged from military rule in 1965. Despite the convenient rhetoric, the demonstrations weren't about democracy or human rights; they were about jobs. Since the time of Ataturk, both military and civil governments had focused on geopolitical issues rather than on relieving economic or social problems, but now the post-war aid lifelines were drying up. Increasing discontent among youth groups and trade unions reflected concerns over declining economic prospects, not about social or government reform.

Out of the potpourri of protest groups, university-age youths in Turkey found themselves ever more drawn towards a group that was different. The group that became known as Dev-Genç wasn't a forum for debating macroeconomic principles. It sought not merely to change or enhance the system, but to revolutionize it to serve the people of Turkey: in other words, to turn the system upside down..

Dev-Genç began in 1965 as an avowedly Marxist-Leninist cell calling itself the Federation of Thought Clubs (FKF). Over time, an umbrella organization arose to coordinate activities between FKF and other similar groups; that organization was the Revolutionary Youth Federation of Turkey, more simply known as the Revolutionary Youth (Turkish: Dev-Genç).

While the FKF and similar organizations may have provided some innocent social activities for youths, they were true to their names in fomenting violent action. University campuses in Turkey became the frontline for Turkish struggles against the system, and the movement spread with each protest.

For the most part, Kurdish students could not participate in these protests on a nationwide basis or even in the national capital, because most Kurds were confined to the Kurdish area in the southeast part of Turkey. On the other hand, this provided more opportunity for Kurdish organizers to become a close-knit group well-known to their constituents, hardly known at all to the Turkish government, and able to spot government agents instantly simply because they were outsiders.

Chapter 6. From Rhetoric to Revolution

Abdullah Öcalan, however, was lucky enough to secure a government appointment which permitted (indeed, required) him to leave Turkish Kurdistan to take up a position in Istanbul. Soon after his arrival he discovered and joined Dev-Genç.

The student disturbances peaked during the landmark protests against a visit to Turkey in February 1969 by the American Sixth Fleet. In clearing the streets, the security forces killed a young revolutionary by the name of Vedat Demircioglu at Istanbul Technical University. That further infuriated the revolutionary youth movement, which saw him as a murdered martyr and organized even more protests that culminated in the First Bloody Sunday. Later in the year, Dev-Genç members set US Ambassador Robert Komer's car on fire while he was visiting an Ankara university campus

Dev-Genç and other groups claimed that their intent was only "social changes to relieve problems they didn't cause but only inherited." Their preference for violence and violent demise shows an agenda that went far beyond that. It was revolution for the sake of revolution. These confrontations with the US had nothing to do with the issues that the students saw in their own government, but they were tactically exciting and generated a lot of publicity.

They also proved to be a strategic disaster, as the US now devoted resources to a response. It was not the sort of response the hooligans had hoped for. CIA agent Aldrich Ames, who would go on to infamy when he was uncovered as a Soviet mole, discovered and revealed to the Turkish government the identities of a vast number of Dev-Genç members, including Ulash Bardakçi, Mahir Çayan, and Cihan Alptekin.

Organizing Dissent

After the 1971 Turkish coup d'état, the Turkish Government banned Dev-Genç and arrested its alleged members. Of these, 226 members were tried at Ankara Military Court, 154 at Istanbul Military Court, and 34 at Diyarbakir Military Court.

The revolutionary youth movement of Turkey gave birth to true heroes, notably Deniz Gezmish, Mahir Cayan, Ibrahim Kaypakkaya and Sinan Cemgil, all of whom have (posthumously) found their way to the top rank of revolutionary role models.

Chapter 6. From Rhetoric to Revolution

- Deniz Gezmish was a Marxist-Leninist revolutionary and also the leader of Dev-Genç. He was executed by hanging on 6 May 1972 in Ankara Central Prison, along with Huseyin Inan and Yusuf Aslan.

- Another revolutionary, Ibrahim Kaypakkaya, was imprisoned and treated to horrific torture before expiring in prison.

- Mahir Çayan was a Turkish politician and the leader of the People's Liberation Party-Front of Turkey, a violent revolutionary group. He escaped from prison in October 1971. In March 1972, in an attempt to obtain hostages to trade to stop the impending execution of his comrades, he launched a raid on an isolated British compound on Turkey's northeast coast near Unye. The response may have been more than he had counted on, because it happened that this compound was isolated due to its role as a "black" facility, meaning that it was an unacknowledged and very sensitive facility operated by the British GCHQ (an intelligence and security organization responsible for providing signals intelligence, known as SIGINT, to the British government). Çayan captured three of the GCHQ staff members and took them to the inland village of Kizildere. After a search, Turkish Special Forces located the group in the Mayor's house at Kizildere and surrounded it. After lengthy negotiations conducted personally by the Interior Minister, an extensive firefight broke out in which all three of the GCHQ staff were killed in the firefight. Only one of the twelve kidnappers survived.

The revolutionary groups celebrated these martyrs and used them to inspire their troops and future recruits. Their standard for heroism is not achieving victory despite adversity; it is of resisting the inevitable to the point of death. If anything, they had too many heroes. The revolutionaries had hoped to create fundamental change in the Turkish system. They ended up putting an end only to themselves.

Dev-Genç did continue for some time as an underground organization after it was banned. In its brief moment of publicity, the activities of Dev-Genç and its fellow organizations within the FKF, coupled with public outrage at the Government's usual over-reaction to mundane annoyances, affected millions of youth in Turkey. Beyond its own existence, it inspired various offshoots, including Devrimci Yol, the Revolutionary Workers and Peasants Party of Turkey, and the Kurdistan Workers' Party (PKK).

Chapter 6. From Rhetoric to Revolution

Enter Öcalan

During this period, Abdullah Öcalan was just being introduced to Dev-Genç. How did he avoid getting caught up in the roundup?

Some writers have suggested that the Turkish authorities were already using him as an asset and ensured that he would not be caught up in the dragnet. A more likely reason is that at this point he was an extremely small fish, only 3 years out of high school and still in university. Of course, this was also true of most Dev-Genç leaders.

After Abdullah Öcalan graduated from a Turkish vocational high school in Ankara (Ankara Tapu-Kadastro Meslek Lisesi) in 1968, he obtained a government position in the Diyarbakir Title Deeds Office. He was relocated one month later to Bakirkoy, a part of Istanbul. While assigned in Istanbul, he enrolled in the Istanbul Law Faculty but, after the first year, he transferred to Ankara University to study political science.

In his short stay in Istanbul, he found ways to involve himself in several subversive activities. He participated in political demonstrations (then, as now, a more provocative act in Turkey than it would have been in the West) and as a result of those demonstrations he found himself being tried by a martial law court. Perhaps because of his status as a public employee, the public prosecutor urged the harshest possible sentence.

Then some odd things happened. First, he was acquitted by the military court. That was unusual enough, and in this case there was no doubt that he had actually committed this offense. Then, despite being over the required age and having a record of anti-government activity, he was awarded a scholarship by the Ministry of Finance to study for a finance degree. This in turn was irregular because he was permitted to transfer between government departments without first passing the examinations required to qualify for that agency's specialty. Capping it all off, he was transferred back to the capital, again despite his record of agitation. These oddities are the basis for a belief that persists in some quarters that this transfer was actually endorsed because the Turkish intelligence service was grooming him to infiltrate Dev-Genç.

If that was the case, it was a decision that then-President Süleyman Demirel and his successors would later regret. The PKK was to become a much greater threat to the state than Dev-Genç had ever dreamed of being.

Chapter 6. From Rhetoric to Revolution

Öcalan joined the Ankara Higher Education Association (AYOD), itself one of the several political offshoots of the Dev-Genç. He reached the leadership circle very quickly because of his energy and his effectiveness as an organizer. Once on the inside, he demanded that if Dev-Genç was really about being freedom fighters, then it must recognize in its written plan the freedom of the Kurdish people living in Turkey. That idea was rejected immediately by most of the Turkish leadership of Dev-Genç. Instead, they promised to give Kurdish people freedom after Turkey's liberation from capitalism and imperialism. That seemed unlikely to occur in the foreseeable future.

Abdullah Öcalan worked with the leadership of Dev-Genç in constant efforts to get them to recognize some of the Kurdish rights and interests, rather than simply demanding that Kurds support them unconditionally.

Kurdish Leader Öcalan and co-founder Cemil Bayik, in the early days

He reminded the other leaders of how the Kurds had helped the Ottoman royal family to build their Ottoman Empire. For Western readers, it might seem somewhat bizarre to refer to a debt of honor from some 500 years earlier, but for both Turks and Kurds it was apparently a perfectly reasonable observation. The Kurds, as a large minority, had persuaded other principalities to join in with the Ottomans on the basis that the Empire would provide a home country for every Muslim. In reality, the Ottoman Empire ended up serving only Turks.

Chapter 6. From Rhetoric to Revolution

Closer to home and closer to the modern day, the Kurdish people had helped Mustafa Kemal Ataturk to establish the modern Republic of Turkey. Nearly the entire Arab world joined the UK and France against Ataturk, it was only the Kurds who stood with him. But later, while proclaiming that his intention was to build a new and better Turkey for citizens, he betrayed his only loyal ally (the Kurds) and did not follow through for them, and the country soon returned to being for Turks only.

After several years of this effort, it became clear that Dev-Genç had no interest in any Kurdish issues, or even in letting Kurds act as equal partners within it. Öcalan decided to found his own Kurdish youth movement.

The new organization was named the Apoist Youth Movement, Apo being Abdullah Öcalan's nickname.

One of its core principles from the outset was to follow the lead of Mao Tse-Tung (now known as Mao Zedong) and reject Russian sponsorship. It had not escaped Öcalan's attention that all of the national movements that had started out with Russian guidance and money had ended up becoming slave states in the Soviet Empire. Öcalan was determined not to let that happen to Kurdistan.

The Apoist movement was nothing much in the beginning, but for Öcalan it did create the unintended consequence of having him off the scene and below the radar during the 1971 coup. That gave him a decade to create a loyal following and solid base that could weather difficulties. Over time, the Apoist youth movement spawned so many related organizations, some of which exercised considerable power, that the term became a more generic reference to all of those groups working for Kurdish visibility and autonomy within an overall socialist framework.

The first cadres of the Apoist Youth Movement that formed the nucleus of the PKK organization were idealistic, motivated and very young, mostly between the ages of 20 to 25, including Öcalan himself. They had little experience of the hard realities of actual life without parental assistance. They had few resources. They didn't really even have any rational foundation or agenda for the establishment of their mass movement. Consequently, the group bent itself entirely to the guidance of its leader, Abdullah Öcalan, and over time it found its place as the leading player in the Kurdish cause.

The PKK that Abdullah Öcalan started with a group of a handful of loyal friends has now become a struggle taken up by millions of Kurds worldwide demanding the liberation of the Kurdish people in their own lands from the

Chapter 6. From Rhetoric to Revolution

Persian, Arab, and Turkish occupiers. They are not just demanding it with pointless speeches: they are winning their right to self-respect with their blood and courage on the battlefields of Iraq and Syria.

****

The Apoists also had a hidden gem whose value they surely could not have fully appreciated at that time: a new recruit by the name of Sakine Cansiz.

These years of global revolutionary spirit drew tens of thousands of young women, still innocent enough of real life to retain their ideals of a world filled with peace, love and understanding. They followed the siren call of young men (in those days, the leaders were all men) who were intense, articulate, or in many cases simply good-looking. Some of these young gurus were sincere but naive. Some were cynically using the unwitting tools that offered themselves as the cannon-fodder for ambition.

In most cases, when the thrills and the tear gas wore off, the charismatic leader would be captured, killed or bought off, and their revolutionary cells would just dry up. In the West, the women camp followers would be able to put those years behind them and return to a humdrum existence in playing a productive role in the social order.

In Turkey, simply returning home was a less likely outcome. Some would be killed or maimed by police actions before or after their arrest. Many would learn that their families had been abused as surrogates in their absence. Most found themselves, as the possessors of extensive police records, permanently excluded from the possibility of any substantive participation in the society at large, condemned to eking out an existence on the fringes.

A few would find themselves fighting for their cause in reality, which very few women revolutionaries in any country would ever undergo. Of those, a very small number, truly one in a million, would distinguish themselves such as to ascend to a higher plane than they could ever have imagined.

That is what happened to one ordinary high-school girl in Turkey, happy to hand out amateurish flyers urging a few people to show up for furtive meetings, anything to win a favorable glance from The Leader. The same girl, for the "crime" of handing out those flyers, would be confined in the most forbidding prison in Turkey -- while the objects of this loyalty were safely ensconced three countries away. That young girl would grow quickly and shockingly to womanhood in conditions only imagined by Dante and Bosch but brought convincingly to life by the wardens of the modern yet medieval state of Turkey. That young woman would emerge from that prison, damaged

Chapter 6. From Rhetoric to Revolution

in body but not in spirit, the one in a million who transcended these horrific events to become the embodiment of the Kurdish experience.

That woman was Sakine Cansiz. The rest of the book is her story.

Chapter 7. Sakine Meets Apo

One of the cells of the Apoist movement operated from Kirakos, known in Turkish as Batman. That, in turn, is a part of other progressively larger villages that become the municipality of Dersim (called Tunceli by Turks). It might be a rather remote area, but a Kurdish group such as the Apoists had to set up some representation there because, as the town from which Zoroaster came, it is the religious and ethnic center of the Kurds.

Dersim lies in the Munzur Valley, surrounded by the Munzur Mountain range, whose ruggedness had provided its Kurdish inhabitants with a form of protection in turn from the Mongolian Turks, from Islamic Arabs, and now from hyper-nationalist Turks. Isolation has some advantages. The air in the valley is free from pollution; the Munzur River, unlike most in Turkey, runs freely, beautiful and drinkable. Wildlife abounds, and there are 1,518 registered species of plants growing in the Munzur Valley; the perfume of wild flowering plants covers the region during the spring season.

In this ideal place, in those idealistic years, earnest organizers of the Apoist Youth Movement held meetings not too different from those urging "give peace a chance" in Europe and America. They explained the movement, its ideals and its goals to any who were interested.

One such meeting was attended by a girl named Sakine Cansiz. She was not even a "young woman" yet; she had no idea of who she was or what the world was about. In a Turkey that was rapidly becoming less secular and more Islamic, she was not expected to have ambitions or even much of a self-image, and she harbored no great intention of being anything more than her family had foreseen for her. She was just a schoolgirl, joining other young people randomly attending such a meeting out of a feeling of intrigue or excitement, or perhaps just for something to do in this quiet community.

She would become the most famous and revered inhabitant of Dersim, perhaps even of all Kurdistan, since Zoroaster himself. But at this moment, she is just a schoolgirl, about to have her eyes opened to her own reality.

****

Sakine Cansiz was born to Ismail and Zeynep Cansız in 1958 in Taxti-Xalil village, another of the very minor appendages of Dersim. She had five brothers and two sisters, and the family lived on the ridge above the village in a modest home surrounded by stores of wood they collected to use for heating

Chapter 7. Sakine Meets Apo

and cooking during the long, cold and snowy winters of this mountainous region.

Young Sakine Cansiz

Her father was a military officer who wanted the family to blend in with the military and government communities in which he circulated. She went to a regular Turkish school without knowing at all that her family came from a Zaza Kurd background, let alone having any idea of what that might have meant.

That is itself was somewhat remarkable. In 1938, only 20 years previously, Dersim had been the epicenter of some of the strongest resistance to the increasing centralization of Turkish rule. In response, it had become the site of the largest internal deployment of Turkish troops. Reading between the lines of the edicts issued at the time, Dersim was subjected to heavy ethnic cleansing to reduce the proportion of non-Turkic inhabitants. In other words, the idea was to get rid of as many of the Kurds as possible, particularly any who might cause trouble.

Why the focus on Dersim? In the Kurdish language, Dêsim means "the motherland", a title earned by being the birthplace of the prophet Zoroaster. The town had become Dersim over the centuries. In suppressing Kurdish protests, the Turks also sought to eliminate Kurdish ethnic symbology, and they renamed the city as Tunceli, "the bronze mine". It might be so on the official maps, but nobody owned any of those; in spoken Kurdish, the motherland it was and remained.

Zazas and Alawites

When Islam arrived in this motherland centuries earlier, their new religion appeared to feature killing off everyone who would not sign up for it. The Kurds publicly endorsed it by taking on the most prominent aspects that happened to coincide with their original religion, but many of them didn't discard many elements of their much longer-held beliefs. Instead, they fashioned a compromise of sorts between their ancient Zoroastrian religion and that of the new religion, and this combination was known as Zaza.

The Zazas and their Syrian cousins, the Alawites, have always been highly secretive, which is probably wise, considering that the punishment in Islam for heresy is instant death and that the basic tenets of Zazaism have little to do with the Islamic faith. Its doctrines are centered around the concept of a holy Trinity, it incorporates the Gnostic texts rejected by the contemporary decisions of the early Christian church, it celebrates a form of mass with consecrated wine, and it reveres Mary Magdalen. It also includes a belief in reincarnation, with progression up or down the scale towards becoming an enlightened being depending on one's behavior in the previous life. In other words, it incorporates the major tenets of all the religions that dotted the Middle East in the year 1000 when Zazaism was born.

While these mashed-up beliefs are considered very odd, they are not unprecedented. The practices of Zaza are based on Sufi elements of the *Bektashi tariqa* (path) and are quite similar to the practices laid down by the Shi'ite Safavid dynasty that for two centuries would rule the area that forms today's Iran.

Zazaism was formalized in the late 13th century and spread, as religions do, also taking on the names of Alevism and Qizilbash. The adherents were periodically subjected to ethnic cleansing by whichever Turkic faction had the upper hand and desired more land. Not surprisingly, many Zazas or Alevis fled Anatolia, as the Turks had intended, and a variant of the religion appeared in the adjoining lands (i.e. in today's Syria), where it became known as Alawism.

Chapter 7. Sakine Meets Apo

Modern Muslims remain split as to whether Alawism constitutes legitimate Islamic worship or not. It seems likely that it is tolerated within Islam on geopolitical rather than religious grounds; Alawites happen to control the strategically-positioned state of Syria, which has a frontier with Israel and has oil.

That worked for the Alawites in Syria; life was not so rosy for the Zazas in Turkey. In Anatolia in the 1960s, the Turkish government continued to repress Kurds. Muslim prayers were required to be conducted in Arabic, a language that meant no more to the average Kurd (or even to the average Turk) than Catholic High Masses said in Latin mean to the average Christian in Europe or America. Cansiz' family got around that restriction when they secretly practiced the Zaza faith, sneaking in Kurdish variations on the standard Shi'a prayers:

"Oh Ana Fatima, oh St. Ali, St. Hasan, St. Huseyin, liberate Kurdistan and Dersim, oh almighty god ....".

Even this provides a measure of irony. The Shi'a saints had been canonized precisely because, in their living roles as political and religious leaders in their physical lives, they were responsible for the suppression of the Kurds and of Zoroastrianism in the first place.

Sakine Awakens

Sakine was no different from many other Kurds in being unaware of her history and culture. That is part of the Gülen agenda, because a culture without a language or history cannot last very long. As part of the Turkification program that began in the 1930s and continues to this day, the estimated 30 million Kurds in Turkey speak only Turkish at work, at school, and even (with the threat of spies everywhere) in the home. Only a few households dare to mix in some Kurdish with the Turkish.

Children who bring Kurdish to school are sternly corrected, and it may well result in an investigation of the parents. Children everywhere create relentless peer pressure to fit in. In Turkey, those who don't speak proper Turkish are ridiculed by their schoolmates until they too rebuke their parents and resist any effort to take them away from the mainstream of their schoolmates.

Of course, all this Turkification won't really matter. In two thousand years, the Turks have never accepted ethnic Kurds as real Turks, no matter how

Chapter 7. Sakine Meets Apo

nicely they speak the language. It's just a carrot to help the Kurds oppress themselves into submission.

Until a certain night in high school, a girl named Sakine Cansiz was simply the child of a father who only wanted to avoid jeopardizing his military position. She was unaware that she was a Kurd, unaware that her home town was the epicenter of both Kurdish nationalism or of the original Zoroastrian faith, and unaware of the events of the Dersim massacre or of the government's continuing lower-intensity repressive activity since then. She was just going out for an evening to relieve the boredom.

On that day in high school, Sakine Cansiz heard about the Turkish youth movement as a group involved in human rights in general, not Kurdish issues, and she had the chance to attend a secret meeting in a neighbor's house.

In a later interview, she related how this had transpired.

[Editor's note: Either Sakine Cansiz tended to express herself in the stilted Maoist style she had studied for over 25 years, or perhaps the only records we have in English suffered in the translation by Maoist-trained members of the PKK cadre. Throughout this book, we've cleaned up the words where they're clearly mistranslated, but we've left the style in place to give a better flavor of how she and/or they thought and spoke about things.]

Most of the following material comes from a lengthy interview captured (not quite identically) on Kurdish Question.com and on Kurdish Info.com (another case in point of the murkiness of the original source of so much of the cross-posted material about the Kurds).

- http://kurdishquestion.com/oldarticle.php?aid=the-foundation-of-the-pkk-in-the-words-of-sakine-cansiz, and
- http://www.kurdishinfo.com/pkk-foundation-sakine-cansizs-words.

"There was an intense repression in Dersim where there was a public sympathy for the revolutionary movement and its leaders and brave fighters. It was in 1969 that people in Dersim started to raise some questions in their minds when the city refused to give permission to perform a theater play about Pir Sultan Abdal, one of the Zaza Kurdish Alevi saints. The denial led to unrest in which a civilian, Mehmet Kilan, was killed, and other people were arrested under martial law. All these events began to create some awareness in general, but there was still no awakening regarding patriotism and Kurdishness. Dersim was really more of a left-wing territory in general, mostly following the leftism of the Republican People's Party (Turkish: Cumhuriyet Halk Partisi,

Chapter 7. Sakine Meets Apo

CHP), whose leader Karaoglan was Kurdish but denied it [Ed: a nickname for Bulent Ecevit, who served several short terms as Prime Minister of Turkey]."

At one of the early meetings Sakine attended, the organizer brought up the Dersim Massacre and explained how Ataturk had sent troops to repress the Zaza Kurds and installed puppet regional governments. Sakine went home shocked. She had known nothing about the Dersim Massacre, or even about the Zazas, and she confronted her parents for concealing this.

Now she learned from her parents that her family, as with almost every Kurdish family in Dersim, had lost many members in the 1937 massacres. She discovered that they were Zazas rather than mainstream Muslims. They told her that this must remain in the past; they could not afford to be exposed to the Turkish military and political authorities. They were citizens of Turkey, and they must speak only the Turkish language, even inside the house, to avoid slipping up.

Sakine Cansiz attended more meetings to find out more about her people's past and present as well as the history of dissident movements. Over time, she began to meet the revolutionary leaders who had been living in her neighborhood all along.

Speaking of those cadre members, she noted: "*Those people's way of life had an effect on the other residents in the neighborhood who would describe those people as 'entirely different'. They were very serious in their relations, their visits, their sense of dress and everything else. I built a relationship with those people, but I was always out of the ordinary in their circle as I was making a point of different issues.*" The other issue being, we assume, feminism, a concept that had not been part of Öcalan's philosophy until that point.

"*I was later told that comrade Mazlum told his comrades to take a close interest in me, saying that I could be a good revolutionary fighter. He told them that they were wrong about me.*"

After those early meetings, one of the Apoists then dared a visit to the Cansiz house, where he told them about the history of Kurdistan. That comrade was Mazlum Doğan, one of the PKK founders. Only seven years later, he would burn himself to death during the Kurdish New Year (Newroz) in protest of the treatment of inmates at the Diyarbakir Prison. One of those inmates at the time would be Sakine Cansız. It was only a few years into the future; for now, he was just an earnest and charismatic young man with big ideas.

Chapter 7. Sakine Meets Apo

After her own death, Sakine Cansız's friends would be asked by the media how they remembered her in those early days. Yemosh Guzel said, "*We grew up together. She was quite brave, determined and modest. She never did make concessions about any of her ideas. However, she respected different thoughts. She struggled alone against lots of people, and she was very strong like that.*"

Her classmate Cemal Soylemez said, "*She always guided all of us in the school. In the 1970s, left-socialist organizations were new. Cansız was always at the front line. She had a revolutionary ideology. She was always trying to organize. She never accepted injustice or inequity. She affected all of us with her unique behavior and attitude.*"

Urban Revolutionists

Beyond all the cheerful stories, the scene had a darker side. The Apoist revolutionary movement's chosen means of fighting for the rights of the Kurds in Turkey was to participate in violent unrest in Ankara. Her family opposed her involvement with the group, and they tried to force her to stop.

If she had been detected, her father's career and maybe even his life would be endangered, but she could not endure the hypocrisy. Before finishing high school, she fled without her family's permission to Ankara.

It wasn't an ugly separation. There was respect on both sides. Speaking of the need to lead a double life, her mother said "I broke her heart too much ..." Her father said "The way she comported herself was very decent; her style, the way she talks ... She wanted to be a revolutionist and leaving home was her only solution".

Sakine didn't see herself quite so kindly. In a later interview, she said: "*Maybe it was just my weakness that I failed to convince the family and to provide proper conditions so that I could stay and join the fight there.*"

That was perfectly normal for an Islamic woman. She would grow in her convictions and mental toughness. for the meantime, she was still a schoolgirl. Once in Ankara, she connected with the Apoists; soon after her arrival she met their leader, in a scene that sounds like something that was a bit of an anti-climax but was in fact the beginning of a lifelong devotion.

She had been speaking with a student who had been an organizer in Dersim. "'We have friends here,' he said, showing me the group sitting under the trees. The leader was also there, and he was wearing glasses." That leader was Abdullah Öcalan. In a first taste of one of Sakine's trademarks, she

Chapter 7. Sakine Meets Apo

seemed almost oblivious to the great man himself and much more taken with the Marxist dialectic.

"That was the first time I saw the leader. We later gathered at the campus near the Faculty of Law. The leader was in a discussion with some people from other left-wing groups. We listened to the arguments of the leader with great attention."

She finished her high school education while establishing friendships with Kesire Yildirim (the future wife of Abdullah Öcalan) and other comrades. She was trained by Öcalan and another co-founder, Ali Haydar Kaytan, learning how to recruit new members.

The group spent much of its effort in 1975 honing its political message. Later in that year, the various revolutionary organizations concluded that the government pressures were just too intense in the capital city. At a meeting at Dikmen, they decided to spread out in 1976, seeing one another only as training activities permitted. She was, after Kesire Yildirim, the second woman inducted as a formal member of the Apoist movement. She traveled to other regions and stayed with other families while organizing new members.

In the late 1970s she would marry an engineer and briefly carried the surname of Polat. Not much is known about that marriage, even the dates, but she had divorced by the time the PKK formed in 1979.

In 1977 she earned her first arrest and prison stay in Izmir for Kurdish activism. Upon her release she found the Apoists in a somber mood.

After the Dikmen meeting, Haki Karer had decided to return to Kurdistan and went to Dilok, where he had been invited by Alaattin Kapan to take part in a discussion. Kapan was a member of STERKA SOR, a revolutionary organization; only later would it become clear that the group was operating under the control of MIT, the Turkish Government intelligence service. On March 18, 1977, Karer was gunned down while sitting at a coffee shop.

Karer's role as an icon of the Kurdish struggle was particularly important to the Apoists because he was not actually a Kurd. The Apoists and later the PKK would always have to endure criticism that they weren't about peace and democracy, just about Kurdish nationalism.

Cansiz dismissed that accusation:

"Despite our ideology against primitive-nationalist circles, other social-chauvinist and denier groups would continuously accuse us of nationalism. In this respect, these comrades set an example in our movement. We all found the

Chapter 7. Sakine Meets Apo

death of comrade Haki quite difficult, particularly his being killed by an agent provocateur. I cried when I saw their posters."

It was the first time the targeting came close to reaching the leader himself. There would be many other attempts.

Kerer's death was followed by the 1977 killing of Kurdish scholar Musa Anter and PKK member Aydın Gul by Halkin Kurtulushu, a member of the "Gendarmerie for Intelligence and Counter-Terrorism" (JITEM).

At this point, Öcalan and his followers began re-assessing the situation. In the traditional convoluted Marxist style, Cansiz explained: *"We had been engaged in an ideological struggle from the very beginning against denial, social-chauvinistic impression, primitive and nationalist approaches ... We developed more intense criticism of our own positions, as we felt the need to give a much sharper ideological fight. The other leftists were talking about an internationalist duty and brotherhood with the Kurdish people, but on the other hand they were participating in killing our comrades."*

Birth of the PKK

By 1978 Öcalan had realized that his group was not going to gain the Kurds any measure of political autonomy as a result of cooperation with other equally small groups that were unreliable and mostly bigoted about Kurds in the first place. What the Kurds needed was a voice in the political process, and to grow strong enough to exercise that voice. They would also need to be strong enough to deter violence from other leftist groups.

Öcalan gathered his little band, which numbered only a few dozen people who were truly committed to the organization, as opposed to the 200-300 people who might show up randomly for exciting and provocative events, to discuss the possibilities in re-organizing for a political strategy and forming a political party.

The Apoists grew as their message became more focused on Kurdishness instead of wild protest. By 1977 they had graduated from being campus radicals to seeking support from all levels of Kurdish society.

"The main obstacle our movement faced was denial by Kurdish groups of their true situations, which then prevented us from even speaking with them, let alone asking them to let us represent them.

The fight against fascist circles in Elazig also had an influence on groups inside these circles, which were made up of Kurds organized by the MHP

Chapter 7. Sakine Meets Apo

(Nationalist Movement Party). A group of around 70 people severed their ties with the nationalist circle while on the other hand some other groups from the Turkish left wing and KUK (Nationalist Libertarians of Kurdistan) movement also joined our organization. Our struggle also led to disintegration in other structures."

In simpler language, the movement was growing, but many of the recruits were coming from other revolutionary groups. Those groups were armed and dangerous, and didn't appreciate having to defend their membership rolls.

That leads to the one topic that has made Kurdish resistance successful and yet prevented it from gaining worldwide acceptance: the matter of whether the PKK is a violent extremist group. Sakine didn't back away from it, while claiming that it was all about self-defense.

"As all these groups were standing against us, we gave an effective total struggle against these circles in all areas to protect our own presence. We intensely discussed the ways of the struggle, and the leader always put forward a pattern of fighting basing on the mass and people."

A total struggle. The Apoists were under violent attack, not only from the government and from their fellow revolutionaries, and they would fight back.

Although they were forced to battle with other activists, the Apoists were otherwise simply inviting Kurds to learn about their history and culture. They were posing no actual problem for the government, other than ignoring rules that such assemblies were illegal, yet the violent intimidation and repression escalated.

It became obvious to Öcalan that the Turkish government would never recognize Kurdish rights and would never stop repressing them until they gave up all aspects of Kurdish identity. He also realized that since the Turkish government wasn't listening to popular demands, activist groups were wasting their time with protests, and with such fragmented opposition, force wasn't going to work either.

The Apoists needed a way to jog the political machine, and to do so they needed to show enough political strength to become part of the government themselves. He decided to convert his conversation circles (and, let's be honest, his gang of agitators) into a genuine political party that would attempt to gain enough representation to force a governing coalition to recognize some of the Kurds' more immediate issues.

Twenty-two of the leading members of the Apoist revolutionary movement (including Kesire Yildirim and Sakine Cansiz) met from 25-27 November 1978

Chapter 7. Sakine Meets Apo

near Diyarbakir in the village of Fis for a formal establishment of a legitimate political party, the Partiya Karkerên Kurdistanê (PKK), which in English means the Kurdistan Workers' Party. The number was chosen to ensure that the meeting was able to maintain a low profile, in the face of pressure that Sakine described as "the remarkable security problem" from both the government and other revolutionary forces.

Öcalan's wife, Kesire Yildirim, had already explored the political route. She and other future PKK leaders had founded the "Ankara group" in 1975 and they now merged it into the PKK. Later, she found herself constantly opposing Abdullah Öcalan's ideas and policies, which led her in 1987 to leave the PKK, divorce Öcalan, and seek refuge in Sweden.

Cansiz represented Elazig Province in that first meeting of Öcalan's group, and as such became one of the founding members of the PKK. She was also on a small committee that drafted a historical background paper and compiled a detailed report on that first Congress. The founders established by-laws based on Marxist ideology, although those by-laws would evolve over time to conform to Abdullah Öcalan's own ideological journeys.

The deliberations weren't just ritual speeches. "*Some among us dissociated themselves from the movement as they couldn't take up the challenge, but the others were completely determined to fight in the revolutionary way for Kurdistan with no concerns or doubts ...*"

"*Everything was being read and watched with great attention. You could breathe the atmosphere of great experience and responsibility there. You could feel the responsibility, which seemed to be getting heavier every passing moment. The environment gave rise to a feeling that the revolution wasn't going to be easy and needed to be led with great patience and attention.*"

Matters under debate included the initial leadership team and a short-term action plan leading up to the public launching on the next Newroz festival. Curiously, in selecting the party name, they consciously avoided the use of "Communist", deciding eventually on the Kurdistan Workers' Party.

After the Congress ended, Cansiz returned to her role in "propaganda-agitation work", which was the production of notices, leaflets and other materials for use in all the regional offices. She enjoyed the work and the communities. Politics, in other words, can be fun, at least sometimes. In late 1979 she was arrested again, although she was soon released. Perhaps it prepared her for what was soon to follow.

Chapter 7. Sakine Meets Apo

Politics By Other Means

The PKK had no illusions about actual independence, nor the likelihood of taking over formal power even within Kurdistan in any short timeframe. They doubted that the Turkish government would allow them to run for office or be seated in the first place, let alone achieve positions of influence within the government. The expected no substantial support from the Turkish population at large beyond Kurdistan. So, despite its intent to be a political force, the fledgling PKK decided that it had little to lose by provocations. Any publicity, as they say, is good publicity. Accordingly, the PKK was associated with insurgent violence from day one of its existence.

Sakine said: "*Our purpose was to announce the Congress with an expansive act targeting reactionary centers, particularly some tribal structures [Ed.: government offices] that applied intense pressure on the people. However, we delayed our act because of the arrest of some of us. It was only the leading staff that knew about the Congress, and they still kept it secret inside the organization. Still, others were feeling that we were advancing towards a new organization and structuring.*"

Translated: they had been planning some violent action to generate publicity for the organization's launch. Even at this low level of activity, the government's antennae had twitched, and the organization had to lie low while the heat was on. That opened the door for the intelligence services to beat them to the bottom of the death spiral.

On May 18, 1978, Kurdish landowners who were loyal to the Turkish government killed Halil Çavgun, another "Revolutionaries of Kurdistan" leader. On December 25, 1978, the Grey Wolves, a Turkish nationalist extremist group, killed 109 Alevi Turks and Kurds, injuring an additional 176 people, in Kahramanmarash at an event that became known as the Marash Massacre.

The Grey Wolves organization was established by Colonel Alparslan in the 1960s. It was then, and is today, routinely described as ultra-nationalist and as one of the most neo-fascist forces in the world. Formally a youth organization with close links to the Nationalist Movement Party (MHP), it has been described as MHP's "militant youth arm", as a "paramilitary and terrorist wing", or, when deniability is required, the "unofficial militant arm".

Their most infamous assault was the attempt on Pope John Paul II's life in 1981 by Grey Wolves member Mehmet Ali Agca; the masterminds behind that attack were not identified, and the organization's role remains unclear. Due

Chapter 7. Sakine Meets Apo

to these attacks, scholars and journalists have described the Grey Wolves as a terrorist organization. No matter what you call it, what the Grey Wolves do (among other things) is to kill or terrorize anyone, in Turkey or beyond, who opposes their political sponsors.

The Gray Wolves had not achieved international notoriety until the attack on the Pope, but the Kurds knew just who they were. These wolves had been harrying the Kurdish population for years before the formation of the PKK. They fielded the main nationalist force during the political violence in 1976–80, becoming a "death squad" that killed leftist Turks and a large number of Kurds in a series of street killings and gun battles. According to authorities, 220 of its members carried out 694 murders of left-wing and liberal activists and intellectuals. Attacks on university students were commonplace. They certainly killed hundreds of Alevi Kurds and Turks in the Marash massacre of 1978, and they are alleged to have been behind the Taksim Square massacre of 1977.

Cansiz assessed the Marash event as follows: "*The massacre aimed to intimidate our movement. Had they been able to find some other ground and had we failed to take precautions and respond to it with our struggle, they may have tried doing the same thing in some other places too.*"

In addition to massacring over 100 Alawite civilians, which was widely reported and was so far beyond the pale that the Turkish government felt compelled to respond with prosecutions, the Gray Wolves had planned to attack Kurds as well. The PKK had seen this coming and prepared sufficient armed strength to fend off the planned attacks of that day or, as Cansiz makes it sound, to have conducted a pre-emptive strike. Whichever way it actually happened, it apparently deterred further action by the Gray Wolves.

The PKK didn't have the means or the platform needed to capitalize on this tragedy (and, unbeknownst to them, they would not have the time). In assessing its situation in 1980, the PKK had clearly miscalculated what it took to be effective. Not only did it hold a grand total of zero seats in the legislature, but it seems to have had no more than a few hundred adherents at best, with a core membership numbered in dozens. It viewed the other Kurdish and/or revolutionary parties as much more significant threats to its existence than the Turkish government that was the main oppressor.

Its leaders may have felt frustrated that the Turkish government either did not know of their existence or did not particularly care. That assumption would prove to be quite wrong.

Chapter 7. Sakine Meets Apo

Less than two years after the founding of the PKK, the military under General Kenan Evren staged its most aggressive coup ever on 12 September 1980, deposing the elected government of Süleyman Demirel and the Justice Party.

In each case in recent history when the Turkish army has intervened in politics (1960-1965, 1971-1973, and 1980-1988, plus an abortive fiasco in 2016), the pretext has been the need to defend the country against a perceived threat from internal enemies.

According to the Turkish military, the 1980 coup was provoked because the core Kemalist values were being endangered by enemies of the Republic of Turkey: Turkish leftists and Turkish Kurds.

To defeat this rampant threat, the Turkish military government arrested 650,000 people, and most of the leftist and Kurdish detainees were either beaten or tortured. The Turkish army and police killed over 500 people and kept 85,000 people under detention for an extended period. Many of those who went through it are still alive, if not well, and they serve as the collective memory of those abuses and torture sessions for the rest of the Kurdish and Turkish people.

It turned out that the Apoists had not been ignored after all: one of the groups specifically targeted was the PKK. The government's aim was not just to remove the PKK's leadership, nor to shut the PKK down altogether as an operable entry. It was to take its members - all of its members, of whatever rank or position - out of circulation completely, even the ones who simply handed out leaflets.

Not long after graduating from high school, Sakine Cansiz, distributor of pamphlets that nobody would really read written by a few dozen radical youths grandly-styling themselves as a movement, was arrested again in the sweep that followed the 1980 coup. This time she was treated as a dangerous enemy of the state. Thanks to that very treatment, that is exactly what she would eventually become. From that moment of great testing, she emerged as a heroine of the Kurdish people.

Chapter 8. The Painful Price of Becoming a Legend

Sakine Cansiz was the assassin's prize target because she was not just any Kurd activist.

In her life, she would make an indelible mark among Turkey's Kurds as a founder of the Kurdish separatist movement and an unbreakable spirit who endured a decade of torture in a Turkish prison. She would go on from there to become a ground-breaker for women's rights to the fullest measure, including equal participation in party leadership and in actual combat, where she would prove herself as a heroic warrior whose women's units had inarguably distinguished themselves in open warfare. Eventually, she would one day become the public face of the Kurds in Europe, being introduced into the highest circles of the Western governments.

All of that would be quite a ride for a country girl, but first she had to endure a trial by ordeal.

****

The military coup of 1980 had, among other objectives, the final eradication of the already-reeling Turkish revolutionary youth movements. As with earlier coups, Turkish state police and troops suppressed dissent in the streets with maximum brutality. One difference this time was that the repression also occurred inside the Kurdistan region, which the Turks had occupied since the establishment of the Ottoman Empire over 500 years earlier. The Kurds' nascent Apoist youth movement was caught up in that effort and was almost quashed.

Most of the dissident movements could not withstand this kind of pressure. The leaders who could move quickly enough fled to Europe in a strategic step to maintain their existence. The Apoist leaders decided to remain in the vicinity to retain both popular credibility and some possibility of taking direct action. Abdullah Öcalan and the majority of the PKK leadership took refuge in the Palestinian camp in Lebanon's Bekaa Valley, which was under the direct control of the Syrian military. From there, they directed the efforts of the remaining cadres of the PKK.

The Syrian Government helped the PKK to build up its forces in the hope of using them against Turkey to take back control of the Turkish-Syrian border region. Ironically, this is exactly what would happen, but not for another 25 years; when it did, it would be a part of a campaign to defeat the Syrian government rather than helping it.

Chapter 8: The Painful Price

The PKK and the Armenian Secret Army for the Liberation of Armenia (ASALA) declared a temporary alliance in Lebanon in order to cooperate in opposing the Turkish Government. On November 10, 1980, a bomb exploded outside the Turkish Consulate in Strasbourg, France, causing significant material damage but no injuries. In a telephone call to the Agence France-Press office, a spokesman said the blast was a joint operation and marked the start of a "fruitful collaboration" between ASALA and the PKK. On September 24, 1981, ASALA attacked the Turkish consulate in Paris; their demands included the release of five Kurdish revolutionary fighters.

Sponsorship always has its price. Just as the PKK was hitting its stride with setting up guerrilla operations in the remote mountains on the Turkish border, the Syrians decided on June 6, 1982 to launch the First Lebanon War. They demanded that the PKK concentrate its forces back in the Bekaa Valley and fight against Israel alongside the Palestinian Liberation Organization (PLO) and Syria. The PKK might have endorsed the idea as part of the general Muslim hatred of Israel, but it forced a substantial time-out in preparing to conduct operations against Turkey.

The High Price of Loyalty

Meanwhile, a significant number of PKK cadre members remained in Turkey after the 1980 coup. Those who evaded the ensuing mass arrests intended to continue the struggle within the heart of the enemy's territory, but they saw that the movement could not exist without followers, and they would lose their following if they remained too remote to maintain credibility. They had to remain in the open enough to remain visible, which allowed the government to resume its targeting of PKK leaders. Most of the remaining PKK leadership was arrested during 1980, among them Sakine Cansiz and Mazlum Doğan, along with numerous people who had nothing to do with the PKK but were collected for good measure.

Many of the PKK leaders and other detainees lost their lives in prison, not by random accidents or the occasional out-of-control jailers, but by the orchestrated actions of officials of Turkish government agencies carrying out government programs. Some survived after years of torture and abuses. Sakine Cansiz was one of these.

Part of the problem with applying normal standards to the Turkish situation is deciding where the standard operating practices end and the torture begins. Ordinary criminal suspects are blindfolded and handcuffed immediately, and get beat up after they are booked into detention. They are

Chapter 8: The Painful Price

stripped naked during interrogation, sexually abused and left like that, often being hosed with ice-cold water and left on the concrete floors of cells that are quite exposed to the harsh conditions of winter. If they get sick or die, that's their fault for being criminals.

That's not a description of what used to happen with maximum-security offenders in Diyarbakir in 1980. It describes standard police procedure in handling the average pickpocket or car thief anywhere in Turkey in 2016.

Kurdish scholar Welat Zeydanlioglu wrote an article about Diyarbakir prison under the title of "Torture and Turkification in the Diyarbakir Military Prison", which is recommended for further reading. He is the founder and Coordinator of the Kurdish Studies Network, a global research network for scholars working in Kurdish Studies. He wrote,

"As always, the richness of testimonies is greatest on the side of the victims and very rare from the torturers or their superiors. Recently, the former Turkish General Kenan Evren, who led the 12 September 1980 Turkish coup d'état, revealed that torture had indeed been a routine practice both before and after the coup in detention centers as well as in prisons across Turkey. However, Evren argued that torture in prisons following the coup was nothing more than the correctional officers taking revenge on prisoners who had ruled the prisons and mistreated them before the coup. Evren's simplistic account fails to explain the sheer systematic brutality of the torture practiced in Turkey against leftists in general and in Diyarbakir against Kurds in particular."

It also fails to explain how the Kurds, shut out of most public employment, and present inside the prisons only in the role of prisoners, were able to abuse their Turkish captors.

Cansiz' fellow captive, Mazlum Doğan, was born in 1955 in Karakoçan in Elazig Province. He finished high school in Elâzığ and then enrolled at the Hacettepe University in Ankara in 1974. In 1976 he joined the Kurdish student movement, the precursor of the PKK. He was the one who had urged the Apoists to take in Sakine Cansiz as a member despite their (and her) misgivings. He was a member of the Central Committee of the Kurdistan Workers' Party (PKK) and the first chief editor of the PKK party newspaper Serxwebun. Eventually, the Turkish government arrested him on charges that he was leading a terrorist organization, had taken part in the liberation of a PKK comrade from a state hospital in Diyarbakir, and forged identity documents. As a leader of a group that even styles itself as revolutionaries, most of the charges are accurate.

Chapter 8: The Painful Price

March 21st is the festival of Newroz (New Year) in the Aryan religion, and as such is a holy day for the Kurdish people, although the governments of Turkey and Arab countries forbid them from celebrating it. The Iranian government does accept celebration of Newroz as a non-religious spring festival.

On March 21, 1982, while the Kurdish people celebrated the Newroz festival, Mazlum Doğan lit up his own body as a Newroz bonfire in his cell at the Diyarbakir Prison to protest Turkish violence against the Kurdish people.

With this act, Doğan tried to stimulate awareness of the inhumane conditions at the Diyarbakir Prison and other jails in Turkey. He succeeded in death in achieving that which he could not do it in life: awakening the consciousness of the entire Kurdish population.

Since then, on March 21 of every year, the Kurdish Movement worldwide honors Mazlum Doğan's life. The PKK organization has named its elite school after him, and several Kurdish youth festivals around Europe also share his name.

Doğan was the first of the imprisoned PKK leaders to give his life voluntarily to draw attention to the cause of the Kurdish people. His suicide was the start of several hunger strikes and resistance campaigns run by prisoners of conscience in Turkey.

On May 7, 1982, PKK members Ferhat Kurtay, Necmi Onen, Mahmut Zengin and Eshref Anyik also burned themselves to death in Diyarbakir Prison.

On July 14, 1982, PKK members in Diyarbakir Prison started a hunger strike that would last for 75 days. The Turkish authorities did not relent, and so Kemal Pir died on September 7, M. Hayri Durmush died on September 12, Akif Yılmaz died on September 15, and Ali Çiçek died on September 17.

The Women's Program

The women didn't get any better treatment. Much to the contrary, the wardens viewed them as having exceeded their station and needing to be taught a severe lesson. Most of the women ranged in age only from 19 to 22 years old, just the right age to be the target for a sadistic pervert, which appeared to be the primary job qualification for many of the staff at Diyarbakir.

Chapter 8: The Painful Price

One of the women arrested at the same time as Sakine Cansiz in 1980 was Gültan Kisanak. In later years she would be elected to represent the Diyarbakir constituency in the national legislature as a member of the Peace and Democracy Party (BDP), a pro-Kurdish political party, and we emphasize here "political". Although she had been through the same horrific treatment as Sakine Cansiz, Kisanak had chosen to use the open political process to try and improve conditions for the Kurds. Eventually, she would become the Mayor of Diyarbakir in 2014.

In 2016, she and her Deputy Mayor would again be arrested on the grounds of being members of the PKK. That is quite absurd, since she had spent an entire career preaching that the PKK's violent approach is the wrong path. Nonetheless, she is facing charges that would amount to over 230 years in prison, assuming that any trial ever occurs. At the time of publication of this book in 2017, a year later, no trial date has been set, but the government already has what it wants. With their offices "vacated", it replaced two independent-minded elected officials with appointed trustees who could be counted on not to contradict the increasingly autocratic President Erdoğan.

Kisanak had long resisted talking about her experiences in the infamous Diyarbakir Prison (which has since closed), hoping that a positive outlook would yield more future benefits than trying to re-litigate the past. In 2012, she had a bitter and highly public disagreement with Bülent Arinç, Deputy Prime Minister of the Islamist AKP party, over his dismissal of Kurdish concerns over the Uludere incident (described in more detail in Chapter 11). Infuriated by this lack of interest in a situation that was rocking the nation, Kisanak decided to publicize the reasons why Kurds were so opposed to efforts to increase the power of the central government. For almost the first time since 1980, she opened up her personal story in 2012 to reporter Goksel Bozkurt about Diyarbakir Prison.

Others had told these stories before, but that mostly happened in hidden conversations deep within the Kurdish community. That grapevine was the means by which Sakine Cansiz had become a legend among the Kurds, but only among the Kurds. Kisanak's legitimate political role allowed her to be the first to get her message out onto the national and international stage without having to resort to violence just to get media attention.

Gültan Kisanak felt that Bülent Arınç, as Deputy PM (the title for the Party's leading member in the ruling coalition in the legislature), had a responsibility to prevent the whitewashing of these incidents, or at least to speak up about them if and when they did occur. When he refused to do so,

Chapter 8: The Painful Price

she spoke out in her own turn, charging that Arınç had not only known about but actively supported all the incidents since 1980. In order to illustrate how bad the situation was she started speaking about the outrages that she, the 85 other women, and Sakine Cansiz had experienced while imprisoned by the Turks in Diyarbakir.

Gültan Kisanak is an Alevi Muslim Kurd, born on 15 June 1961 in Elazig. She graduated from the Ege University Communication Faculty in Journalism and Public Relations. Kisanak worked for various newspapers as a journalist and ran several projects as coordinator and consultant for the Baglar Municipality Social Project in Diyarbakir. Running as an independent candidate, she was elected as the MP for Diyarbakir on 22 July 2007. To take her seat, she joined the Democratic Society Party (DTP), which in December 2009 rebranded itself as the Peace and Democracy Party (Barish ve Demokrasi Partisi, BDP). During the BDP's first Congress on February 2010, Gültan Kisanak was elected co-chair of the party along with Selahattin Demirtash.

She didn't build her career on lurid tales of what had happened in Diyarbakir Prison, even though it was right in her own district. In fact, she never mentioned it. She had made a successful career as a person who gets things done. Some people knew (certainly the Kurds knew) about her back-story of having been tortured by the Turks, but she never brought it up. In other words, Kisanak is very much a public figure with credibility and *gravitas*. When she speaks, people take her seriously.

Kisanak was detained in the southeastern province of Diyarbakir in July of 1980, just before the coup occurred, while she was a 19-year-old university student at Diclc University. After the military coup, she was sent to Diyarbakir prison with 85 other women. Few of them had radical political views. Most of them were not members of any organization at all; they were mostly just young university students, like Kisanak. Their principal offenses were that they were women who had been trying to get an education, and they were Kurds.

Unfortunately for them, Diyarbakir had just acquired the latest in modern conveniences: a brand-new prison constructed by the Ministry of Justice as an E-Type (maximum security) prison in the heartland of the Kurdish area. Once martial law was declared a part of the 1980 coup, the prison was transferred to the military until they returned it to civil authorities in 1988. A typical cell was 1.5 by 2 meters (45 inches wide and 6 feet long), or about the

Chapter 8: The Painful Price

size of a normal coffin. Those weren't the isolation cells; two people occupied them. In the isolation cells, the height was also about 45 inches.

The Ankara-Hürriyet Daily Newspaper reported that over the course of two years, Kisanak saw her family only four times, each meeting lasting only three minutes. It was six months before her family found out she was alive.

There were probably many occasions when she wished she was. The Turks are considered even by the Arabs to be specialists in the matter of torture. Perhaps their long history of cruelty harks back to their days as victims of the Mongol horde, who were themselves no slouches in that department. Whatever the reasons, torturing people who are merely annoying appears to be a generally acceptable practice, even for duly constituted members of the legislature. Deputy Risa Nur was arrested and tortured in 1910; when he was eventually returned to his post in the parliament, it voted 96-73 not to hold any investigations on the incident.

Gültan Kisanak was one of six women who went through severe torture. Sakine Cansiz was another.

Kisanak said, "*When I got into the Diyarbakir prison, I said 'I am not Turkish, I am Kurdish'. That alone got me sent to confinement in the doghouse for six months. They would put our skirts over our head, leaving us naked, and they would require us to walk like that, prison ward by prison ward. We experienced all forms of torture, including electric, but by far the most serious and disgusting was sexual torture. When they raped the women, then they would walk them around to another ward showing off their bloody skirts! Then they were masturbating when we came out of the bathroom!!*"

As horrific as that was for these women, it wasn't the worst torture of all. "*One woman had 11-year-old twin sons. The Turks made the mother listen to the sounds her children made while the Turks tortured them*".

Cansiz, Kisanak, and the other women were unable to take a proper bath for two years and barely ate anything. "*We tried to clean ourselves with cold water and a single torn piece of cloth that we had to keep for two years. We were constantly ill and wounded,*" Kisanak said. She added, "*Our mouths were full of blood, and they were forcing us to beg for their permission: Sir, could you please excuse us to wash our face? But we did not say that!*"

Kisanak's testimony went on: "*The women in the Diyarbakir prison were subjected to physical, verbal and psychological abuses. The Turkish correctional officers were always insulting, cursing and harassing us women and always finding an excuse to torture us. They used sticks, bayonets, electric cables, bandoliers, police clubs, planks, and hosepipes to torment us women. They would use every one of those items above indiscriminately on people regardless of their genders."*

Human Rights Watch has published a short book entitled "Turkey Torture and Mistreatment in Pre-trial Detention by Anti-Terror Police". It is available at:

https://books.google.com/books/about/Turkey.html?id=rgvZnAAACAAJ),

The book documents a variety of torture methods still being used in Turkey. Five main techniques seem to predominate among the anti-terror police: electric shock; hanging by the arms in a variety of positions; spraying with high-pressure water; sexually-oriented abuses such as squeezing breasts or testicles; and beating with fists, nightsticks, or sandbags. Often, these techniques are used in concert. Blindfolding, poor food, stripping the suspect naked, extremely cold or hot conditions, lack of medical care and cramped, decrepit cell conditions are also standard. Note again the present tense: we may be sure that these techniques were also available 35 years ago.

Other reports indicated that the Turks waterboarded their prisoners, increasing the atrocity of the practice by using sewer water. In a 2011 documentary, Cansiz (who, like Kisanak, recoiled from discussing her time in Diyarbakir) also recounted some of the tortures she had suffered in the Diyarbakir, including a beating endured while being forced to wade through neck-high sewage water.

Kisanak and the other surviving women pointed the finger at prison commander Esat Oktay Yildiran as the one personally responsible for her and the other women's pain.

"He was responsible for the trauma I endure to this day," Kisanak said. *"Every single moment we were under great torture there".*

Kisanak recalled: *"Commander Yildiran came to the ward one day with a group of soldiers and they ordered us to stand at attention. I resisted, so commander Yildiran attacked me and insulted me and tried to choke me using my scarf. He wrapped it around my neck very hard and I was not able to breathe. He started torturing me physically after that. My life was nothing but blood and tears for two years without ceasing. He was full of hate toward Kurds, and abused us women violently. He really enjoyed torturing us. And the other Turkish soldiers did not have any sympathy for us either."*

Yildiran was the prison commander and, most unusually, he was executed in Istanbul in 1988 (i.e. after the military government restored control to a

Chapter 8: The Painful Price

civilian government) for the tortures he inflicted and the crimes he committed against the prisoners. But the Turks had thousands of others there and elsewhere just like him, bent on making the Kurds pay for being Kurdish by torturing and/or killing as many of them as they could get their hands on.

In March 1995, Azimet Köylüotmlu, who was then the State Minister for Human Rights, revealed that eighteen different torture methods were still being used in Turkey. Virtually all detainees who report being tortured were beaten, and the majorities who are systematically tortured were blindfolded, often for long periods of time.

Some of those who were tortured in prison were, once released, no longer ready for battling the regime openly. But they shared their experiences at the hands of the Turks with the Kurdish people, and they shared stories of the bravery and unbreakable will of other PKK leaders, including the one who was a woman: Sakine Cansiz.

Sakine Cansiz had been arrested, along with most of the other PKK leaders, just after the 1980 Turkish coup d'état. Consider the horrors reported by Kisanak over a two-year period; Cansiz would endure 10. She went through the worst kind of torture from 1980 to 1991 without breaking down. Her only weapon was the teaching of Kurdish leader Abdullah Öcalan on how to resist the enemies of Kurds and Kurdistan. She endured pain and suffering for her people, and it simply made her more determined that, if and when this imprisonment ended, she would work harder than ever for the freedom of Kurdish women and women of the world as a whole.

Sakine Cansız said, *"After those years in prison, cheating death so many times, I reached for the happiest and beautiful part of my life source"*.

Neither woman mentioned in their interviews that one of the acts the Turks had undertaken for their amusement had been to cut off one of Sakine's breasts.

In 2013, Kisanak eulogized Sakine's bravery. *"She spat in the face of her torturers"*.

One PKK commander who was also in prison with her remembered: *"Sakine's manner, her tough line, that was another thing. Once when she was walking through the corridor on her way to the court for the trial, the way she walked was completely another thing. She was walking with dignity; her head always up, never down!"*

Chapter 8: The Painful Price

Kisanak said that much of the current rage that Kurds feel is the direct result of the pointless abuse and torture that group of women underwent in Diyarbakir.

The leaders who emerged amongst the imprisoned Kurdish women, including Sakine Cansiz and Gulten Kisanak, decided that they needed an independent women's organization that could focus on women's' issues. Both realized that in the Turkish culture simply setting up an organization of women was a waste of time. It would not be taken seriously, if it was even allowed to exist at all. It would need a larger context to operate from.

Kisanak, as we have noted, would choose the more optimistic path of trying to build respect for women from within a more traditional setting. Upon her release she would become a journalist and then enter politics as an individual woman within an established party.

Sakine, who had acquired the status of leader of all the imprisoned Kurds, both male and female, believed that the need could only be met by setting up a separate identifiable entity within an existing party. As was to be the case often in her remaining life, she took a more direct response to the problem. At the time, the only political party that was then interested in Kurdish causes of any kind was the Kurdistan Workers' Party (PKK). Her release did not come until 1991, almost 3 years after the military junta turned control of the government (and the prison) back to civilian authorities. When it did, she rejoined the still-outlawed PKK and became a guerilla fighter. By the time she arrived there, as a result of the stories already spread by the other surviving women who had been released years earlier, she was already a household name among the Kurds.

Chapter 9. Guerrilla Leader

After her release in 1991, Sakine Cansiz was smuggled out of Turkey, passing through Syria to the PKK camps in Lebanon's Bekaa Valley. The PKK is not the only organization that has used it; Hezbollah had occupied the area long before.

Only 30 kilometers east of Beirut, this massive valley, lying between Mount Lebanon to the west and the Anti-Lebanon Mountains to the east, is 75 miles long and 10 miles wide and forms the eastern half of the country of Lebanon. The north-easternmost extension of the Great Rift Valley, it stretches from the plains of Homs in Syria to a narrow point that becomes the Sea of Galilee and the Jordan Valley. The area has a Mediterranean climate with wet, often snowy winters and dry, warm summers. The region receives limited rainfall, but two rivers originate in the valley: the Orontes (Asi), which flows north into Syria and Turkey, and the Litani, which flows south and then west to the Mediterranean Sea. If you're going to be spending months outdoors, you can do a lot worse.

Sakine stayed there for some time undergoing military training. Reunited at last with Abdullah Öcalan, with whom she had founded the PKK, she met with him almost daily.

An Equal Role for Women

She told Öcalan about the idea that the women in Diyarbakir Prison had developed of forming an independent Woman's Liberation Movement. Abdullah Öcalan was always interested in new ideas and sought to listen attentively to any PKK member; he considered her suggestion seriously and promised to research these issues in greater depth. For the time being, he asked her to recruit and lead Kurdish women, using the stories of the struggles of those 85 women in the Diyarbakir prison.

The idea wasn't completely novel for Öcalan. The PKK had already opened its arms to the participation of women during the years that Sakine had been imprisoned.

In the first years of the PKK, there were only two women in the Party leadership, one of whom (Sakine) had been in prison for most of that time and just released. In those years, there had been few women anywhere in the organization: life as a guerrilla, or more specifically a guerrilla camp follower, is not an easy sell for a recruiter in a culture that has for 1500 years been

Chapter 9. Guerilla Leader

built around the assumption that a woman's only legitimate place is in the home. But Öcalan had discovered that those women that did join the PKK were driven by an insurmountable desire for the liberation both of fellow Kurds and of fellow women. Their enthusiasm made them highly effective in recruiting other committed members, and women members played a significant role in growing the PKK into a mass movement.

While Sakine was in Diyarbakir, the PKK had given up on the political process, since there was none. The country was being governed by a military junta that had as one of its specific objectives the elimination of groups such as the PKK it had also taken to ever-more stringent methods of repressing the Kurdish population in general. The PKK launched its guerrilla war on 15 August 1984, and Kurdish women began arriving in the ranks of the PKK following that declaration.

When women joined the PKK after hearing the initial stories in the recruitment sessions, just as Sakine and the others had done, they had absorbed the Marxist-Leninist rhetoric about universal equality, but the leaders of the PKK itself, who knew no other way, still reflected the feudal characteristics of Turkish and Kurdish society of the time. The women reasoned that if they were going to risk their own lives in the struggle, they wanted to be treated with respect and to participate in the decisions that affected their very lives. If they couldn't do so in the councils of the PKK as a whole, then they would form their own organizations that would contribute to the PKK mission while allowing them to make their own decisions.

Their initial steps in this direction had to conform to what was possible. In 1987, Öcalan's approved he formation of the Women's Kurdistan Liberation Union (Yekitiya Azadiya Jinen Kurdistan, "YAJK"). The first revolutionary and liberationist movement of the women of Kurdistan, the YAJK aspired to recruit not only Kurdish women but also revolutionary-minded women from all over the world.

Apo spelled out what the PKK wanted out of its women members in these early days. In the stiff, self-conscious prose of Maoist handbooks:

- *YAJK means the attainment of the highest possible sentiments for one's country. This means that even if everyone gives up on his or her country, YAJK continues the struggle.*

- *YAJK is a reality of war. Here there is a national liberationist war. YAJK is well aware that this war is the fundamental component of its existence. War is a basic principle for YAJK. However, this does not*

Chapter 9. Guerilla Leader

> *only mean aggressive war; this war is internal as much as it is external.*
>
> - *YAJK is a partisan force. It is entirely devoted to the principles and ideals of the party (PKK). Without the struggle of the PKK, it is clear that the women's liberation movement could not have taken these major strides. Therefore, the devotion and internalization of the PKK are an important responsibility for YAJK.*

The PKK wasn't looking for women to serve as "guerrilla groupies" like the earnest college girls in the Western countries, swooning over romantic pictures of Che Guevara, making pointless speeches in the safety of their campus, and styling themselves the Liberation Front for This or That.

The PKK may have been what it claimed to be: a political party that was forced by the lack of other alternatives to take up arms to defend itself. It is equally true that, subsequent to that decision, it was and remains to this day an actual fighting guerrilla force. Ostensibly it intends to further its objectives through formal political actions if and when permitted to do so, but that opportunity has not arisen.

Entrance to the PKK required active participation in the guerrilla campaign, living hard under field conditions at all times. At this point in the development of the Kurdish and PKK cultures, the women served as active assistants to the actual guerrilla fighters. They were the administrators of the camps, and not just in a secretarial sense: they conducted the training programs for male guerrilla fighters,. Nonetheless, an actual combat role for women remained unthinkable.

The women felt that this situation completely erased their own identity and failed to recognize their own contribution to the Kurdish cause. For the first few years, that could not change. Still, there was an unanticipated benefit. In playing this immediate supporting role, the Kurdish women were becoming very familiar not just with the hardships of field life but also with all of the actions necessary to form, equip, train and support a fighting force. Eventually it occurred to them that they were learning exactly what they needed to know to form their own combat units. All they needed was the opening to do so, and it appeared in the form of Sakine Cansiz.

Sakine returned to the PKK in 1992. Because of her reputation from the prison, she was soon accepted as a leader among the roughly 50 women who had joined the PKK forces before her arrival. With them, she went through

Chapter 9. Guerilla Leader

hard training to cover many of the contingencies they might have to face when deployed more directly into the battlegrounds in Turkey.

Sakine Cansiz at work in PKK Headquarters. [Photo: YouTube: RojevTV]

She also took advantage of her long relationship with Öcalan to press him daily for a meaningful independent role for women, both in the PKK and also in Kurdish society for those territories that the PKK might someday control.

The First Unit of Women

In 1992, Öcalan wasn't ready for a discussion of full equality in every aspect of Kurdish life. The culture simply could not move fast enough to accept that. What he could do was to conduct a pilot project.

He allowed Sakine to form one fighting unit of women and see how this idea of women fighters was going to work out. He also wanted to make sure that the women who'd already been in the field for years didn't resent this move, and took a vote among them before proceeding.

Chapter 9. Guerilla Leader

He then sent Sakine and most of the other women in her cadre to serve under his brother Commander Osman Öcalan. They passed through Syria and the territories in Kurdistan that were controlled by the peshmerga, which were Iraqi Kurdish tribal forces controlled by Massoud Barzani.

This was right after the first Gulf War, in which the US had activated the Iraqi Kurds with promises of independence when Saddam Hussein was brought to heel. Turkey, which had little interest in those promises and definitely did not want any formal Kurdish state on its borders, had decided to co-opt the Iraqi Kurds into a deal in which the Turks would stop attacking them if they would stay on their side of the border and prevent other Kurds from attacking Turkey. In fact, the Turks would even allow the peshmerga to cross into Turkey if they were in hot pursuit of such groups.

Barzani's forces were actively patrolling the area to prevent guerrilla groups from reaching the PKK bases in the Qandil (or Kandil) Mountain range but, with no other route available, the PKK's trainees had no choice but to run this gauntlet. The peshmerga, thanks to years of self-defense against Saddam Hussein, were quite good at their jobs. Fortunately for the trainees, so were the PKK leaders.

Some may have seen the whole venture as romantic. They would discover that there is very little romantic in an actual war, especially against an enemy at least as well-armed and well-trained as oneself.

A German citizen of Turkish origin was leaving his work at a car repair shop one day when he saw another Turkish man kill a young Kurd for hanging a poster denouncing Turkey's war against its Kurdish citizens. After learning what was going on in Turkey, he decided to join the PKK forces to fight for the Kurdish people's rights in Kurdistan. He was sent to the PKK camp in Lebanon, finished training and took this same route to the Qandil Mountains. En route, his group was ambushed by Barzani forces, and many PKK members were killed. He himself took a Barzani bullet in his chest, but survived and returned to Germany. He said: "*I went to Kurdistan to help the Kurds, but the Kurds almost killed me.*"

Sakine's group made it through the peshmerga's patrol zones and reached the Qandil mountain range, where they were integrated into the People's Defense Forces (Kurdish: Hêzên Parastina Gel [HPG]) as an independent unit of Kurdish women.

The Qandil Mountains are located not far south of Mount Ararat, precisely at the point where the borders of northwestern Iran, northeastern Iraqi

Chapter 9. Guerilla Leader

Kurdistan, and a small tentacle of Turkey all come together. It's an ideal location for skipping across jurisdictions, especially in a situation where the three governments don't have much love for one another. Slipping across these borders, Sakine's unit deployed into Turkey and settled into the Botan region, just south of Lake Van.

The PKK's female fighters under Cansiz' command made headlines in the mid-1990s through a series of suicide bombings and ambushes of Turkish military and police convoys in the Botan region that killed dozens of security force members. Some posed as pregnant women, disguising bombs strapped to their bellies and blowing themselves up in the faces of those who were used to abusing Kurdish women daily in that region. The Turkish army and police became fearful of getting close to Kurdish women. That alone was a reversal of the usual situation.

Impressed with the results of the 1993 trial, Öcalan gave the order to form a women's army. By 1995, they had enough numbers and experience to recruit and train separate units of female guerrillas, under the leadership of a commandant completely separate from Osman Öcalan's HPG organization. This first women's army operated under the banner of the YAJK organization that the PKK women had founded earlier.

Kurdish leader Murat Karayilan said of Sakine's units: "In the year 1994 Sara [*Sakine's PKK code-name*] stayed in Botan, the attacks were very intense, and she was in the most effective battalion".

Women did not require Sakine Cansiz' personal leadership to be effective fighters. Women in other units performed bravely too, and several of them carried out a series of suicide attacks in the mid-1990s. In one such attack, in 1996, Güler Otaç (cover name: Bermal), Zeynep Kinaci (cover name: Zilan) and Leyla Kaplan (cover name: Rewshen) combined in a single attack against soldiers and policemen.

Sakine Cansiz's women recruits were prominent among PKK suicide bombers who committed several acts of terrorism in the early 1990s. During this conflict, which reached a peak in the mid-1990s, the Turkish government responded with even more sweeping atrocities, including many large-scale massacres of civilians. Reasoning that the PKK could not hide among the populace and draw support from it if there was no populace among whom to hide and no means of support for them to draw on, the government embarked on a scorched earth policy similar to that employed by the British in 1902 to defeat the Boers in South Africa.

Chapter 9. Guerilla Leader

The only defense of this approach, really, was that it had been successful. A major difference was that the British were actually invading the Boer Republic, and didn't view the inhabitants as its citizens. Nor, as a result of this treatment, would the Boers ever really consider themselves citizens of the British empire. For the same reasons, the Kurds find it increasingly difficult to visualize themselves as full citizens of a country whose government actively and unceasingly destroys their fields and homes in the hope of catching a few dozen bandits. These are actions aimed at the entire Kurdish population.

In an ethnic cleansing project on a mammoth scale, thousands of villages were destroyed and fields ravaged in the mostly Kurdish areas in the east and southeast of Turkey. Hundreds of thousands of Kurds who now lacked the ability to sustain a rural community fled to cities in other parts of the country. Today, in 2017, it is estimated that over five million Kurds thus displaced now reside in refugee camps outside Istanbul and Ankara.

While there may be overtones of resentment that the PKK's actions may have precipitated this problem, the Kurds reserve far more anger for the government that carried it out with apparently neither any intent nor subsequently any plan to provide a means for those citizens caught in the crossfire to create new lives under the rule of law. When you make it impossible for someone to live lawfully, they must behave like the outlaws they have become. So the PKK continues to grow.

What Women Won

When YAJK was formed, its 700 women comprised around 12 percent of the estimated 5,500 PKK fighters at that time. Since then, many more have been actively involved with the PKK, which claims that over 100,000 more women have returned to their homes and families after receiving combat training in Kurdistan. There they will be better able to protect their families and their villages against the next round of attacks by the Turkish government or nationalist mobs.

The 1990s were a difficult time for the PKK, which was designated as a terrorist organization by the US and NATO. That permitted Turkey to assemble a global coalition of intelligence agencies to gather information about the PKK, and the Turks were able to inflict some serious damage to the organization both through active combat measures and through the devastation of the Kurdish homeland described earlier.

Chapter 9. Guerilla Leader

The brightest sparks in that gloomy period came from the women, who continued to prove themselves in combat, and eventually they precipitated in 2014 the international recognition that the Kurds so desperately needed.

These women were recently arrived in the eyes of the world, but they had been in operation for over 20 years. Since their initial operations in 1994, the bravery of Sakine Cansiz and her women fighters, who gained a reputation for fighting to the very end in difficult situations, made a huge difference in lifting the morale of the rest of the HPG. PKK military commanders recognized the capacity and value of women fighters.

The PKK leaders weren't the only ones to notice. Word of this charismatic figure eventually got around to the international media. This was the kind of story they loved. A photograph from that period shows a young woman in guerrilla fatigues, long hair tied back, toting a machine gun. The scene is in one of the PKK guerrilla training camps at the height of the Kurdish rebellion. The woman is Sakine Cansiz. She stands next to Abdullah Öcalan, showing her senior role in the insurgency.

Sakine Cansiz et le leader du PKK, Abdullah Öcalan, en 1995

Sakine Cansiz with Abdullah Öcalan (Photograph: AFP)

As promised, Öcalan studied the issue of women's combat units thoroughly while assessing the initial results of Sakine's pilot effort. By the mid-1990s it had become obvious that women could indeed fight and in doing

Chapter 9. Guerilla Leader

so should be treated equally with male fighters. By 1997 he had come to a much broader conclusion: not only were they fighting, but in a much larger sense women were making contributions equal to or greater than those of men in a wide array of PKK activities.

In the usual incomprehensible Maoist style, he issued a new policy on the matter: *"A woman's army is not only a requirement for the war against the patriarchal system but is also an element in opposition to sexist mindsets within the PKK freedom movement. Instead of traditional lifestyles and relationships, relationships based on freedom must be adopted; the free choice must overcome the synthetic dependence of women on men."*

With this pronouncement, and others that followed, Abdullah Öcalan placed the PKK on a path to a radical change in the way that Middle Eastern societies looked at women. The new PKK philosophy sets it dramatically apart from every other society in the region (except, ironically, for the hated Israel). The following chapter provides more details of this ultra-feminist view; for the moment, we leave Sakine in her role as battlefield commander.

In the year 2000, the PKK re-organized itself; in the process, the women's military organization became known as YJA-STAR. (In Kurdish, the YJA stands for Yekîneyên Jinên Azad, meaning Units of Free Women. The suffix STAR is a reference to the Zoroastrian goddess Ishtar). The YJA runs a strong personality-cult around Abdullah Öcalan and pays homage to the martyrdom around the figures of Beritan and Zilan (further described at the end of the chapter). The Germans Andrea Wolf and Uta Schneiderbanger are also honored as martyrs.

Sakine didn't see these units as simply a bunch of trained killers. She wanted to prepare her cadres to reintegrate into Turkey and carry on political organizing.

A women's organizer said: *"Sara was impressed with the level of debate of the women delegates. She held my hand and said 'Could you imagine bringing even 5-6 women together in the beginning? Now they are all educated and can discuss very well'. Sara was always ready to leave as if she would go tomorrow, and she worked very hard as if she would stay forever"*.

Sakine Cansiz told her organization: *"As an individual, I love to fight for rights. I do not believe that when you arrive at a certain level, you can give up the fight. In my utopia, you must struggle for freedom all your life. In a liberated Kurdistan, the struggle must be glorious"*.

Chapter 9. Guerilla Leader

Commander Cansiz with one of her patrols (Photo: KurdishQuestion.com)

****

The spirit and bravery of those early recruits and heroines have not been lost on the modern generation.

To some Kurdish women, joining the PKK was an escape from the Kurdish culture's rigid social mores – forced marriages, honor killings and other restrictive practices that remain rife in southeastern Turkey just as they do in the rest of the Islamic world. Many others joined the PKK inspired by a dream of a separate state for Kurds. Some had more specific desires to avenge Kurds killed, imprisoned or tortured by Turkish security forces. Today, the PKK's liberation ideology becomes more widely known, and more importantly it is being proven in practice in PKK-controlled territories in Syria and the Turkish borderlands. Large numbers of educated women are joining PKK in the hope of establishing a country with peace and freedom for all based on the rule of law.

Chapter 9. Guerilla Leader

Whether their motives are martial or social, all the women undergo the same rigorous training as men in camps in the mountains of northern Iraq, but they train and live separately from male comrades. The PKK bars relations between female and male fighters, fearing a weakening of the cause, and in fact has been known to execute fighters who "fell in love" for breaking the group's strict rules.

At the height of the conflict between the PKK and the Turkish security forces, an estimated 20 to 25 percent of the group's fighters were women, according to Nihat Ali Ozcan, a terrorism expert at the Ankara-based Economic Policy Research Foundation of Turkey.

There is no doubting their effectiveness, and it's not just in hit-and-run raids. The Kurds in Syria first gained attention during the crisis around Sinjar, in 2014. A later chapter on events in Syria provides more details about that battle. In this chapter about the rejection by Kurdish women of their treatment by Islamists, a summary will suffice.

The province of Sinjar was home to an offshoot of Islam and Kurdism known as the Yazidi. Unlike many areas of Arabic Syria, the inhabitants resisted the arrival of ISIS and their Islamic fundamentalism. In an unconcealed (in fact, broadcasted) response, ISIS began carrying out a reprisal in which pretty enough women were raped and then taken off to be sold as sex slaves; the less-pretty women were sent to join the men and boys in mass executions. The international media eventually picked up the story of the Yazidis' ongoing resistance, while the Western powers, including the US, fretted but did nothing.

The situation worsened as ISIS herded the entire area's population into an avowed killing field. The Yazidis were doomed.

Suddenly, PKK forces appeared and cut through the ISIS lines to extricate their fellow Kurds. What went largely unreported (incredibly so, given the newsworthiness) was that the rescuers were not just PKK fighters. They were the battalions of women that Sakine Cansiz had trained and led. The ISIS troops well-armed and well-trained, and had defeated all of the other state-sponsored military forces in the area. The women swatted them aside like so many flies.

A YJA-STAR guerrilla, Viyan, had a unique perspective on the events in Sinjar. She came from an Armenian family, which had migrated, to the city of Kobanê in Rojava (former North Syria) following the 1915 Armenian massacres by the Turks.

Chapter 9. Guerilla Leader

Viyan has participated in countless battles within the Rojava Revolution (the uprising against the government of Syrian dictator Bashar al-Assad) and has been wounded many times, most recently in the village of Sününe in Sinjar.

As a Yazidi herself, Viyan has learned the history that is not allowed to be taught in the schools. She learned by oral tradition, listening to her grandmothers' stories that were told generation after generation. The Yazidis count and remember each of the 72 massacres by the Ottoman Islamic Empire against them ever since the Turks took over that part of Kurdistan. The majority of Kurds in Kurdistan used to be Yazidi, but after Islamist purges killed most of them over the centuries, there are only some small communities left, mostly in the Sinjar region. Yazidis also exist in Armenia and Russia, and they travel to Sinjar to visit the Zoroastrian holy places on Sinjar Mountain.

Because the Kurds are repressed everywhere, and Yazidis more so than the rest, they've learned to defend themselves. It was natural for many to join up with the PKK, the only organization that seemed to be after the same objective.

Viyan was a resident of Sinjar who had actually been part of an YJA-STAR unit that operates around Diyarbakir in Turkey. She happened to be recuperating at home in Sinjar from a wound received in Turkey, and was getting well enough to help respond when ISIS attacked.

She joined the defense units in Sinjar, and told of her experiences in Sinjar: "When I came face to face with the ISIS gang and we opened fire on each other, the stories that my grandmother had told me passed through my mind in an instant as if it were a film. It was as if I had become my grandmother and there was a feeling that the massacre I was living through had become a part of the killings about which my grandmother told me. As the people passed across the border, I could not stop myself from thinking about those kidnapped women, and I made a thousand promises to my conscience that I would do everything in my power so that the children I was carrying in my wounded arm would never again see such a massacre."

"Indeed, I became a part of my grandmother's stories."

Sakine Cansiz' training stood the test of time. In March 2016, Turkish security forces killed 15 women Kurdish rebel fighters in a clash in a forested area in southeast Turkey, believed to be the largest one-day casualty toll for women guerrilla fighters. A Turkish security official, speaking on condition of

Chapter 9. Guerilla Leader

anonymity because the government forbids any discussion of the fighting, said security forces did not realize they were fighting women until all were killed and they recovered the bodies.

The women of the PKK have earned with blood the right to be treated with respect and equally with the men with whom they have shared the fighting. And so the PKK, unique among all organizations in all countries in the Islamic world (and perhaps unique among all countries in the entire world), has taken steps in that exact direction.

Within the areas controlled by the PKK or affiliated Kurdish factions, such that a de facto government exists, the Kurds have indeed set up societies in which women have fully equal rights. Many Syrians, not just the Kurds, are flocking to join in.

Heroines and Martyrs

The following stories show a great deal of individual initiative and courage, but it was Sakine Cansiz who molded the group and its fighting spirit. Perhaps they would have been just as brave without her, but without her, they would never have been allowed to go into combat in the first place.

Fair warning: this section is about women getting killed and blowing themselves up. As noted from the outset, there is ample evidence that the PKK has engaged in violent activities; they would not deny it. The question is whether there is any other means by which citizens *can* combat a repressive government that has no compunction about applying excessive force on the slightest pretext.

Beritan

One of their first casualties would quickly become a heroine and inspirational icon of the PKK.

Gülnaz Karatash had the PKK code-name Beritan, which is how the PKK ranks remember her today. The family originally came from Mazgirt in the province of Tunceli (Dersim), near Sakine's home town, but she was born in 1971 in Solhan, in the province of Bingol in Turkey. Also like Sakine, her father was a government official. In 1989, she enrolled in the college of economics at the University of Istanbul, and in 1990 joined the PKK. After a short imprisonment, Gülnaz Karatash became radicalized and moved to the guerrilla side of the movement.

Chapter 9. Guerilla Leader

Beritan wrote that the *"Revolution is growing freedom; we are fighting, and victory will be guaranteed."*

In 1992, the Barzani Kurdish tribal forces of Iraq (Peshmerga), which are allied with Turkey, received the permission of the Turkish forces to cross the Turkish border and pursue the PKK in the area of Shemdinan-Turkey-Iraq border. They surrounded Commander Karatash and her women's unit, and the Peshmerga called on them to surrender. Commander Karatash told her group to move out one by one while she stayed behind to fight the Peshmerga. The Peshmerga continued to call on her to surrender and promised her "one of us would marry you, you will live like a rose". She fought until she ran out of bullets. Then, to escape capture, she threw herself off the rock cliff to meet her death and to gain her place in PKK history as a martyr and an example of true courage.

PKK producer Halil Dag made a film entitled "Beritan" about her bravery and her death. She is memorialized every year.

Zilan

Zeynep Kinaci (codename Zilan) was born 10 August 1971 in the village of Elmali near Malatya in Turkey. She attended elementary and middle school in Malatya. She completed the vocational education of health in Haydarpasha. She studied psychology at the İnönü University in Malatya and worked as a radiologist in the state hospital. In 1994, she joined the PKK and worked for the organization in Adana for one year. In 1995 she joined the women's guerrilla forces, whereupon the Turks arrested her husband.

On 30 June 1996, she killed at least six Turkish soldiers during a military parade at the city center of Tunceli through an act of suicide.

Zilan, according to the PKK, left a farewell letter:

"I want to be the expression of the liberation struggle of my people. Against the policy of imperialism to enslave women, I would like to ignite the bomb on my body and, at the same time, show all my rage and be the symbol of the resistance of the Kurdish woman. My desire is a fulfilled life through great action."

The suicide attack ("fedai eylem" in Kurdish), was then presented as a "good example of a well-planned military attack" in PKK military training courses. Since then, she has been an icon of the PKK, which portrays her attack as an example of "significant resistance" rather than suicide. For

Chapter 9. Guerilla Leader

instance, in the Ruhr area in Germany, the PKK holds an annual women's festival that bears her name: the International Zilan Women's Festival.

Ronahi (Andrea Wolf)

Andrea Wolf (cover name: Ronahî) was born 15 January 1965 in Munich in what was then West Germany. In her high school, Andrea Wolf was a school speaker. Later, she became a member of an SPD (German Socialist Party) youth group and a helper at the Jugendrotkreuz (Youth's Red Cross). The SPD soon opened doors for her and her twin brother Tom to contacts with the more extreme elements of the left-wing scene, which in turn led to their first arrests in the early 1980s. After conducting a house occupation, she received a day in custody. Participation in a demonstration on 4 April 1981 led to four more days of custody.

She and Tom joined the Leisure 81 Autonomous Movement shortly after that. In October 1981, she and her brother received sentences of 18 months' imprisonment because of their involvement in arson attacks on a branch of the Dresdner Bank and a high school, as well as for several instances of graffiti. They actually served about six months. In November 1984 Tom Wolf died by a presumed suicide after a fall from a window. Following regular participation in demonstrations against fascism and globalization, Andrea Wolf committed herself to the successful protests against the activation of the Wackersdorf nuclear reprocessing plant.

With that victory behind it, radical activity declined in Munich, so Wolf moved to Frankfurt. There, in the summer of 1987, she began further house occupations in support of a hunger strike by female detainees in Berlin. In September 1987, she was charged with planning several bomb attacks; the evidence must have been flimsy because she was released with two months of probation. Wolf then joined the No Peace Autonomous Group. She committed further house occupations to show solidarity with members of the Red Army Faction (RAF) who were also conducting a hunger strike.

In addition to these direct actions, Wolf also took up studies to develop her own ideas about revolutionary struggle. In 1990, she spoke at a demonstration on the significance of being branded as a criminal member of a terrorist organization (Section 129a of the Penal Code) and was the founding member of a discussion forum on political detention.

During protests against the 1992 World Economic Summit in Munich, she made contact with foreign left-radical groups, mainly from Central America and Kurdistan. In 1993, Wolf traveled to El Salvador for several weeks to

Chapter 9. Guerilla Leader

expand contacts with the local resistance fighters against the military dictatorship of that time. In 1994, she made another political trip, this time to the USA and Guatemala, where her mother had been living since the death of Tom Wolf.

After her return, the investigating authorities linked Andrea Wolf with the RAF's strike with explosives against the Weiterstadt Prison. She denied her participation in this event or being a member of the RAF, but the investigation process revealed that one of her close friends, Klaus Steinmetz, was actually a police informant. Some of Andrea Wolf's political companions had already been accusing her of recklessness in approaching establishment figures and possibly revealing secrets. The RAF was not an organization to cross lightly. When an arrest warrant was issued against her in the summer of 1995, she found herself with both the RAF and the authorities after her, leaving her with few places in Germany to turn to for help. She went to ground and prepared for an escape to Kurdistan.

By the end of 1996, she had finally fled Germany and joined the PKK, choosing as a cover name the word Ronahî, meaning Light. After spending a few weeks with the PKK, she joined the YAJK, received military training, and was sent into the fight. Her initial battles were against the Kurdish peshmerga; later she would fight against the Turkish army.

On 23 October 1998, Andrea Wolf was captured by a Turkish army unit and disappeared. Over time, rumors emerged that she had been murdered by an officer.

Her mother and a circle of supporters, including the PKK family of those PKK members who died with her, demanded that Turkey explain the deaths of Andrea Wolf and others. When Turkey failed to initiate an appropriate investigation, the mother complained to the European Court of Human Rights. After several years of proceedings, the ECHR condemned Turkey in June 2010 "because it did not conduct an adequate and efficient investigation into the fate of the applicant's daughter." It seemed obvious from such stories as had surfaced that Andrea Wolf was killed only after her capture, but as the ECHR noted, this supposition "was based on legitimate suspicions, but not by evidence". There was no further investigation by the court into the matter of torture and killing. Since it denied that any related event had ever taken place, there was never any investigation by the Turkish government at all.

According to a report of the Human Rights Association, the corpse of Andrea Wolf was found in 2011 in a mass grave with 40 other bodies of PKK fighters, in a cave near the village of Andiçen in the Çatak district. The cave

Chapter 9. Guerilla Leader

was subsequently blown up, but Andrea Wolf lived on as Ronahi, a martyr to the cause of Kurdish rights.

Vian Jaff (also known as Vian Soran)

The mantle has passed from the women who were inspired by Sakine Cansiz' direct leadership to a new generation of Kurdish women who have been inspired by her life story.

Laila Wali was born in 1981 in the city of Sulaymaniyah in-Iraq. There she attended primary and secondary school and then left school in order to join the PKK's struggle for women's rights. She believed that the PKK was the only organization making any effort to achieve the rights of Kurdish people or women. Under the codename of Vian Jaff (sometimes as Vian Soran), she became one of the most active women in the movement

Later on, she became a member of the PCDK, a legitimate Kurdish political party organization in South Kurdistan (northern Iraq) that was nonetheless affiliated with the PKK. She worked in PCDK's media team and started to write about Kurdish women. On the fourth conference of PCDK, she became a member of the Party of Free Women, called YJA-STAR in Turkey but known in Iraq as PJA.

On 2 February 2006, she immolated herself for freedom, leaving a message to the world that "There is no life without Öcalan." She bequeathed her soul, body, courage, bravery, words, pens, papers, etc., to Kurdish women.

Chapter 10. Crusader for Women's Equality

"In Kurdistan to be Kurdish was banned, to be Kurdish was made to be a source of shame. This for women meant no identity and a deeper exploitation of labor. Persecution and violence had become fate."

Sakine Cansiz' story is compelling on its own merits. If you're reading this book as a simple history, or a political thriller, this chapter may be a break in the flow. That very disconnect in the pace of the story is the element that changed Sakine Cansiz from a brave survivor and fierce guerrilla (of whom the PKK has many) into a transformative figure who has galvanized a nation.

How she survived her ordeal in Diyarbakir is something we normal people will never understand. Obviously, she had super-human moral strength. Had we been able to survive even much less abuse, many of us might have done what we do every day when things don't go well: lie low, lick our wounds and hope for the whole grisly episode to go away. Only a few would find a way to get across Turkey and into Syria to rejoin the PKK and seek a violent revenge on the Turks. Perhaps that horrific experience enabled her to see how limited such a response actually was. She must have been spared from that ordeal to serve a much higher calling, and that is what she did.

She recalled the conversations in prison with the other women, many of whom did not survive, and she resolved to honor their memories. One of Sakine Cansiz' greatest legacies to the PKK is the conversion of a conservative culture to a political approach that is actually being practiced on the ground today. If it takes root, it might even serve as the solution for the chaos wrought by 75 years of failed Levantine governments.

From the time of her release from prison and arrival in Lebanon, Sakine Cansiz started lobbying Abdullah Öcalan about recognizing the proper role of modern women in the PKK, and about defining the proper role for women in the Kurdish society that the PKK should launch if it ever gained power.

Sakine wasn't the only one pressing for this, but she was the one who influenced Öcalan to take the subject seriously.

Roadblock to Understanding

Öcalan was not an instant convert. He undertook a methodical approach to studying the issue, and it took him from 1992 to 1997 for him to evolve an understanding of the potential of a broad role for women. His caution was

Chapter 10. Crusader for Equality

driven by the size of the ideological hurdle he had to overcome. Adopting a feminist view of the world is to reject many of the fundamental principles of Islamic society. Because there is no separation of church, state or society in Islam, to reject a long-standing social arrangement is to reject the precepts of the religion itself, and that is heresy, in the most literal sense. In Islam, heretics can be and often are placed under a *fatwa* authorizing any person to kill them with divine blessings.

As an insurgent leader, Öcalan did have the macabre advantage of being under a death sentence anyway, but, as a devout Muslim, he was naturally hesitant to take the road of heresy. Besides, in a purely pragmatic light, the mission of the PKK depended on collecting adherents from amongst the Kurds, who are generally conservative Muslims, and collecting sympathizers from other elements of non-Kurdish but definitely Islamic communities. It's a lot harder to recruit if you start by overturning someone's long-held beliefs.

To the Western world, the most notable and unreasonable of Islamic practices is its vicious treatment of women. Islam is not alone in having enslaved women based on religious laws that they claim to have received directly from the deity. Most world religions, especially Abrahamic religions (Judaism, Christianity, and Islam), have similar histories. The difference is that the other religions have moved on in the past 1400 years, whereas even the most tolerant branch of Islam has evolved very little in that time. Even during the height of the Islamic culture in the 13th and 14th centuries, when scientists and doctors were the marvel of the age, women shared no part in that enlightenment. Since then, the religion has regressed in most areas to its pre-medieval value system. That may be a testament to the integrity of their belief system, but the beliefs themselves do no credit to the religion.

This is one of the main issues that Turkish religious figures have with the Kurds. Every Kurdish community pays more respect to its women than even the most enlightened Islamic leader. PKK leader Abdullah Öcalan has published laws to grant women equal rights to men in every field, which makes them even more progressive than Western countries. This came about because of the influence of PKK co-founder Sakine Cansiz.

There are PKK-oriented parties and even elected officials in Iran, Iraq, and Syria. There are even some in Turkey itself. These leaders use Abdullah Öcalan's philosophies as guidance for their organizations. One of the key requirements, taking the Marxist Commissar approach one step further, is that it is mandatory for political and military organizations to have one man and one woman with equal power as leaders for those organizations.

Chapter 10. Crusader for Equality

Under Kurdish law, women may hold office, own and inherit property, and hold jobs beyond mother and housekeeper. Kurdish men aren't worried that the woman will run off as soon as she has scraped together a few coins. The PKK has reversed Islam's shameful practice of punishing the female in the case of a domestic dispute, regardless of actual fault. It has banned "honor killing", a concept in which the judicial system accepts without question the husband's word with regard to possible crimes of thought, speech or deed by the wife. Today, in the region of Syria where Öcalan-based governing entities have taken charge, Kurdish judges have handed down a life sentence to a Kurdish husband for killing his wife.

In short, PKK laws and practices implement the vision of defending the role of women in a more open society.

This is a novel concept even for the Kurds. In most other Islamic communities, it goes beyond being intolerable. It's blasphemy.

The PKK's policy pronouncements are not just exercises in public relations. They've been proven in action. The PKK does not control any governments, but it does exercise a de facto martial law in those areas of Syria that it has liberated from the Assad regime or ISIS, and it has long served as a shadow government in the wilder Turkish mountain areas. In those areas the PKK governments have implemented the party's policies. Even the military units follow these precepts.

The true testament to the Kurds' basic sincerity is that they are attracting numerous converts even in the non-Kurdish areas of Syria that fall under their control.

Moving Forward On the Women's Liberation Ideology

Since Sakine's arrival, her stories of the women suffering in the Diyarbakir Military Prison had provided Öcalan with much food for thought. She told the leader about the desire of the women's leaders to form their own political party and independent PKK military forces, which would prove how much they deserved to be liberated from male domination. Öcalan listened to Sakine Cansiz carefully. He heard what she went through with those 85 women in prison and realized the strength it must have taken to survive on behalf of a cause that barely recognized their existence.

From thinking about the initial demands for an equal role as combatants, he broadened his thinking to an interest in a meaningful ideology as to the role of women in the larger party context; eventually he considered an

Chapter 10. Crusader for Equality

ideology that would be suitable across all societies. He wanted to come up with an approach that would be better even than the experience of women in modern countries.

The leaders among the women decided to hold the first Women's Congress of the PKK at the end of 1992. Among other things, it resolved that women should have the right to marry or to refuse to marry, and it resolved that the women should create their own political party. Abdullah Öcalan had not approved this meeting or its agenda in advance. When it ended, he reviewed the actions of the Congress and was greatly concerned that their demands for a separate organization could wind up pulling the PKK apart to the point that it was no longer sustainable. He decided to annul the actions of that first Congress, which in itself speaks volumes about the status of women in the PKK at that time. Still, the women of the PKK were the only Muslim women anywhere who could express an opinion at all without incurring the risk of being put to death for doing so.

Öcalan, while troubled, was listening. In 1993, under the urging of Sakine Cansız (and no doubt others), he authorized the formation of the first women's combat units, a major step in defying conventional thinking not just within Islam but in every global society.

On 8 March 1995, the first officially-sanctioned Congress of PKK Women took place in Metina in South Kurdistan (northern Iraq). The Women's Congress elected 23 members of the executive board and formally created a Kurdish women's organization to implement their ideas. That organization is TAJK (Kurdish: Tevgera Azadiya Jinên Kurdistan, which means the Freedom Movement of the Women of Kurdistan). The TAJK inducted as its first official heroine Gülnaz Karataş, the one who leaped off a cliff to escape being captured by the Iraqi Peshmerga forces of Barzani and Talabani.

On 8 March 1998, Abdullah Öcalan finished his promised study of women and announced the Women's Liberation Ideology.

It took time to get there, but Abdullah Öcalan's plan for female freedom is unique. No government and no party in any country have proposed a program that offers such complete equality for women. It is a workable plan that has met acceptance even in the conservative Kurdish culture.

One might look cynically at a women's emancipation proclamation prepared, authorized and delivered by a man, with input but little participation from women. It might suggest that women did not really have the equality of role that this very document purports to offer. But the reality

Chapter 10. Crusader for Equality

is that the prisoner cannot mandate himself to be free. Was Lincoln's freeing of the slaves illegitimate because he was not himself black or enslaved?

The question is not who wrote the paper; the question is whether the existing power structure walks the talk. Do its efforts to reform itself meet up with its proclamations?

Women's Unity Poster

Women have received Öcalan's neo-feminist ideology with great enthusiasm, as evidenced by its power in recruiting new women members for the PKK. Beyond generic adherence to international Communism, YJA-STAR publications emphasize women's liberation and ecological renewals. An element particular to Islam is the PKK's stand against the sharia-based "honor code" that allows men to take extreme measures against the women in their families for little or no reason with no recourse. That issue is one of the YJA-STAR's most powerful recruitment tools.

The Eureka moment in the evolution of Öcalan's thinking was the realization that it is simply impossible to maintain strict adherence to a conservative Islamist dogma while trying to develop policies and programs that respect women. These concepts are completely irreconcilable. This is one reason that it took Öcalan as long as it did to adopt his approach: it required shedding a significant part of his own value system.

The Aryan religion that descended from Mithraism had actually provided a rather modern view of women, allowing them to hold property and maintain a

Chapter 10. Crusader for Equality

role in public affairs. While Zoroastrianism had officially died out under the Muslim tidal wave, much of it was retained through Kurdish sects such as Alawism, Zazaism, the Yarsan and the Yazidi. Elements of it permeated the Kurdish culture even among those who thought of themselves as devout Muslims. That is what enables Kurds to think beyond the oppressive dogma that parades itself as religion in this part of the world.

The fall of Aryanism came at the hand of its counterpart, the Indian-origin Deva religions. The abuse of women was a cardinal feature of those religions, going back 12,000 years to the era of Deva religion and thence to Abraham, who is claimed as forefather to three of the world's great religions. Among those Abrahamic offshoots, the Judaic religion in its Torah form did not recognize women's rights, nor did early Christianity. Muhammed's Islam, being derived from those earlier religions as well as possibly having a close relationship with Shiva, didn't pay any regard to women's rights either. Öcalan certainly wasn't going to abandon Islam altogether (in fact, one of the primary reasons that Kurds broke with Ataturk was that many Kurds did not want to embrace the secular state), but he *was* about to create a modernized version of it.

It is (once again) ironic, really, that Islamic countries consider the PKK's guerrilla activities against corrupt and oppressive regimes to be uncivilized. Those same regimes, under the control of Islamist clerics, condone and underwrite the random killing of people who are not Muslims, or for that matter of Muslims who are not "their kind" of Muslim. All of the various versions of Islamic religious teaching endorse all this behavior for themselves while condemning it in others. By now, everyone in the West is aware that there is little peaceful about the Islamic religion.

Fewer people are aware of how hateful it is towards women, going far beyond the obvious requirements to wear hajibs and burkas. It endorses men's rights to commit all forms of abuse and actual crimes. Most Islamist clerics and the governments they advise or run deny all rights to women, kidnap them for marriage or sale, and maintain a relatively open market on them as sex slaves. Women are considered as property, and may not own any; therefore, they cannot escape an abusive household (which by Western standards describes most Islamic households in this part of the world)

Living in the mountains of Kurdistan without the oversight of government or mullahs, and without depending on communities or families, gave the PKK militants, both male and female, the freedom of perspective. Without that, they could not even have conceived of the idea of breaking away from the

Chapter 10. Crusader for Equality

dominant traditions. In this atmosphere of freedom, they were able to construct new values and thought systems.

For female militants, this carried extra significance. The ability to perform military actions and the capacity to defend themselves empowered them to establish their own thoughts, and that breakthrough brought about significant developments for female PKK militants.

Millions of Kurdish women around the world are regularly taking the streets to struggle for their freedom. These are the values that have derived from significant resistance in the last 38 years of the PKK existence. The Kurdistan Woman's Liberation Movement maintains a core statement to motivate itself, *"In Kurdistan to be Kurdish was banned, to be Kurdish was made to be a source of shame. This for women meant no identity and a deeper exploitation of labor; persecution and violence had become fate."*

The women of Kurdistan never accepted any of these conditions as their destiny. To reject them meant that they had to construct a new means of obtaining their freedom. Some, like Gültan Kisanak (the legislator, mayor and now political prisoner) tried the conventional route, discovering only too late that it led only to co-optation and eventual betrayal. In Turkey, and in much of the Islamic world, the only other route available is through the organizations considered the most radical (by Islamic standards) because they actually do endorse the view of women as a force for good rather than a group to be oppressed.

The PKK is just such an organization, but as we have seen, it didn't get there overnight. Öcalan had to evolve in his thinking to get to the point that he was able to align his political movement behind women's interest. In turn, they had to learn how to work with him to get their chance of using that movement as their vehicle.

It takes a long time to change even a small organization. The women weren't asking for just a small change in the way the PKK conducted itself. Starting to think in their way required throwing off traditions that are nearly 1500 years old and baked into every fragment of every social interaction, under possible penalty of death for infractions. That's not just a matter of changing your mind.

Fortunately, Abdullah Öcalan didn't have as far to travel as most Turkish or Kurdish men. It wasn't that he started out to be a messianic being; in fact, he was on track to be quite the opposite: a government actuary. What could be less revolutionary? However, in his early studies under a more or less open

Chapter 10. Crusader for Equality

secular Turkish government, he began to see the need to get rid of the larger Turkish society's backward traditions and lifestyle. In doing so, he was pushed further and further out of the mainstream of Turkish thought and Turkish society until he had to carry out his insights through secret cells, which took him even further out of the social network until he abandoned it altogether in taking up the life of an outlaw.

Only then, with his whole social framework being thrown open to question and examination, was he able to perceive how much of "the culture" was merely a mechanism for control. That is what freed him to philosophize as to what it might mean to live freely with women and to live with free women.

None of this was revealed overnight. Female recruits learned to discard their former selves and become fighters. Male fighters learned to respect the capability, bravery and sometimes savagery of their female counterparts. Öcalan observed this taking place while he was learning, thinking, and evaluating possible outcomes and consequences. What emerged was truly revolutionary.

Öcalan's new doctrine goes far beyond a simple ambition to achieve equality between the sexes. Rather, it aims to reorganize the whole of society by renovating the matriarchal order of life that existed in natural communities. He summarized this aim in saying, "*Women, reborn to freedom, will drive the general liberation, enlightenment, and justice in all upper and lower institutions of society*". Öcalan came to believe that only a liberated society could be considered truly democratic.

The following paragraphs describe the PKK's new view on women. Unfortunately it is always difficult to translate the Maoist styling of extreme harangues preferred by so many revolutionary groups, but rendering it in a style more compatible with Western readers simply dilutes the message without adding anything to it. So, in Öcalan's own words:

Woman's Freedom will play a stabilizing and equalizing role in forming the new civilization, and she will take her place under respectable, free and equal conditions. To achieve this, the necessary theoretical, programmatic, and organizational and implementation work must be done. The reality of woman is a more concrete and analyzable phenomenon than concepts such as "proletariat" and "oppressed nation." The extent to which society can be thoroughly transformed is determined by the extent of the transformation attained by women.

Chapter 10. Crusader for Equality

Similarly, the level of women's freedom and equality determines liberty and equality of all sections of society. Thus, the democratization of woman is decisive for the permanent establishment of democracy and secularism. For a democratic nation, woman's freedom is of great importance too, as liberated woman constitutes liberated society. Liberated society, in turn, constitutes the democratic nation. Moreover, the need to reverse the role of man is of revolutionary importance.

The Basic Principles of the PKK Women's Liberation Ideology

I. Patriotism: "Before everything women's ideology cannot exist without land. The art of harvest and the art of production are connected to women's artistry. This means that the first principle of the women's ideology is a woman's connection to the land she is born on; in other words, patriotism."

II. The principle of free thought and free will: "The second principle is the woman's ability to think freely and develop a free will in her participations to social life. If this ideology is to succeed, women must be able to live as they wish and make their decisions accordingly. We must trust in their decisions and respect their will. This is an essential principle for this ideology."

III. A sharing has life-based on freedom and the principle of organization: "For any of the above to materialize, an organizational structure is vital. An unorganized individual is nothing. The first social structures are organized around women. Women must take their organizational structures seriously, as men have in their organizations. Women must internalize the values of their organization – this is what today we are doing in the YAJK".

IV. The principle of resistance: "Women must see life as a domain for resistance. This is because without resistance women are being kept captive between four walls. Women are being burdened into non-productivity by being confined to simple tasks; therefore, to counter this, women must empower themselves by resisting in every possible way.

Since the year 2000, Öcalan's new democratic, ecological and gender-equality paradigm has been an essential component of the YAJK's educational seminars that teach about the history of the women's struggle in Kurdistan. It is a powerfully effective part of the recruiting approach to Kurdish women. Perhaps just as important to the Kurdish cause in the long run, the focus on gender equality has opened the doors for the women of Kurdistan to many women's groups around the world. It may not be as apparent or as exciting as blowing up police cars, but creating a supportive

Chapter 10. Crusader for Equality

worldwide community may end up being the most durable way to keep Kurdish issues in the forefront of world attention.

In 2005, the women of Kurdistan formed a democratic umbrella organization called the High Women's Council of the Kurdish Women's Movement (KJB, which in Kurdish is Koma Jinên Bilind). The KJB includes four fundamental components:

1- The women's ideological movement, PAJK

2- The women's social movement, YJA (the Free Women's Union)

3- The women's self-defense force, YJA-STAR

4- The young women's organization

These four primary groups all organize and plan their work independently but come together in the formation of wider strategies.

Jineology

The latest development in PKK thinking about gender and roles is called Jineology. The original version of this word is Kurdish and is derived from the Kurdish word for woman, jin, and the globally-recognized "-ology" to imply a scientific approach.

Öcalan devised Jineology to describe the knowledge needed to fill the gaps in that understanding, as the current social sciences have proven themselves incapable of doing.

Jineology is built on the principle that without the freedom of women within society and without a real consciousness surrounding women, no society can call itself free. Öcalan wanted women to depend on themselves as the guide to study for self-liberation from ancient laws enforced with the chain of legal enslavement by men.

Jineology is formed on the criticism that existing scientific disciplines are structured within the framework of capitalist modernity and therefore are extremely divided and fragmented. Jineology, on the other hand, foresees a wholesome approach to humanity, society and the universe. This is why, rather than being a new scientific discipline, Jineology is a new epistemological approach fueled by a conscience of freedom.

For those readers anxious to delve further into this line of thought, there's more material on the PKK's website about its stands on women's issues: see

Chapter 10. Crusader for Equality

http://www.pkkonline.com/en/index.php?sys=article&artID=231.

Its women members always have in mind the friends and family members they seek to liberate from the oppression they face on a daily basis at home in Turkey.

Öcalan may be ponderous and sanctimonious in his rhetoric about women needing to throw off the yoke of slavery to men, and it may sound ridiculous to those readers fortunate enough to live in a Western democracy. Although Islam certainly espouses this treatment, it's not really about Islam especially. There are only a handful of countries on the globe that do **not** treat the female gender quite literally as slaves.

Turkey has neither more nor less to answer for in that matter than any other country in the region, but that's an exceedingly low standard to meet. Turkey, which had many years of success as a secular society in which women were free to contribute, should know better.

The PKK's stand on these issues is unique in the region, and to some degree, as Öcalan says, unique in the world. As an illegal organization representing a country that doesn't yet exist, there's only so much the PKK can do.

Continuing Abuses of Women

In the decade of 2011-2020, Turkey may have given up on achieving membership in the European Union. It believes with some justification that the continuing refusal since the 1980s to accept Turkey as a member, despite all the reforms made, while admitting many much newer and equally shaky states from the former Soviet Union, proves that the oh-so-liberal Europeans are, behind the cosmopolitan facade, closet racists or jingoist who want nothing to do with a bunch of dark-skinned Muslims. Over time, Erdoğan greatly reduced Turkey's chances of such acceptance in his ever-more transparent march towards totalitarianism.

Another anomaly in Turkey's desire to be seen as European is its attitude toward the role of women in society. Under the AKP, the country is sliding rapidly backward to the same standard as the rest of those countries when it comes to the treatment of women.

Recall that the offenses of the warden at Diyarbakir were so egregious that he was eventually executed for his crimes. That doesn't mean the abuses

Chapter 10. Crusader for Equality

have stopped. Nor are they much less egregious. The only real difference is that Erdoğan has given up on trying to win the hearts and minds of the Kurds, and so there's no more incentive to do anything about these abuses and no consequence for doing it. So the offenses go unreported and uninvestigated, and the abuse continues.

Abuses by Turkish officials isn't confined to the hidden spaces behind high prison walls. Rape especially goes unreported and unpunished, even when it occurs essentially in public, because of the Islamic "honor" code that blames the victim and the victim's family rather than the attacker.

Duygu Kasakolu was detained in Istanbul in 2013; she was sexually tortured while blindfolded in the police vehicle. Duygu told the story of how she survived the torture: by remembering the struggle of her childhood heroine Sakine Cansız, the Kurdish woman fighter and politician assassinated while battling for the rights of Kurds and for women everywhere.

The Legal Aid Bureau Against Harassment and Rape under Arrest (an entity that is sponsored by the government to investigate such offenses) prepared a report on state-perpetrated sexual torture between the years of 1997 and 2013, indicating that at least 393 women had applied for help related to sexual molestation while under arrest. Commenting on the recent rise in sexual torture in Turkey, Duygu Kasakolu, a survivor of this type of behavior at the hands of the police, called for women everywhere to report their stories without shame and struggle against these attacks.

For Duygu, Sakine's "life of fighting" (as the title of her autobiography put it) inspired her own resistance against sexual torture. Duygu first encountered harassment from police at Karabuk University, where local police often harassed Kurdish women students. While she was staying in a dormitory, police often made threatening remarks, telling her and other women students that they "had her number." In the same period, a man began sexually harassing Duygu. She knew that even if she complained to police, nothing would change, so she had to move to Istanbul.

At a 2013 protest, Duygu was struck in the head with an unknown projectile and was then arrested while trying to help a friend wounded by police. She was put into a vehicle with two other people. "They took me to a dark, closed place. There's one sentence I remember very clearly: 'we have handled a lot of Alevi and Kurdish women like you. We'll handle you too, and you'll like it.'" One policeman, angered when Duygu broke into hysterical laughter, cut her breasts with a knife, saying, "This scar is so I'll always be able to find you again."

Chapter 10. Crusader for Equality

"When they did this, Sakine Cansız came into my head. Comrade Sara was tortured in the Diyarbakir prison by guards cutting off her breast. But she wasn't intimidated, and she continued to struggle," said Duygu. "Even if I couldn't do as much as her, I needed not to be undone by this torture; I needed to resist."

Sakine Cansız was a childhood hero of Duygu's. After she was released in atrocious physical condition, she says that Sakine Cansız' resistance gave her the courage to report the police who harassed her. However, her struggle was largely fruitless, as she could not remember any exact details from the attack, in which she was blindfolded.

"In spite of them, I continue to be out there on the streets," said Duygu. "Recently, there's been a big rise in sexual torture. Women need not be ashamed. These disgusting things they've experienced are not because of them." She called on women to continue their struggle in the face of harassment.

Not much can be clear in a society where the government withholds or distorts all official information. Nonetheless, the facts on the ground speak for themselves. It is very clear that continuing these abuses against half of the country.s population, Turkish and Kurdish women alike, will continue to build popular support for the PKK over a period of many years when that support would otherwise have withered away.

Chapter 11. Sakine the Diplomat

By the late 1990s, Sakine Cansiz had built an impressive reputation among the Kurds for her exploits as a guerrilla leader. The shift in the PKK's thinking to female equality, implemented through 1998, was widely credited to her influence. She had been brave in prison, fearless and effective in combat, and tireless in pursuing Öcalan to the new understanding of the potential of women.

Looking at her career in retrospect, her various metamorphoses had been forced on her by external circumstances; her achievement lay in turning those situations to successful, if unanticipated, conclusions. In 1999, the PKK was presented with a dramatic shift, and before long Sakine would once again be presented with a high-stakes conundrum.

The Capture of Öcalan

After the 1980 coup, Abdullah Öcalan began operating out of the Bekaa Valley in Lebanon, which was in turn controlled by Syria. At its peak, the PKK deployed over 8,000 fighters in its war against Turkey, and most of them trained here.

With the transition of power back to a democratic government in 1988, Turkey was in a better position to demand that the international community support its efforts at self-government. Over time, Turkey persuaded many countries to declare the PKK to be a terrorist organization. Nonetheless, through the late 1990s, Sakine's units and those of the mainline PKK exacted ever-more intensive pressure against Turkish forces.

In 1998, the Turkish government felt sufficiently sure of itself at home (although it was in fact about to be handed a major election defeat by the AKP in 2000) that it also felt able to bluster on the world stage. Turkey demanded that the Syrians hand Öcalan over, or it would invade and do the job for them. The US and various NATO-EU members supported their fellow NATO member Turkey's threats.

Öcalan didn't want to burn bridges with Syria, one of the few countries that were openly supporting the PKK. He was also concerned that if a conflict over the PKK should occur, the millions of non-combatant Kurds were the ones who would suffer reprisals at the hands of their governments, while Öcalan himself might be thousands of miles away. It might also render *non*

Chapter 11. Sakine the Diplomat

grata the hundreds of thousands of Kurds who were exiled in Western countries, where they too would then be at risk.

Öcalan decided to buy peace for Assad by vacating the Bekaa Valley bases, and when he did so, the Turkish military units on the Syrian border did indeed stand down from their invasion posture (but not from their pursuit of the PKK). He could have relocated to join his combat units in their mountain holdfasts in Iraq and Iran. Iraq's Kurdish peshmerga, subsidized by its support from the US government, would likely have stepped up efforts to find and eliminate him. Iran would not have been impressed with Turkish threats, and many PKK bands operated from Iran regularly, but setting up a noticeable presence could change all that. The radical Shi'ite regime, well-known for its aggressive approach to non-Shi'a groups all across the Middle East, would certainly not provide a safe haven for a sizeable force. Iran had both the military capability and the disregard for human rights needed to root out an insurgent group. Besides, the PKK forces had been doing very well for themselves over the past few years even with their leadership being several hundred miles away. Öcalan chose instead to depart from the fray altogether, holing up in the sanctuary of friendly embassies.

That strategy did not last long. Once his basing plan shifted from a field operation to dependence on bureaucrats in diplomatic pin-stripes, he was out of his element. The US and EU threatened sanctions on one country after another, and one by one they folded. He hopscotched down the countries of the eastern coastline of Africa, and by the end of 1998 he had shifted as far as the Kenyan capital of Nairobi, where he was a guest of the Greek embassy. Again the US and European pressure built, and the Greeks asked him to make other plans. On 2 February, 1999, Öcalan departed the diplomatic sanctuary of the embassy compound.

Within minutes, he disappeared and was next seen in the custody of the Turkish government. As with any good covert operation, we can't be sure exactly who carried out the mission; Kurdish sources believe that only the Americans or the Israelis had the necessary intelligence, logistics and tactical know-how to pull it off. Öcalan was soon facing trial by military courts on a massive array of charges that, as the leader of the PKK and its armed elements, were irrefutable.

Fortunately for him, Turkey was at that moment actively seeking entry to the European Union, which banned capital punishment, and so this sentence, while imposed, was not carried out, and eventually Turkey too would do away with the death sentence. Instead, Öcalan was confined as the

[123]

Chapter 11. Sakine the Diplomat

only prisoner on a small island with a guard force of over 1,000 soldiers, and on that island Öcalan remains to this day.

Division in the PKK

The PKK had to devise ways to lead itself in the absence of its leader. Öcalan might have given the Turks the idea that the PKK was on the edge of collapse when as early as August 5, 1999 he called from his imprisonment for the PKK to stand down in Turkey and seek a peaceful settlement for Kurdish rights. Although it does re-publish Öcalan's periodic calls for a peaceful resolution of Kurdish issues, the Turkish government has never taken any tangible actions to implement that peace, with the exception of some brief personal overtures by then-Prime Minister Erdoğan at the start of the AKP regime. On paper, the government formed a commission to investigate war crimes on both sides. There is no evidence that the commission has ever met.

Instead, since 1999 the Turks have set their sights on the opposite objective: the elimination of every member of the PKK organization.

The Turkish government would prefer to eliminate every vestige of Kurdish nationalism wherever it might be found, in order to resolve once and for all its concerns over the long-term consequences of a large and intractable Kurdistan forming out of various smaller enclaves. That simply wasn't practical. In view of the general support for the Kurds from the western allies, and the active armed support from the US, Turkey had little option but to concede the existence of the Kurdish homeland in Iraq. With the PKK driven out of Lebanon, Turkey's rationale for an intervention in Syria was also extinguished.

Unable to come up with a plan to engage the PKK directly outside Turkey, the Turks decided instead to capitalize on the removal of the binding force of Öcalan's leadership. They hired a wide range of people inside Turkey and abroad, first to divide the PKK organization internally and then to destroy it permanently.

The first fissure within the PKK came from its own self-appraisal. Somebody had tipped someone off as to Öcalan's movements. Now the first round in the Turkish strategy would start paying off: the organization would turn against itself in the effort to find out who the traitor was.

In the wake of Öcalan's arrest, the PKK launched an investigation as to who had betrayed the PKK organization and enabled Öcalan's arrest. To lead this investigation they recalled the representatives in Europe, Kani Yilmaz

Chapter 11. Sakine the Diplomat

and Ali Haidar, who could not have been involved because they had not possessed the necessary information.

The other four members of the PKK Presidential Council were senior and long serving PKK leaders: Murat Karayillan (Cemal), Cemil Bayik (Cuma), Osman Öcalan (Ferhat) and Duran Kalkan (Abbas). They met with Kani and Haidar in the PKK base in the Qandil mountains to review the situation, but they never uncovered, or at least never disclosed, any information about who might have been involved in the betrayal of Öcalan.

Cemil Bayik at BBC interview, posted on YouTube.

Another consequence of this reflection period was that the PKK elected to follow Öcalan's call to stand down and negotiate. The Turkish Government published this call and the PKK's acceptance widely. Beyond that, it made no conciliatory response; instead, it unveiled the second step in the wedging strategy.

In return for accepting the existence of the Iraqi Kurdish regional government near its borders, the Turks had some years earlier co-opted Barzani and Talabani into working aggressively against the PKK organization. Now Jalal Talabani, in turn, sought out the PKK members who had separated themselves at the time of the earlier ceasefire, and he successfully recruited Osman Öcalan. He was not only the younger brother of Kurdish leader Abdullah Öcalan but also one of the major leaders of the PKK forces in the

Chapter 11. Sakine the Diplomat

Qandil Mountains. In that capacity, he had been the commander of the force to which the first of Sakine Cansiz' women's units were initially attached.

Nine years younger than his brother Abdullah, he was born in 1958 in the small village of Omerli, in Ourfa province. After studying at teachers' training college, he became a member of the PKK in 1978 and spent two years in Libya, thus escaping the 1980 roundup. He joined the central committee in 1986 and the executive committee in the 1990s, but he had suffered disgrace in 1992 after signing a truce with the two main Iraqi Kurdish parties, Massoud Barzani's KDP and Jalal Talabani's PUK. For that apostasy he was jailed by the PKK until he recanted. Having thus been "re-educated" in proper Maoist style, he was restored to his former position. Apparently he never forgave his brother Abdullah for this, and began his own subversive efforts as soon as Abdullah was safely in a Turkish prison.

Journalist Chris Kutschera reported in 2005 that "*while the European Court of Human Rights (ECHR) ruled the trial of Abdulla Öcalan had been unfair, some of the former PKK leader's closest lieutenants were establishing a new political organization, the Patriotic and Democratic Party of Kurdistan, and voicing serious criticism of their former leader. They accuse Öcalan of being a 'despot comparable to Stalin or Hitler', who, they claim, ordered the murder of a number of dissidents*".

See: https://www.chris-kutschera.com/A/pkk_dissidents.htm).

These accusations are remarkable in view of the cult status that the PKK afforded its leader even while he was in the Beka'a Valley and they were hundreds of miles apart in Qandil. Even today, after he has been isolated in prison for more than 15 years, PKK-dominated communities display banners, posters and portraits of Öcalan on every available surface.

On the other hand, we also have Sakine Cansiz' casual remark that guerrillas who broke the PKK's rules were executed. She didn't specify whether that occurred in the Beka'a or in Qandil; quite likely it was both. In its early years, the PKK code of conduct was very severe. Recruits who joined the organization were required to swear a loyalty oath vowing on the strength of their own lives not to betray the PKK or its principles. More recently, the PKK has loosened its policies, ending the practice of hunting down and killing defectors, let alone those who just wanted to stop being a guerrilla. Or so they say; who would know?

The other leaders of this internal dissident group were equally highly-placed. Shahnaz Altun had risen from raw recruit to become a military

Chapter 11. Sakine the Diplomat

commander at the head of a battalion of 150 women fighters. Nizamettin Tas (codenamed "Botan") was one of the most well-regarded of the PKK's military commanders. He became a member of its central committee in 1986, and was commander of all PKK armed forces in the 1990s.

Osman Öcalan

With 14 other cadre members and about 30 fighters, these three left the PKK headquarters at Qandil, making their way through the mountains of Iraqi Kurdistan to find asylum and protection in the area controlled by Jalal Talabani's PUK. On 21 October 2004, at Said Sadik, near Suleimania, they founded the Patriotic and Democratic Party, which was open to working with the Massoud Barzani group towards establishing a cooperative federation of Kurdish enclaves. Once those became viable, the cadre would worry about whether and how to re-assemble them into a unitary nation later on.

This group of defectors also disclosed many secrets of the PKK's organization, financing and military tactics to Jalal Talabani and Massoud Barzani. They, in turn, shared these secrets with Turkey and anyone else who would give them money. It gave a formidable advantage to the Turks and the peshmerga in hunting the PKK down, and it would be several years before the PKK was able to reconstitute itself.

The PKK has not forgotten or forgiven this group. Quitting is one thing; selling out the organization and its secrets is another. They have survived only by making themselves scarce, deep inside the Barzani enclave. Whether they are eventually proven right, or whether the PKK will catch up with them, will be known over time. In either case, as we know, the Kurds will not forget even if it is a very, very long time.

Chapter 11. Sakine the Diplomat

****

Back at the PKK headquarters, Murat Karayılan and other PKK leaders picked up the pieces and worked to rebuild the party that the defectors had sold out.

Murat Karayılan was a very strong leader and would become the de facto head of the PKK. With Cemil Bayik, Sakine Cansiz, Dr. Bahoz Erdal and others, he drove the PKK to survive the betrayal by Osman Öcalan.

The defections to Barzani failed to achieve Turkey's goal. PKK organizations began to regroup in 2002-2003 and since then have grown rapidly in Kurdistan, militarily, financially and politically.

For a brief period, the regrouping was facilitated by upheavals in the Turkish government between 2000 and 2004.

At the start of this timeframe, Öcalan had declared the ceasefire with the government in the hope of a peaceful resolution process. The Assembly of Turkish-American Associations, an entity similar to a Chamber of Commerce but run by the Turkish government, has stated that the PKK did little to implement this initiative, turning in no arms and continuing to recruit for its force of an estimated 5,000 guerillas, but conceded that the volume of attacks did diminish considerably.

2002 brought the radical change in Turkey that many hoped for. A financial crash in 2001 had erased voter confidence in any of the old-guard political parties that had participated in the coalition government that followed military rule, and every single incumbent delegate was removed from office. The big winner was the AKP, which took two-thirds of the seats.

Erdoğan himself could not take office as Prime Minister because of last-minute dirty tricks by the outgoing government. Erdoğan had not always been a strong Islamist; he was opposed to the previous government because of its corruption and ineffectiveness, not because of its secularism. In fact, he would continue most of its policies once he got into office. Nonetheless, because he had founded an opposition party, the government's response was to jail him in 1998 on dubious charges of anti-secular activities.

That was humiliating but it could have been a lucky break. His party remained in opposition as the government's performance slid ever more quickly downhill. If the politicians didn't notice or care, the people did.

On the eve of the 2002 election, Erdoğan himself was served with new and even more specious charges that prevented him from standing as a candidate.

Chapter 11. Sakine the Diplomat

He may have had more empathy than most Turks for the PKK's issues with the vagaries of the government's use of the legal system! He had to wait until winning a by-election in 2003 before he could enter Parliament and take office as Prime Minister. Ironically enough, the seat that came open was in a heavily Kurdish district that gave him 67% of the vote. Most of them would come to regret that choice.

As part of the 2002 campaign, Erdoğan had extended olive branches to the Kurds, to business leaders, and to moderates of various sorts -- in fact, to anyone who was not a member of the ruling party at the time. After an initial period of optimism, the Kurds observed that nothing much changed, even though they had directly assisted Erdoğan into the Premiership.

In 2003, the new government published the "Law on Reintegration into Society", providing amnesty to any member of the PKK who had not been involved in actual crimes. However, most of the PKK's active followers had come to the PKK precisely because, much like Erdoğan himself, the government had jailed them or a family member for specious "crimes". They were only been released at all because the charges were so specious that not even the Turkish justice system would acknowledge the charges, but the charges remained on their records nonetheless. It should come as little surprise that there were few takers on that offer. Given this caveat in the amnesty, the actual fighters themselves were obviously not covered at all, so there was no point in them turning themselves in.

As we now know, whatever his initial intentions with regard to the Kurds, Erdoğan was playing a much bigger game. During the earliest years of his administration, he had three parallel and related priorities. One was to enter the European Union as a means of boosting the Turkish economy. The second was the re-establishment of a religious government through the AKP. The third was an alliance with the principal recognized Islamist entity in Turkey, the Gülen group described earlier, to get rid of the other competing parties. To the extent that they didn't interfere with the goals, the Kurds were the least of his problems.

The PKK, alleging a complete lack of a serious response to Kurdish issues, declared the combat moratorium at an end in 2004. However, the leadership split over this decision too, with several more insisting that the PKK was not positioned for such a choice. It had only half the strength of its peak years; more importantly, it had no state sponsor to provide logistical and financial shelter. Those who advocated accommodation departed the party.

Chapter 11. Sakine the Diplomat

As a result of the defection of a good portion of its leadership and the troops loyal to them, and the ongoing dispute among the remaining leaders as to the proper approach to take, the PKK's strength was reduced even further. Its operations were reduced from platoon-sized combat operations to raids conducted by small teams that avoided direct engagement. Drawing on the lessons rapidly being learned in Iraq, they placed land-mines and conducted random hit-and-run raids to harass and intimidate the Turkish soldiers rather than aiming to cause any real damage.

With the reduced scale of operations, the PKK seldom made enough of a splash to attract any attention, and the supporters outside the immediate theater began to lose interest in the cause. Since that overseas base was the source of the vast majority of the PKK's revenues, that situation needed to be turned around.

Diplomatic Mission

Running an ongoing organization, even one dedicated to personal sacrifice and socialist minimalism such as the PKK, takes money. The Assembly of American-Turkish Associations, mentioned earlier, notes some of the PKKs activities as:

- Financing its terrorist strength
- Running media outlets (dailies, periodicals, TV and radio channels) and
- Carrying out anti-Turkish propaganda activities in many parts of the world

The PKK's revenue sources include:

- Revenues obtained from the "special nights" organized by affiliates.
- Sales of publications etc.
- Revenues obtained from commercial establishments belonging to or otherwise affiliated with the organization.

The AATA claims that the PKK is also in the business of extortion, collecting "protection money" from non-affiliated (i.e. Turkish) businesses. That is true, if distorted. The PKK views these transactions as simply collecting taxes in areas where it exercises de facto control, making the activities just as legitimate as those coerced by any other government in any country.

Chapter 11. Sakine the Diplomat

More significantly, the AATA suggests that the PKK is also in the businesses of drug-trafficking, arms-smuggling and trafficking in human beings. The arms smuggling is true almost by definition for an illegal guerilla group, but the charges of drug-running and human trafficking are found only in Turkish surrogate sources. In fact, the US embassy's alarm evidenced in the cable cited in the Appendix would suggest that the authorities believe the PKK is already raising far too much money through the overt channels that diplomatic action cannot interdict.

A popular movement, by definition, requires popular support, but as a rule the oppressed people who launch a popular movement are poor and in danger of losing at any moment whatever meager resources they may have. It's very hard for them to produce actual cash to support the insurgency's needs. The government makes that harder by wresting property away from Kurds at every opportunity; in the meantime, the taxes that it raises from Kurdish people are largely used to support the same military apparatus that suppresses them.

To survive in opposition to a powerful nation-state, such a movement needs access to an independent financial supply

Many of the most natural allies, i.e. the Islamic countries in the region, have supported all sorts of terrorist-style organizations. The Kurds disqualified themselves in those eyes when Öcalan began espousing philosophies that actively disputed Islam and its laws. The only places where potential donors have sufficient quantities of disposable income are the western economies of Europe and America. These countries have, technically speaking, outlawed the PKK. Then again, they had also done that with the IRA, which nonetheless derived considerable support from citizens of those countries.

The Kurdish diaspora was not large in the USA. Although the American government got the Kurds stirred up in Iraq, few of them made it back to the US and few people in the US heard anything about it. To the extent that any interaction was there, the experience of many veterans in Iraq tilted American sympathies towards the peshmerga rather than to the Turkish or Syrian Kurds. Until 2013, hardly anybody in the US even knew that there *were* any Kurdish populations outside Iraq.

The necessary financial and political conditions merged in Europe. The economies are wealthy enough that significant donations are possible even for working-class people, and several European countries have permitted the entry of some substantial Kurdish populations. Politically, while the banned

Chapter 11. Sakine the Diplomat

PKK cannot have formal contacts with the various government entities, the PKK leadership has been able to build effective relationships with European government leaders. This facilitates activism and fund-raising.

Émigrés also benefit from the general economic prosperity in their adoptive countries. Unlike many government-funded entities, the PKK needs very little funding to support its operations. Living off the land and in the shadows, and not trying to confront the government forces strength-for-strength, the PKK purchases modest amounts of food and simple weaponry, although the net costs are increased by having to make those purchases on the black market and smuggle them into the operational area. Relatively small donations, by western standards of personal giving, can provide sufficient funds to meet the PKK's needs ... as long as the donors are so inclined.

In 2005, they were not so inclined. Despite the creation of a favorable political environment in which to operate, the news was not good at the street level. The rate of enrolment in the PKK among the over one million Kurds living in Europe declined rapidly after Öcalan's arrest. After their own resurgence in 2004, the Iraqi Kurds began siphoning off potential PKK followers with promises of an eventual share in the Iraqi oil money when Kurdistan would become autonomous.

Events in Turkey, at least at the public level, seemed to suggest that perhaps the issue was on the wane. Since 2003, the AKP had relaxed a few of the governmental policies, including the much-despised prohibition on teaching children the Kurdish language at all. During the national elections in 2005, Erdoğan had come to Kurdistan and openly acknowledged the existence of, and the need to resolve, "the Kurdish question". In 2007 the state-run TV network would begin work on putting together a Kurdish-language channel.

Not long before this, Americans of Irish descent had started to believe that the Anglo-Irish situation would resolve itself once the peace process appeared to be gaining traction, even though it was not finalized. In that case, donations to fund combat operations seemed like condoning pointless mayhem. In the end, the drying up of donations appeared to lead in turn to the drying up of the conflict itself.

Now European-based Kurds who had found a way to make a less risky living in a less-contentious environment such as France, Belgium or Germany started to entertain the same doubts. It looked as though there could well be peace, and it was clear that the Turkish government would remain firmly in place. In fact, the pin-prick bombings and drive-by shootings that the

Chapter 11. Sakine the Diplomat

reduced-strength PKK was able to mount were starting to look like little more than sour grapes, and the associated casualties to be no longer justified.

Crowds tend to follow a winner. Even Kurds.

The PKK might have been able to find one government or another somewhere around the world anxious to stir up trouble for Turkey. Finding one that didn't like Iraq or Syria would have been simple. But the PKK leaders were anxious to avoid become dependent on any one source of easy money. They had come to this conclusion after observing their nemesis in Iraq, the Barzani family, which had opposed the Ba'athists throughout the 1960s and 1970s and had received the support of the US, Israel and the Shah of Iran. In 1976, the morally-scrupulous but naïve Carter administration decided to cut off funding to Barzani, whose accounting for that money was highly opaque, and to start undermining the Shah. The money supply disappeared and Barzani's strength foundered. Iraqi Kurds, far from being liberated, became the recipients for many years of even more brutal repression by the Ba'ath regime in retaliation. The PKK took it as a point of strategic importance to keep their funding needs at a tolerable level that could be met by grass-roots fund-raising.

Now the grass roots were drying up. The PKK had to find a way to get back into the consciousness of the European Kurdish community. If it could not do so promptly, it would wither away.

Once again, the PKK depended on Sakine Cansiz to provide the vital spark at the right moment.

By this time, as a result of her own story followed by many years of the daring exploits of her women's guerrilla units, Sakine Cansiz had achieved a powerful reputation throughout Kurdistan and the dispersed émigré community. Murat Karayilan, the acting leader, had served as the PKK's voice in Europe for several years before being recalled to lead the PKK after the schism; now he dispatched Cansiz to Europe to fill his earlier role there. The idea was that she would inspire the donor base there as she had done in building a formidable organization of fighting women.

Just because your enemy prints propaganda doesn't mean it isn't sometimes true. The Turkish Hürriyet newspaper stated that she was actually transferred to Europe as the result of a split within the PKK over the matter of the execution of PKK member Mehmet Shener. The PKK was quite open about its practice of executing defectors and traitors, but Sakine objected strenuously to that decision. This time, her objections were overridden

Chapter 11. Sakine the Diplomat

because it was known that she was having an affair with Shener. The fact that she of all people was now placing her personal feelings over the good of the organization may have caused the PKK leadership to worry about her continued reliability. Some of these leaders, as noted earlier, hadn't bought into the equality philosophy and resented having a woman in the leadership councils at all; they may well have seen the mission to Europe as a nice clean way to remove an irritant. Whether any of the back-stories are true does not really matter. The important thing was that the PKK needed the money, and Sakine looked like the best way to get it turned back on.

She moved secretly to Europe in 2005. Although several writers have suggested that she arrived in Germany in 2007, there are video clips of her conducting television interviews in Paris in 2006 (see https://www.youtube.com/watch?v=o2yEZwsC254). That date would also be more consistent with the US raising official concerns by 2007 that she was getting too good at her job.

On arrival, she applied for refugee status in Germany, claiming that she had quit the PKK organization because of internal conflict and now feared for her life. However, she also declined to cooperate with German intelligence services by providing detailed information on the PKK's activities, and she was therefore imprisoned briefly in Germany. The Turks learned of her presence and demanded to extradite her; the Germans declined to do that, but also declined to grant her refugee status. An apparent setback, this turned out to be quite fortunate: the Germans had to release her and allow her to move along.

She departed for France, where she was officially accepted as a refugee. From a base in France, she was able to revitalize Kurdish civic organizations, especially the women's groups, across Europe. Her messages to them were focused on the need to retain their Kurdish character, which she would then portray using the philosophies that Abdullah Öcalan had published. This approach resonated strongly among these exiled Kurds, and with the new enthusiasm came an increase in the flow of funds to the PKK.

Recall that the 2004 split in the PKK had been over a matter of tactics. The results since then appeared to validate that the risk-averse approach wasn't working. It wasn't annoying the Turks much, and it wasn't exciting the donors enough. In addition, because it was very clearly a nuisance campaign rather than a proper insurgency, nations that had hedged earlier were climbing on board the terrorist designation wagon.

Chapter 11. Sakine the Diplomat

In 2007, the PKK changed gears again; we cannot know whether Sakine's reports from the fund-raising front had anything to do with that. The PKK sought to raise its profile by launching fewer but much larger and better-planned attacks. On October 7th, 2007, they ambushed a Turkish commando patrol, in itself an act of some daring since these were combat-hardened troops who were actively patrolling for these same PKK guerillas. The PKK killed 13 soldiers, more than their total for the previous year and the most in any battle in over a decade (i.e. since before the original 1999 ceasefire). On October 21st, they followed this up with an attack by almost 200 fighters on an army outpost at Daglica near the Turkish-Iraqi border. Of the 50 Turkish soldiers, 12 were killed, 17 wounded and 8 taken off as prisoners. Those prisoners were released when a Turkish Parliamentary delegation came to Iraq to met with the PKK. Now they felt they were getting the respect they had been seeking.

Now, too, the funds started coming back.

Sakine had proven to be a superb organizer, diplomat, and fund-raiser, and achieved a level of legitimacy beyond any of the PKK's previous experience. Among the evidence developed during the later murder investigation, it was revealed that she had held several secret meetings with French President François Hollande. This is even more impressive in view of the fact that France was one of the nations that had declared the PKK to be a terrorist organization. PKK sources also reported that the Turkish security services had become aware of these same meetings, and the Turkish government, in turn, stepped up the pressure to cut the PKK off from the international community.

In 2006-2007, the US had been struggling with its campaign in Iraq. The US airbases in Turkey were essential to the overall logistics effort, and on the ground the peshmerga (who had their own goals of a pan-Kurdish state which would be ruled by them rather than the PKK) remained the only reliable elements of those who were cooperating with the US forces. To please both the peshmerga and the Turks, the US continued to treat the PKK as a terrorist organization.

In 2007, the US Ambassador in Ankara sent a cable that would make its way to Wikileaks; a copy is provided in the Appendix to this book. It confirms that U.S. officials had already identified Cansiz as one of the outlawed PKK's top two "most notorious financiers" in Europe, high praise considering that she had only just gotten started. They wanted her captured to stop the flow of money to the rebels.

Chapter 11. Sakine the Diplomat

"We must redouble our efforts to shut down the financial flows from Europe into PKK headquarters" in northern Iraq, the cable reads. *"We need to narrow our focus by identifying and going after the two top targets of Riza Altun and Sakine Cansiz."*

"We can help by ... coordinating with law enforcement and intelligence counterparts in Europe, to ensure these two terrorists are incarcerated," it says.

The cable goes on to suggest that the PKK raises money in Europe through fundraising and business activities as well as drugs, smuggling, and extortion. The first two points are indeed correct: the Kurds are raising money the old-fashioned way, by asking for it and by earning it. Whether the ambassador had any intelligence-based reason for adding the other two charges we cannot know, but it seems no coincidence that the verbiage in that part of the cable is identical to the talking points floated by the AATA (an arm of the Turkish government) earlier in the year.

Sakine's success notwithstanding, the PKK could only pull off so many attacks, and this level of violence the Turks were able to contain, no doubt with a measure of annoyance since they were undertaking what they considered to be a generous effort to move fairly quickly towards more even-handed treatment. The PKK considered those efforts to be mostly window-dressing when they were not downright disingenuous. This is, after all, a struggle that has been going on for 2500 years.

By 2009, in another bid to bring an end to the conflict, Erdoğan authorized negotiations with Öcalan and (in a significant throwaway remark) "PKK's executives in Europe". With Murat Karayilan remaining back at PKK headquarters, there is only one such executive in Europe: Sakine Cansiz.

This is worth noting on a couple of levels. First, it confirms Sakine's stature within the Kurdish community. First, since she was "just a woman," it is remarkable that the Turks accepted the idea of including her at all. Even more impressive is the fact that her participation appeared to be more or less a condition for having the talks at all.

A darker angle would resurface in December 2013. By insisting that she be present, the Turkish government would be able to locate her very precisely at least from time to time, since she would have to appear when negotiations were required. The MIT could start figuring out how to conduct surveillance on her more effectively.

Later in 2009, PKK soldiers were permitted to surrender themselves (without their weapons) and receive an amnesty. Based on the apparent

Chapter 11. Sakine the Diplomat

sincerity of the ongoing negotiations and the success of this initial amnesty, the PKK declared another ceasefire. The dream of an independent homeland either within or separate from Turkey appeared to be receding, but some measure of respect within the Turkish polity appeared to be taking shape.

If you've been following along with the story over the past 4000 years, you might expect that the wheel would turn and reverse expectations. That reversal was completed by 2011.

The next chapter will provide more details of events in Syria. For the moment we have only to point out that, for both the PKK and the Turkish government, the sudden change in the situation in Syria changed the game completely.

Thanks to Barack Obama's catastrophic bungling of the situation in Iraq and of the opening rounds of what would turn into the Syrian civil war, a completely unknown group called (among other things) ISIS arose in 2011. From that point forward, all bets were off.

From the PKK's viewpoint, opportunity beckoned. They had been conducting operations against Turkey from bases in northern Syria and western Iraq since 1980; many of the guerrillas were not even Turkish and, for many, Syria was their home turf. The peshmerga were not yet involved in Syria. If the Syrian government fell, there would be a power vacuum over a decent-sized chunk of land that was largely inhabited by ethnic Kurds, Alawite Syrians (who, as we have already noted, were in essence a variant of Zazas) and other similar oddments. If those residents could organize themselves, they could be left standing when the dust settled.

The PKK simply had to follow the same playbook that Barzani and Talibani had used in Iraq: prove themselves in combat against an enemy that the Western armies and the host government didn't seem able or willing to handle. Once the previous regime fell and chaos ensued, there would be pressure to restore order so that, among other things, the oil would resume flowing to the west. Then the Kurds just had to hold what they could while the western powers forced a coalition government onto the Syrians.

After that, they could play out the scenario of Afghanistan and Iraq again in Syria. The Kurds' combat record would open the door to the western powers, who would in turn support Kurdish demands for some sort of semi-legitimate role in the future of Syria. From there, they would be in position to join up with other Kurdish communities across the Levant somehow,

Chapter 11. Sakine the Diplomat

sometime. After all, time is no object when you've been waiting for 2500 years.

What more could a tattered guerrilla group want?

Return to Normalcy: Turks vs. Kurds

The Erdoğan government would prefer the world to believe that all would have been well had the PKK simply refrained from further attacks. In reality, the Turks saw essentially the same picture that the PKK was grasping, and they did not like what they saw. Beginning in 2011, the government started seeing the signs that one of their most-feared scenarios was about to play itself out.

Since they were already working with Barzani, the Turks were perhaps even more aware than the PKK of the extent to which he might be permitted to achieve his ambitions. To keep him on the team, serving as their watchdog against the PKK in the Qandil area, they had fed those ambitions of leading a Pan-Kurdish fiefdom. They felt quite safe allowing him to harbor that fantasy, because it was so absurd ... until 2011, when suddenly it seemed quite realistic. From that moment forward, the Turks started to be more concerned about the emergence of a legitimate (or at least US-subsidized) Kurdish entity in Syria to join the one that as already in place in Iraq. If such an entity did form, the Turks could be sure that the conflict over Turkish Kurdistan would continue indefinitely. The PKK needed to be quashed before it could get entrenched.

That wasn't the only factor. By this time, Erdoğan had consolidated the power of the AKP to the point that his government was selecting which parties and politicians would be allowed to run against them in the elections. The Gülen group alliance was working well, and they and Erdoğan now had the power to begin setting in place the Islamist government Erdoğan had always (except for the brief period between 1998-2005) advocated. As the AKP gave the Gülenists and their school programs and religious institutes free rein in Kurdistan, it was time for the Kurds to decide once and for all whether they preferred to be dead Kurds or live Turks.

The velvet gloves came off; repression of the Kurds inside Turkey resumed under the guise of normal operations. An example of the type of situation that kept the Kurds' tempers boiling was the incident in Uludere.

As described in an earlier chapter, Gültan Kisanak endured much the same treatment as Sakine Cansiz in Diyarbakir Prison. Upon her release, she

Chapter 11. Sakine the Diplomat

took a different path from Cansiz: she tried to work through the establishment process, however dysfunctional it might be. By 2007 she had already succeeded in gaining a seat in the national legislature as an independent, later representing the Peace and Democracy Party (BDP) that the dissident PKK faction had established in 2004.

In 2012, she confronted Deputy Prime Minister Bülent Arinç of the AKP Islamist party, over the subject of the Uludere Incident, also known as the Roboski Massacre. Roboski is the village where the event took place, and Uludere is the province.

It is a case study in the type of justice that the Kurds have been experiencing since the AKP resumed its emphasis on religious and patriotic conformity. It helps to explain why so many of them feel that there simply is no path through the legitimate political system to receiving fair treatment, let alone to have their ethnic traditions respected. When that happens, people believe that they have no choice but to take up arms to defend themselves against a government that is very likely to come in and shoot them to take them off to prison with no due process, no notice and often not even any reason. Such an environment is what more aggressive groups such as the PKK thrive on.

On 28 December 2011, a US drone alerted the US military, who in turn advised the Turks, about a group of smugglers approaching the border from Iraq with a load of cigarettes, tea and diesel oil that they had picked up near the border from Iraqi smugglers. While illegal, it is very common in the area; in truth, it is the only thing that keeps the economy of the region working. Everybody knows exactly how it works so that everybody has the commodities they need and nobody gets hurt.

On this day, however, the Turks immediately demanded that the US remove the drone from the area so it could not observe events further. Then they launched fighter jets to destroy the convoy and kill the survivors while the drone could not observe the action. A total of 34 people in the area (not all of them involved with the smuggling in any way) were killed; not one was wounded. In other words, the jets stayed around long enough to make quite sure of their kills. Unfortunately for the government, without the drone's sharper eyes, the fighter jets had failed to notice quite everybody: a 35th person did survive and made it back to his home village to tell people what had happened.

The funeral attracted over 100 vehicles and over 10,000 attendees. It inspired protests, many of which were met with force and did turn violent, in

Chapter 11. Sakine the Diplomat

cities across Turkey. As word of these events spread, protests occurred in front of Turkish embassies in other cities in Iran, Iraq and Cyprus.

Further inflaming the situation, District Governor Naif Yamuz, while paying condolence visits to the families in the Uludere district, was attacked by a mob of Turks who had travelled there from other parts of Turkey for that very purpose. Five of them were arrested on charges of attempted murder, but they have never been prosecuted.

Bahoz Erdal, the leader of the PKK's military wing, called for a Kurdish uprising in response to the incident, releasing the following statement: "We urge the people of Kurdistan... to react after this massacre and seek a settling of accounts through uprisings."

Selahattin Demirtash, the leader of the Peace and Democracy Party (BDP), which has tried to be the pacifist alternative to the PKK, released a statement claiming that "It's clearly a massacre of civilians, of whom the oldest is 20," but he called for Kurds to respond through democratic means. Demirtas quoted Prime Minister Recep Tayyip Erdoğan's own thoughts on Syrian President Bashar al-Assad: "A leader who kills his own people has lost his legitimacy". He added "Now I say the same thing back to him."

Erdoğan announced that there would be thorough administrative and judicial investigations, and Hüseyin Çelik, the deputy chairman of the ruling AKP party, announced that the families of the victims could be compensated, constituting a "material apology", in the common manner of Islamic law whereby faults are forgiven if enough money changes hands.

Investigations did proceed, in a manner of speaking. The government refused to release any information about the case, but there was a leak of the footage from the drone from 90 minutes before the incident (i.e. at the time that the attack decision was made and the Turks ordered the drone to be turned away). It clearly showed the presence of numerous random civilians in the area. Nonetheless, the legislative committee, personally guided by the government's majority leaders, found nobody at fault.

Most people accepted the absolution of the pilot officers directly involved in the strike, following the rationale that they were just following orders to attack an approved target. The question is, what person would have had the knowledge that this was just a routine smuggling event, would have had direct access to the drone feed at the time (and the ability to demand the drone's removal), and would have had the authority to approve this raid?

Chapter 11. Sakine the Diplomat

There was no effort by anyone to look above the local military commander to determine which general or politician with the authority to direct the Americans' actions had actually directed the drone's removal or authorized the strike. A year later, in 2012, it was discovered that the Chief of the General Staff [i.e. the country's most senior military officer], Necdet Özel, had provided the official authorization. He would certainly have had the relationship with the US military to cause events to happen as they did. Without any investigation of his actions, it cannot be known whether he had also sought Turkish political approval.

As to the promised compensation for the murdered civilians and their families, the Turks paid them back, but not in the manner expected. Three family members were imprisoned for having known about the smuggling activity. The remaining families were, and continue to be, subjected to constant police harassment. No actual compensation has ever been paid to any of the families, nor has any apology been rendered.

This dispute had other untoward consequences. In 2016, an increasingly totalitarian AKP arrested Gültan Kisanak for embarrassing a government minister and disagreeing with the government's position. That's not a matter of reading between the lines; in Turkey, those are actual criminal offenses. No matter how absurd those charges might seem for a country that seeks inclusion in the European Community, in this kangaroo justice system they carry a combined total of 230 years in prison. More practically, her arrest entitled the government to remove her from office and appoint replacements more to their liking with no electoral process. The real issues, of course, are that she is merely a woman, merely a Kurd, and, worst of all possible offenses, a woman speaking truth to an Islamic man.

After 30 years of trying to work within a corrupt and repressive system, Gültan Kisanak's reward has been to find herself right back at the scene of the crime that turned her into an opponent of Turkish despotism in the first place 30 years before. She is back in jail, in Diyarbakir (although not in the same building), on bogus charges. It's unlikely that her attitude towards the AKP will have improved when she gets out, assuming that she does get out at all. It is for that very reason, repeated hundreds or thousands of times, that the PKK exists as an armed force, rather than simply as the political party it tried briefly to become, and its repetition all across Kurdistan is the reason the PKK still gets more recruits than it can afford to sustain.

At the same time the Erdoğan government began demanding that the BKP also be considered a terrorist organization since it was merely a front for the

Chapter 11. Sakine the Diplomat

PKK. This is incorrect as a matter of definition, since the BKP is the group that split off from the PKK in 2004 precisely because its leadership was opposed to the PKK continuing to fight an apparently pointless guerilla war. Instead, they wanted to start operating within the political system, as had been the PKK's original intent. The AKP, in seeking to make that impossible, threatens to drive them back to war.

Chapter 12. Opportunity in Syria

The emblem of the Kurdish nation, and of the PKK for that matter, should be a Phoenix. Destroyed for all practical purposes, they manage time after time to make themselves relevant once again.

Existing, as the Kurds do, in a diaspora makes it very difficult to achieve a critical mass for action that is proportionate to the group's true numbers. Being so spread out does have one advantage: when an opening does come along, it's more likely that someone will be on the ground to take advantage of it. In Syria, in 2011, that moment may have arisen for the Kurds.

To many Westerners, they appeared to be a new arrival on the scene. From the preceding chapters we already know that they have in fact been right there for thousands of years, but the seeds of this particular re-emergence were sown some twenty years earlier, at a time before Öcalan had been captured.

The Fickle Americans

The Kurds had always been fractious under Saddam's Hussein's Ba'athist regime, and (consistent with Kurdish history) a good number chose to fight for Iran in its war with Iraq. They gained one brief moment of international sympathy in 1988 when Saddam Hussein decided to teach them some respect via a massive poison gas attack in which up to 5000 Kurds died. This incident was only a spike in a much larger (but seldom reported) gassing offensive in the region of Anfal from 1997-1990. One-third of all Iraqi Kurds were displaced when their villages were destroyed, and an estimated 100,000 were killed. Two years later, it wasn't hard for the US to convince them to rise up in Saddam's rear areas in return for autonomy in whatever new regime arose after the first Gulf War.

What they got instead was a replay of the First World War scenario. US President George H. Bush decided to halt the war and leave the Iraqi troops (particularly the most vicious of the lot, the Republican Guard) largely unscathed. The intention was to retain enough of a power structure to prevent a return of the Russians and defend itself against Iran. This was precisely the rationale used in 1920, and had the same result: Kurdistan was taken back off the map.

However, the US did establish a no-fly zone over Iraqi Kurdistan which led to the creation of the Kurds' present semi-autonomous region. Unable to

Chapter 12. Opportunity in Syria

conduct direct assaults, Hussein set up an economic embargo that led to many years of near-famine in the region. That situation also led to the establishment of a black market and smuggling ring run by the Barzanis, with the active connivance of both Iraq and Turkey in return for the customary fees.

The next US President, Bill Clinton, focused entirely on maintaining the Camp David accords that had fallen into his lap early in his first term. His domestic opponents correctly saw the Palestinians as career terrorists with no intention of reaching a peaceful solution. To protect his Palestinian treaty, he made sure not to be seen as too soft on terrorists by maintaining the Bush policies against Iraq, including the Kurdistan no-fly zone. This penchant for superficialities led Clinton to acquiesce to Turkish demands to designate the PKK as a terrorist organization; in addition, the Clinton CIA is believed to have actively abetted the 1999 arrest of Abdullah Öcalan. Minor matters to US officials, these hand-waves had major impacts on the Kurdish cause.

Clinton's greatest failure with regard to terrorism was of far, far worse dimensions: he repeatedly failed to accept offers by the states in the region to extradite one Osama bin Ladin, who was wanted internationally and in the US for numerous crimes. On three different occasions, regional governments cornered bin Ladin and offered to hand him over to the US government for trial, and on all three occasions Clinton demurred, leaving bin Ladin at large to plan and carry out the attack of September 11, 2001.

The US became intensively involved in the Middle East, starting with Afghanistan, where it learned that motivated and supported non-governmental forces (in that case, the Northern Alliance) could be very effective at both counter-guerrilla and regime change. As were the Kurds.

In addition, when the US learned that the Taliban government had been actively seeking nuclear material to pass on to Al-Quaeda, it was only logical to take a serious look at Iraq again.

Once again, a Bush would ask the Iraqi Kurds to partner with the US in regime change in return for recognition of a homeland. Once again, when the fighting was over, the US decided that Iraq should not be partitioned completely. The Kurdish Regional Government was instead formally recognized as the smallest of three partners in a dysfunctional government that by its very design must eventually fall increasingly under the control of the Shi'ite faction. In the interim, a robust US military presence sought to secure the country and the civilian government while Iraqis learned how to live together. Despite the inevitable teething pains of democracy in a region

Chapter 12. Opportunity in Syria

where such a concept had never existed, by 2008 Iraq was well on its way to becoming a civilized state.

Bush was succeeded by the diplomatic naïf and Iranian apologist President Obama, whose election campaign was based largely on the idea of abandoning Afghanistan and Iraq immediately if not sooner, regardless of the consequences. But, with bin Laden still at large, he did not have the political support to abandon the fight completely.

It took much longer than he had hoped, but in February 2011, US forces finally located and killed bin Ladin, who had been hiding in Pakistan, and they recovered a considerable amount of intelligence on al-Quaeda operations and operatives on the various computers in his compound. Al-Quaeda was quickly left in tatters.

Meanwhile, Iraq had become as stable as a fledgling democracy can be. Even Afghanistan was starting to behave like a normal country, and in both cases this had occurred while leaving most of the political players in place but with altered job descriptions. Apparently, this drove a sudden realization across most of the people in the Arab world that it was possible for people to rule themselves and still practice some reasonable version of Islam without having to submit to tyrannical clerics. From Teheran to Tunis, the "Arab Spring" of sudden rebellions arose, apparently from nowhere but in reality driven by the success in Iraq. Some resulted in temporary democracies, others in chaos, and others in immediate repression by the government until the situation returned to normal. In Syria, however, the government tried to thread the needle between repression and capitulation, and failed; this delayed the resolution of the issue for several months but also emboldened the opposition.

In the middle of all this, Barack Obama found himself unable to accept the good news surrounding US efforts in that part of the world, or perhaps he just couldn't accept that Bush had been right. He announced that the US would depart Iraq and Afghanistan forthwith, and US forces were immediately for all practical purposes confined to garrison. Both countries started unraveling before the first US boots departed.

In Iraq, Iranian factions began to operate with impunity, and the Kurds were soon facing regular assaults by Iraqi army units and Iranian militias. The Obama administration made it clear that the Kurds were on their own, and things were looking very gloomy for the Kurds when the situation was again upended from a most unexpected direction.

Chapter 12. Opportunity in Syria

The desert areas of the Middle East have always been infested with roaming gangs of bandits. The less effective the government, the more freedom the bandit gangs have to operate, and the more aggressive gangs eventually displace those that aren't as aggressive, not to mention displacing timid or ill-disciplined government forces.

So it was in Iraq and Syria.

In Iraq, the Iranian-backed factions were not the only ones emboldened by the hasty exit of the US troops. Several warlords gathered their forces in the Iraqi desert to contest the claim of leadership. One of these was a relatively small and unknown group variously called ISIS, ISIL or Daesh. It was the most effective of the bandit groups precisely because of its extreme savagery.

At the same time, Syria was spiraling slowly into a formal civil war. The Assad regime had alienated just about all the other countries in the region, most of which were now shipping logistics support, money, volunteers and arms to any rebellious groups they could find in the country. Among those groups were the Syrian Kurds. As the government's hold weakened, large stretches of the country became completely ungoverned, free for the taking by anyone with enough guns and courage to do so. It happened that the initial "turf" held by ISIS (which at the very first was indeed little more than a bandit gang) was the desert area of Iraq that adjoined the Syrian desert.

ISIS was thus already in place to capitalize on the power vacuums created simultaneously in both Syria and Iraq. It expanded rapidly and drafted the local resources and populace to its purposes. Before anyone else could get organized, the contest was over. ISIS set up its own de facto government with an extreme conservative form of Islam enforced by trigger-happy troops. In a part of the world where the military art often consists largely of firing rifles skywards, ISIS shot to kill, and did so with enthusiasm. To emphasize the risk of opposing their regime, ISIS took to conducting grisly executions on the internet. The entire world was horrified, and for once spoke with one voice against the threat. All, that is, but the one person who had the means to do something about it: Barack Obama, who, to justify the continued withdrawal of US forces from the region, dismissed ISIS as "a junior varsity operation".

The longer the rest of the world dithered, and the longer ISIS remained in business, the longer the more extreme parts of the Islamic world came to accept their bluster as reality. Recruits from the legions of unemployed youths began streaming in to join ISIS. Many took advantage of Turkey's challenges in handling a tidal wave of post-Arab Spring refugees. They slipped from Europe or Africa into the refugee camps in Turkey, then moved onward

Chapter 12. Opportunity in Syria

into Syria. In later years, now battle-hardened, they would return via the same routes, again posing as refugees, worming into the soft-hearted and short-sighted Western countries in order to form ISIS sleeper cells there.

The maneuvering of the international community (minus the US) went very slowly while ISIS grew like a cancer. Only one group stepped up to do anything about it: the Kurds.

A good proportion of the areas that ISIS claimed in Syria were Kurdish homelands. Hafez al-Assad, the father of the current dictator, had generally enjoyed a warm relationship with the Kurds and had provided asylum to the PKK leadership after the 1980 coup in Turkey. In fact, although he may not have known it, he was of Kurdish extraction himself, as were most Alawites in Syria. With his country under threat from Turkey in the matter of the Kurdish question, starting from his earliest days in power, Bashar al-Assad had no such overt sympathies for the Kurds. Without the catalyst of US support for a homeland as was found in Iraq, these Kurds had since 1999 been unable to do much more than survive and maintain their community integrity.

They had not been entirely idle, however. Their homelands adjoined the Kurdish homelands in Turkey, where the PKK had gained experience in guerrilla warfare over the prior decades. Much of the northern portion of Syria was the de facto home of the Kurdish guerrilla units, and many of the guerrillas were actually from Syria; speculation remains that Assad did actually tolerate this activity as a small measure of payback for Turkey's threats. The PKK knew every inch of this ground, and they had strong popular support. Now, in ISIS, the Kurds found an oppressor even more vicious than the Assad regime; but, at last, they had the ability to resist.

The Kurds, both those from the Iraqi peshmerga and the units of the PKK, had extensive recent combat experience and didn't have a lot of over-engineering to deal with. They moved to the west from Iraq and to the south from Turkey, and they simply showed up to fight the vicious but lightly armed ISIS mobs. This new branch of the Kurds (new at least to the US) quickly demonstrated that it was effective at fighting ISIS. In the absence of anyone else doing so, the Kurds rapidly gained credibility within US military circles as "the good guys". That's pretty remarkable for an organization that still declares itself to be a Maoist cadre.

As a result, the world was treated to a real box-office attraction: a five-way civil war.

Chapter 12. Opportunity in Syria

- The Syrian government wanted to retain its hold on power, down to the last remaining citizen.

- Various rebel groups, some backed with great enthusiasm by Iran or with the by-now routine ineptitude of the US, opposed the Assad regime while in turn opposing one another.

- Syrian Kurds wanted to recover those lands from ISIS control. They weren't always opposed to the concept of a Syrian government as long as it left them alone.

- Iraqi Kurds wanted to extend their control to incorporate the Syrian Kurds under their umbrella.

- Iranian-sponsored Shiite guerrillas (and disguised army units) were opposed simultaneously to Assad's Alawism, Syrian freedom fighters simply because they were in turn backed by the US, and to the extreme-Sunni ISIS.

The Turks claimed to be opposed to ISIS but were much more opposed to the Turkish-based Kurds. They had already co-opted the Iraqi Kurds as their proxies against the PKK, in return for Turkish acceptance of their families as the rulers of Iraqi Kurdistan.

The US started out by embarrassing itself in the matter of providing support to local resistance forces. An idealistic approach of trying to recruit only those with spotless records to become outlaws had achieved little; the US was never able to produce more than 100 of such paragons, and most of them deserted or were captured within weeks. Its approach also did little to attract the support of existing resistance forces. The majority of the startlingly few local militias who would agree to work with the Americans were elements of the PKK (which were otherwise banned as terrorists).

The US then rendered itself largely irrelevant in the region after Obama failed in 2013 to act in support of his 2012 "red line" proclamation on the use of chemical weapons. That opened the door to the Russians.

For public consumption, the Russians were in the mix because of their opposition to ISIS, the international terrorists. The truth was that they were only engaging against ISIS (which in practice they seldom did) because they were supporting Assad. This was not out of any real affection: they just wanted a Mediterranean port and the opportunity to tweak the nose of America, which, while not actually feeble, had a feeble leader.

Chapter 12. Opportunity in Syria

Only for people as desperate as the Kurds could consider that living in such a chaotic and violent environment would constitute having finally caught a break. When you're a Kurd, everything is relative to the miseries you've already experienced.

The battles against ISIS took the Kurdish troops directly across the areas that happened to have high concentrations of Kurdish inhabitants. That was no accident; the Kurds' priority was on helping their own people. With ISIS removed and the national government obviously powerless in those areas, the Kurds set about governing themselves. A de facto Kurdistan was emerging, reaching from the Iranian border to the Mediterranean, with all of it fronting along the Turkish border. Although the Iraqi, Turkish and Syrian Kurds had significant disagreements amongst themselves, from an outside perspective the "Kurdish held territory" kept growing and the pieces kept coming together. The land of the Medes was re-forming.

Why Were the Kurds in Syria?

There were a great number of Kurds in Syria. Perhaps ten percent were actually Turkish citizens who had fled in response to the unending Turkish assaults on their communities and rights within Turkey. As this century opened, the Turkish government revoked the citizenship of those expatriates unless they returned home to continue living under the oppression that had caused them to flee in the first place. The Turks didn't actually want these non-Turks returning home; they just wanted to secure legal title to the property within Turkey of these Kurdish no-longer-citizens. That didn't make them citizens in Syria either, so in the end they became stateless people with no rights in the country where they had become stranded.

A far greater number of Kurdish residents of Syria were not expatriates or refugees. Millions of them descended from those who were citizens of the Assyrian, Greek and Roman empires, millennia before the Turks and Arabs arrived.

Although Islam overran this part of the world early on, Saladin overthrew the initial Arab regime to establish his Islamic but Kurdish empire, the Ayubbid dynasty, with Damascus as its keystone. Eventually that empire fell to the Ottomans, whose method of rule depended largely on retaining local rulers with all of their wealth and customs providing only that they acknowledge fealty to the Ottoman throne. Thus the inhabitants of Kurdish areas of Asia Minor, while forbidden to practice their original Zoroastrian religion, remained very much ethnic Kurds throughout the Ottoman period.

Chapter 12. Opportunity in Syria

From the 1500s right up to 1920, the Ottomans had ruled modern-day Syria as four separate fiefdoms that comprised the different ethnic regions. As described in the earlier chapter covering the rise of Kemal Ataturk, at the end of World War I the post-War map developed by the Allied powers included the new countries of Kurdistan, Syria and Turkey. None of those countries had ever existed before, being merely ethnic groupings within the Ottoman empire for 500 years and undefined elements of earlier empires before that.

The war-end planning took a different turn as the British and French jockeyed for the most desirable of the conquered territories. The US was excluded because it had never declared was on the Ottomans, and the Russians had declared unconditional peace at the time of the Bolshevik takeover; besides, the other three allies were even then invading Russia in an effort to reinstall the White Russian government.

To preclude providing the French with an overland route to the Persian Gulf and India, the British revised the map to ensure that Iraq would stretch from the Turkish mountains to the Persian Gulf. Had oil already been discovered in the Persian Gulf, the French might have put up more argument, but it had not, so they were much more interested in Syria. That seemed to both sides to be more than fair compensation since the French had played little part in the war in the Middle East, which a junior British officer (T.E. Lawrence) and his Arab allies had captured in its entirety.

With the British taking both Palestine and Iraq, the French sector had to be enlarged to appear somewhat more equal. It was extended to the north and Turkey was extended to the east, so that all four countries (Iraq, Persia, Syria and Turkey) came together at what appeared to be a natural border: the southern edge of the Caucasus Mountains around the area of Lake Van. In the process, the lines that represented the future Kurdistan dropped off the map. The Kurds would have to continue to survive under the rule of others, as they had been doing for 2500 years.

Despite their claims today as to who is and isn't allowed to have a country and "how things have always been", it is important to notice that, except for Israel, until 1946 none of today's squabbling Middle Eastern countries had ever existed at all as independent countries. They were all randomly-drawn areas that were under colonial occupation and administration for 3000 years and more, under different empires. Other than the Persians (Iranians), who are only peripheral players in the Kurdish drama, the last ones to have had any independent identity were the Medes and the Jews, the two groups that

Chapter 12. Opportunity in Syria

all the other regimes in the area continue to try to suppress as illegitimate squatters.

Enter the Assads

Between the World Wars, possibly due to the near-erasure of an entire generation in the trenches, both the British and French decided to shift their approaches for managing their global possessions. The previous method of setting up full governments, expatriate societies and plantations had offered useful employment for the second, third and fourth sons of aristocratic families and for promising lads of the middle class; now it was a drain on an already threadbare treasury. They decided to rely more on delegation to pliant local leaders who could pay for their own thrones and governments.

In Iraq, as early as 1921 the British installed a puppet king who was then allowed to proclaim independence (on a very short leash) in 1932. The French spent several years in negotiations with the inhabitants of Syria , the process being delayed by the inability of those inhabitants to come to agreement amongst themselves. Eventually Syrian independence had to be set aside with the outbreak of the Second World War, at the end of which the League of Nations was deemed defunct, having been replaced by the United Nations. The League mandates under which Palestine and Syria had been governed were also inoperative, and the former Ottoman provinces were released in 1946-1948.

Syria and all the other statelets in the Middle East were no sooner created than they immediately focused their energies on attacking another newly-created state, the only one that was not Islamic. After early Arab attacks on Israel proved humiliating, the United Arab Republic emerged in 1958 in hopes of creating an entity powerful and unified enough to take on Israel effectively. No sooner was it formed than the Egyptians, who controlled the UAR, moved to purge the Ba'ath party, which had been created precisely in pursuit of pan-Arab government, from the UAR government. This was followed by a purge of Syrian nationalists from the UAR military. There seemed to be little reason for Syrians to remain in the union, and with over a hundred miles and the Israeli borders separating the two halves of the UAR, there was no way for Egypt to prevent Syria from issuing its own divorce decree.

The organizers of the 1961 military coup that unraveled the UAR included one Hafez al-Assad, then a mere captain. The purely military government

Chapter 12. Opportunity in Syria

never was able to get its act together, and in 1963 it in turn fell to a coup that restored the rule of the Ba'ath Party.

One of the few things it was able to get around to doing in that short time in power was to pass an edict regarding the Kurds. By 1962, the number of Kurds in Syria was considered to be about 500,000, and that would certainly be an undercount since many of them were in remote communities. In that year the Syrian government revoked the citizenship of 120,000 of those Kurds, who had never claimed to be from anywhere else, nor indeed to have ever gone anywhere but a few miles from the places of their birth, which were in many cases also the places where their ancestors had been born for thousands of years.

Despite its heavy military support, the 1963 Ba'athist government bungled several military adventures, including another disastrous war with Israel in 1968 and the much less-publicized defeat of Syria and its PLO surrogate by Jordan in 1970. Disgusted, the military took matters back into their own hands and installed the now-promoted Colonel Hafez al-Assad as President in 1971, a post he held until his death in 2000.

Kurdish history has been filled for 5000 years with examples of ethnic Kurds building up and then turning against their ethnic kin, and now it was happening again in Syria. The Assads were originally Zaza Kurds (those following the Alawite variant of Islam) and were for that very reason forced out of Turkey into exile in Syria during the Ottoman Empire. Assad's grandfather was on record as having urged the French not to leave Syria to the Arabs, who would trample the rights of each other, let alone those of any other religious or ethnic group.

Thereafter, the Assad family has insisted that they are Arabs and not Kurds, and Hafiz al-Assad probably knew little or nothing of his Kurdish origins. His relations with that community were nonetheless cordial, because he saw them as a source of valuable leverage against the much-distrusted Turks. In 1975, Assad offered the Iraqi Kurdish leader Jalal Talabani a haven in Damascus to found his new Patriotic Union of Kurdistan (PUK). In 1980, as we have learned, Assad settled the PKK in Lebanon, and from then on provided a range of support to the PKK to enable its operations against his regional rival Turkey.

In the late 1990s, perhaps because of Assad's failing health, Turkey became serious about threatening Syria with war over its sponsorship of the PKK. To defuse that possibility, President Hafiz al-Assad asked Kurdish leader Abdullah Öcalan to leave Syria, where he had been based for over 19

Chapter 12. Opportunity in Syria

years. In return, Syria gained a mutual security pact with Turkey, concluded on 20 October 1998 in the Turkish city of Adana. Not only did Assad turn his back on his long-time tool of convenience, but the Syrian government went on to assent to the listing of the PKK as a terrorist organization and withdrew all further support for the PKK. They also agreed to share intelligence about PKK movements with the Turkish Government and to cooperate strategically with Turkey against the PKK organization.

Shortly thereafter, as was already related, Öcalan departed Lebanon on the tour of embassies that ended when he was betrayed and turned over to Turkey.

Hafiz al-Assad's eldest son, Bassel, had died in 1994. The succession passed to Bashar, who had until that time been living a life of relative obscurity and simplicity as a surgeon. Bashar was immersed in a crash course in the institutions of government, including rapid promotion to military command. He also gained some visibility as head of an office that would investigate corruption in response to citizen complaints.

As a physician, Bashar had undergone his specialty training in London. This Western exposure, coupled with the anti-corruption drive, caused some Arab-watchers to assume that he might have absorbed democratic values and be something of a reformer.

They were quite wrong. In an autocracy, only the autocrat is in power; everyone else is by definition a potential opposition member. Every public figure who was not Bashar started falling afoul of the anti-corruption drive. He was therefore unopposed when his father died in 2000. Thereafter, to secure his grip on power, repression flourished throughout Syria, and it fell the hardest on the Kurds to ensure the continuation of Syria's recently-concluded peace deal with Turkey. Meanwhile, the Syrian Kurds began to see their neighbors in Iraq starting (with some measure of American protection) to emerge from the shadows and form a real political unit.

An Identity for Kurds in Syria

While it was probably not part of a premeditated provocation on either side, the flashpoint for the Syrian Kurds came in the unlikely venue of a regional soccer match.

The 2004 Qamishli Soccer Riot occurred shortly after the overthrow of the Saddam Hussein regime in neighboring Iraq. The Ba'athist Arab fans of the visiting team started raising pictures, not of Bashar al-Assad but of Saddam

Chapter 12. Opportunity in Syria

Hussein, who among his many crimes against humanity had earned international sanctions and ultimately owed his downfall to his use of poison gas against Kurdish communities. The host team's largely Kurdish fans did not appreciate this demonstration and raised the Flag of Kurdistan, and before long both groups began throwing stones at each other. The riot escalated to a city-wide conflict that resulted in the Kurds burning down the local Ba'ath Party headquarters and toppling a statue of Hafez al-Assad.

In the end, Syrian Army and Air Force assets had to be used to quell the disturbances, and they arrested hundreds of Kurds. It is probably not true that only Kurds were killed in this cycle of events, although there appear to be no records of any of the Arabs suffering fatalities; it *is* true that only Kurds were arrested. Assad himself would visit the area later and order the release of 312 Kurds as a gesture of a desire for national unity but, in the meantime, his security forces had already begun systematic measures against Kurdish groups across Syria.

Many observers cite that incident as the beginning of Kurdish nationalism and resistance in Syria. In fact it had already begun, although until that point the Kurds had sought channels for a peaceful and political solution.

Sensing the opportunities opened by the US invasion of Iraq, with its open overtures to the Kurdish community there, a group intending to use what passed for a political process in Syria had already come together in 2003 to form the Democratic Union Party (Kurdish: Partiya Yekîtiya Demokrat, PYD) based on the Abdullah Öcalan philosophies. The Carnegie Middle East Center alleges that the PKK actually set the PYD up to get past its own problems with being listed as a terrorist organization. Since the PYD makes no secret of its adherence to Öcalan, that may well be true.

The Syrian government was holding fast to its 1999 agreement with Turkey to root out any form of Kurdish nationalism. No sooner was the PYD formed than the government security forces began hunting it down. The 2004 riots showed the potential strength of ethnic Kurds. It's no coincidence that of the 312 prisoners released in Assad's gesture, none was a member of the PYD.

Small-scale activities persisted after 2004, but the PYD's next major achievement was a set of demonstrations on 2 November 2007 in the cities of Qamishli and Ayn al-Arab (Kurdish: Kobanê) in memory of those who lost their lives in 2004. The events also protested the Syrian government's support for Turkish incursions into Iraq to attack PKK forces based in South Kurdistan (i.e. the Kurdistan Regional Government territory in northern Iraq). The crowd comprised several hundred Kurds, small by the standards of most

Chapter 12. Opportunity in Syria

political demonstrations but significant considering that such events did not occur at all in Assad's domain.

The Syrian security forces, including a unit imported from Damascus, fired teargas to disperse the crowd. Some civilian protesters reportedly began to respond by throwing stones, at which point the Syrian police opened fire with live ammunition, killing one protester and injuring at least two more. The security forces rounded up dozens of Kurds, including men, women and children, regardless of their actual role in the events; many more were detained in an ensuing police crackdown. The police released most of them fairly quickly, but 15 of the apparent leaders, including three PYD party officials, remained imprisoned and were eventually charged.

A special security court would try them and several other PYD members arrested in the next three years. Most received sentences from five to seven years on charges of membership in a "secret organization", although the PYD was in fact a registered political party. Another offense was "seeking to cut off part of Syrian land to join it to another country". One might assume that to be self-evident, given Kurdish aspirations. While it is true that the ultimate dream of most politically-active Kurds is to see a unified Kurdistan someday, that has to be considered in the same manner as Jews saying "next year in Jerusalem": a long-term vision that few are actually working towards or expect to happen. The PYD was committed to working within the Syrian system simply to achieve equal rights as Syrian citizens.

PYD members, based solely on their affiliation with a lawful political party, were detained in often-severe conditions and were not afforded even the limited legal rights available to other Syrian citizens. Many of those released to date have reported being kept in extended solitary confinement, while some were subjected to physical and mental torture. Syrian security forces also often continued to harass activists and their families even following their release. The security forces in Syria commonly use similar methods against many Kurdish prisoners and activists in Syria, but Human Rights Watch has specifically noted that security forces tended to reserve their harshest treatments for PYD members.

The general civil war that arose in Syria in 2011 soon revealed to the Syrian government that its earlier opportunism, coupled with its indiscriminate sponsorship of terror networks of every kind, had left it without friends on any part of the spectrum. Sunni Arab governments everywhere started funneling weapons through Turkey, with the assistance of

Chapter 12. Opportunity in Syria

the US, the EU and Israel. At the same time, Iranian-backed Shi'ite forces filtered through Iraq.

The complications of all the groups operating in Syria is illustrated in the Tammo incident. The Arab elements of the Syrian opposition joined with the Assad regime in accusing the PYD of being responsible for the October 2011 assassination of Mashaal Tammo, who had established a Kurdish party (consisting, apparently, of approximately one member) that wanted to remain part of the country of Syria but was also a member of the Syrian revolution. The PYD has maintained that Tammo was just a Turkish plant, while Mashaal Tammo's son accused the Syrian regime. In October 2012, the Saudi-owned TV channel Al-Arabiya published documents allegedly proving that Bashar al-Assad himself had engaged the Air Force Intelligence Directorate to assassinate Mashaal Tammo.

The PYD was active in the early stages of the civil war, beginning in early 2011 with the outbreak across Syria of antigovernment demonstrations that were loosely coupled with the general phenomenon known as the Arab Spring. The PYD first joined the Kurdish Patriotic Movement in May, participated in the founding of the National Coordination Body for Democratic Change in July, and attended the People's Council of Western Kurdistan in December. Unlike most other Kurdish Syrian parties, it did not join the Kurdish National Council (KNC) when it was formed in October 2011, because the KNC was a creation of the Kurdistan Democratic Party (KDP), which was in turn managed by Iraqi tribal leader Massoud Barzani, one of the leaders of the Iraqi Kurdistan Regional Government. The PYD's intention was to get rid of an overlord, not to switch from one to another.

For the same reason, the PYD declined to affiliate with the Syrian National Council (SNC), a group set up to coordinate across all Syrian rebel organizations, because it had accepted the Barzani group as representing Kurdish interests. The PYD insists that Barzani is actually representing Turkish interests. The SNC's unwillingness to support Kurdish autonomy led all but one of its Kurdish parties to drop out of the Council by February 2012.

Faced with own dissolution, the KNC rethought its strategy. By July 2012, it had found a way to sign an agreement with the Council of Western Kurdistan to form a joint Kurdish Supreme Committee to cooperate on security for Kurdish areas, and to form People's Protection Units (YPG) to provide that security. Under that agreement, cities that fall under the control of Syrian Kurdish forces would be ruled jointly by the PYD and the KNC until elections could be held. However, under Barzani's guidance, the KNC

Chapter 12. Opportunity in Syria

disavowed the idea of elections, preferring to divide Kurdish regions into numerous zones that it would determine unilaterally with no input from the people so affected. The race for dominance of those regions was on.

Barzani meets with Erdoğan to cement the alliance with Turkey
(http://www.Frojavareport.wordpress.com/2013/1118/Ferdogan-and-barzani-cooperating-against-the-rojava-revolution)

Despite the disorganization (or, in the case of the PKK-aligned Kurds, the obsessive over-organization!) and inexperience of the resistance fighters, the government was unable to suppress the insurrection. With minimal popular support and no allies to call on, it was over-stretched. It was forced to reduce its total footprint to something it could defend effectively while re-establishing some form of order. Consolidating around Damascus meant leaving a significant presence only in Qamishli and Al-Hasakah but otherwise withdrawing from most of the more remote areas of the country. Those happened to be Kurdish areas, and that opened the way for the emergence of self-government, if temporary, for the Kurdish people.

Abdelbasset Seida, head of the Barzani-backed Syrian National Council, after a meeting with Turkish Foreign Minister Ahmet Davutoğlu in July 2012, claimed that the Syrian Army's concession of northeastern Syria to the PYD

Chapter 12. Opportunity in Syria

was done in the hope of getting more money and weapons from the Turks. Surrendering half the country to get a few more rifles seems somewhat improbable. The Assad regime's problem was not a lack of weapons or money. It was running out of people willing to fight for it.

The KNC began to accuse the PYD of attacking Kurdish (i.e. pro-Barzani) demonstrators, of kidnapping members of other Kurdish opposition parties, and of setting up armed checkpoints along the border with Turkey. The YPG forces probably did do all of those things in the course of exercising its de facto control of the territories it held. By mid-2012, Reuters was reporting that the towns of Amuda, Derik, Kobane, and Afrin were under PYD control.

As it happened, the move had several unanticipated consequences:

- It emboldened the non-Kurdish resistance, which launched a major offensive against the new core around Damascus.

- It removed the other half of the pincer that Barzani had been using against YPG forces in his battle for control over the Kurdish areas.

- Turkey, instead of providing Syria with more arms and money to fight Kurdish guerrillas, decided to intervene and do the job itself.

In a minor concession after the revolt started gaining steam in 2011, the Syrian government announced that it would restore citizenship to all Kurds. With the government effectively removed from the Kurdish areas, Kurdish citizens of Syria had no practical way to get their documentation restored even if they wanted to do so. As of 2016, only about 6,000 have actually been permitted to take up that offer.

Turkey's intervention on the EU side angered Assad, so in this amnesty, unlike that of 2004, he did release over 640 prisoners who were involved with the PYD, hoping that these Kurds would now start attacking Turkey. In that, at least, he was partially correct. Many of the Kurds who had come from the north to fight the Assad regime did indeed return to the PKK to do battle with Turkey. Those who were Syrian Kurds were already in their homelands, and they remained in Syria to help with the defense against the Syrian government, ISIS, the Iraqi peshmerga and the Turks, all of whom are the enemies of the Syrian Kurds in this crazy five-sided war.

Sinjar and Beyond

While the Kurds were probably the most effective force in Syria, they didn't always win and they didn't always get there in time.

Chapter 12. Opportunity in Syria

In August 2014 ISIS began an offensive against Sinjar, a part of the Nineveh district in northwest Iraq where 3000 years earlier the Kurds (in the form of the Medes) had overthrown the mighty Assyrian empire to start building their own empire. In this same area, ISIS destroyed the remains of Nimrud, including a ziggurat (a structure after which the Tower of Babel is frequently modeled in art) that had until then remained remarkably well-preserved considering that they were thousands of years older than most such sites even in this ancient region. Sinjar was still home to many Yazidis, who are Kurds who still follow a strain of Zoroastrianism.

In a region where being different is very hazardous, the Yazidis had long since formed their own self-defense militias. These were now affiliated with the YPG, a collection of home-grown Syrian Kurdish militias led and trained by many of the alumni of the PKK. The YPG in turn had formed a significant component of the limited force of "vetted" entities that had agreed to join the US-backed force opposing the Assad regime. As a consequence, when ISIS struck, most of these forces were off in the Aleppo area.

Barzani's peshmerga were in place in Iraq, ostensibly on the front lines of the coordinated effort against ISIS at the time. It became apparent to Barzani that the Yazidi Kurds were not interested in being ruled by anyone, even brother Kurds. So he withdrew his peshmerga forces from the integrated front and allowed ISIS to take over that region, in the hope that an unimpeded ISIS would defeat the Syrian Kurds, their YPG, and their female counterparts in the YPJ, who were standing in the way of Barzani's dream of a Levant-wide Kurdistan that he would rule.

Even though it lacked the proper armaments, Sinjar was not totally defenseless. Most of the Yazidis had militia training, either homegrown or through the PKK, as part of their unending need to defend themselves. Although their strength was greatly reduced by the numbers who had gone to fight on behalf of the Americans, a good number of its residents had arms and put up a stout defense. Nonetheless, with no outside forces to complicate matters, ISIS quickly overran the city of 200,000, and most of the inhabitants fled, some 50,000 making for the nearby Sinjar Mountains where ISIS forces trapped them.

ISIS had been interested in the town because of its strategic central location, but they became obsessed with these refugees for two reasons: their anger at facing unaccustomed resistance, and their religious intolerance. The Yazidi men who had resisted were pursued, caught and shot, as was anyone who was around them at the time. The women were treated quite differently.

Chapter 12. Opportunity in Syria

They were rounded up, raped repeatedly, and then transported to other ISIS locations for use as sex slaves. Those who didn't have the looks for such an occupation were rejoined with the men and children in order to be shot.

The US was the only country that could have immediately deployed adequate combat power. Instead, Barack Obama dithered for a week and eventually settled on providing a few drops of food (less than 10 planeloads for 50,000 people), supported with close air cover that did destroy a couple of ISIS armored cars. Much of the food ended up in the hands of ISIS.

As noted in the chapter on Sakine Cansiz' female guerrillas, in the end it was the PKK, and more particularly the female units of the YPJ (one of the PKK's military arms within Syria) that cut a path through ISIS and held it open for the Yazidis to come down from the mountain to safety. Some 35,000 of the 50,000 made it out that way. Only once the YPJ had cleared ISIS off the scene did the peshmerga agree to use their vehicle assets to carry the refugees away to greater safety. When the YPJ had finished clearing the area they melted back into the landscape and went off to resume harrying ISIS and Turks elsewhere. The Yazidis soon returned to their homelands, where they established self-government guided by the PKK ideology (and, no doubt, by PKK cadres).

Walking the Talk: Life in a PKK Territory

Every party with a stake in the Syrian conflict has tried to establish a local government over any territory it controlled.

In the areas that the Iraqi Kurds have liberated from ISIS, the Turkish Government and the peshmerga forces of Massoud Barzani are attempting to establish a Syrian region similar to the Kurdistan Regional Government of Iraq (KRG). In the KRG, each of the dominant families (in the guise of political parties) operate their own army, police, and secret services to serve the Godfather-type warlords of that region. The Kurdish people in Syria are well aware that Barzani is an outsider, an opportunist, and a turncoat. His forces control only the areas that they are able to occupy and quell with force.

The bulk of the Kurdish areas came under the control of the YPG, which ran checkpoints on the main roads and entrances to Kurdish cities to protect the inhabitants from marauding troops of Arabs, Turks and Iraqi Kurds.

In the early years, a key aspect of the success of the YPG was their ability to draw combat-experienced followers from the PKK's other battlefronts (Turkey and Iraq) and to train newer volunteers. The training program

Chapter 12. Opportunity in Syria

followed the lines of the highly-effective programs for both the male units and female units that Sakine Cansiz had set up and run until her move to Europe. With the increasing effectiveness of the Kurdish forces, her reputation continued to grow.

By 2012, the YPG soon became the dominant force in most of the cantons of the territory that the Kurdistan Communities Union (KCK) calls the "Federation of Northern Syria - Rojava" and its cantons. The YPG's sponsor, the PYD, has become the de facto government of Syrian Kurdish districts. In 2010, the PYD elected a chemical engineer by the name of Saleh Muslim as its chairman. In keeping with PKK orthodoxy on the equal role of women, he was joined in 2012 by Asiyah Abdullah as its co-chairwoman.

Being composed almost entirely of Kurds who are actual Syrians, the KPG was able to draw on popular support. Its success went much further than that.

Beyond simply being the "home team", the PYD gained additional support by reason of its ideology, which despite its incomprehensible language has proven to be very attractive to a people used to violent autocracy.

Before looking at the details of the PYD's arrangements, the bottom line is well expressed by a more independent observer. The New York Times has in the past been a lot more interested in pressing for closer US ties with Turkey than it has shown any noticeable concern for the Kurds. Even so, it printed an article in September 2015 that stated:

"For a former diplomat and others who visited the region, they found it to be confusing: the visitors are looking for a hierarchy, the single leader, or signs of a government line, when, in fact, there was none; there were just groups. There was none of that stifling obedience to the party or the obsequious deference to the "big man", a form of government all too evident just across the borders, in Turkey to the north, and the Kurdish regional government of Iraq to the south. The confident assertiveness of young people was striking."

In January 2017, the Washington Post published "*U.S. military aid is fueling big ambitions for Syria's leftist Kurdish militia*", by Liz Sly. The article comprises almost as much space by itself as all Washington Post coverage of the Kurds combined up to that point. The real motivation for the article seemed to be a parting shot by the Post at the departing President Obama. His disastrous Syria policy had been the only matter on which the otherwise fawning Post had deviated from the White House talking points in eight years. The intent of the article, perhaps, was to expose the absurdity of a policy that

Chapter 12. Opportunity in Syria

resulted in the US arming and training factions that fought each other using US advisors; sooner or later, it suggests, US troops or air assets would end up firing on one another.

Sly's article goes into considerable detail in describing how the PYD and Öcalan ideologies are put into practice, including this most telling section:

Manbij offers an illustration of the potential contradictions of the U.S. alliance with the Syrian Kurds. The town, located in the northern Syrian province of Aleppo, is held out by the U.S. military as an example of a successful handover of power by Kurds to Arabs after an area is freed from Islamic State control.

But the Arabs who run Manbij are adherents of the YPG's ideology, making them indistinguishable in Turkey's eyes — and in the eyes of local residents — from the Kurdish force, according to Aaron Stein of the Washington-based Atlantic Council. The YPG-backed Arab force in Manbij has already fought battles with Turkish-backed Arab rebels in the nearby countryside, and Turkey is threatening to launch an offensive to take over the town.

At a recent ceremony for 250 Arab recruits who had just completed training with the U.S. military near Manbij, the newly minted soldiers were told they would be heading not to the Raqqa front lines but to Aleppo, to confront the rebels backed by Turkey, a NATO ally of the United States. As U.S. Special Operations troops looked on, Abu Amjad al-Adnan, commander of the Manbij recruits, rallied the soldiers to take the fight to the forces backed by "terrorist Turkey."

In other words, even Arabs are signing on to the PKK ideology. No doubt they self-select, or are selected, because of their interest in the matter, but the fact is that it shows that this form of governance is not simply by the Kurds, for the Kurds.

So what is this ideology that people of the region are finding so appealing?

The PKK ideology endorses "social equality, justice and the freedom of belief" as well as "pluralism and the freedom of political parties." It describes itself as "striving for a democratic solution that includes the recognition of cultural, national and political rights, and develops and enhances their peaceful struggle to be able to govern themselves in a multicultural, democratic society."

The PYD has called for one military force for Syrian Kurds instead of the multitude of armies controlled by various political parties. It also called for election of the civilian political parties. That's easy talk when one holds no

Chapter 12. Opportunity in Syria

power. To its credit, after attaining power, the PYD has followed through on its rhetoric. It consolidated the various entities into a common police, secret service, and judiciary to serve the people based on the laws of the region.

The PYD also came through on its promises of free elections. In November 2013, the PYD and a few other Kurdish political parties, Arab leaders, and Christian personalities announced the formation of an interim government, dividing the Kurdish region into three non-contiguous autonomous areas or cantons: Afrin, Jazira, and Kobane. Even the media loyal to Barzani, Talabani, and Turkey commented, "*Kurdish rebels are establishing self-rule in war-torn Syria, resembling the Zapatista experience and providing a democratic alternative for the region.*"

Not only has it allowed itself to be democratically elected but (atypically for the region) the PYD has also permitted the existence of dozens of political parties of various degrees of militancy or moderation, even some that are loyal to the Iraqi Kurdish Barzani and Talabani families. These democratic reforms came over the opposition of those very same groups, which wanted direct nomination of governing officials for the simple reason that Barzani, who was not only an Iraqi but one who was already running his own government in Iraq, could count on little support from the Syrian electorate.

One of the most effective tools for bringing legitimacy and citizen involvement to the Kurdish cause is the polyethnic Movement for a Democratic Society (TEV-DEM), formed by the PYD.

According to Zaher Baher of the Haringey Solidarity Group, the TEV-DEM has been "the most successful organ" in Rojava because it has the "determination and power to change things, and it includes many people who believe in working voluntarily at all levels of service to make the event/experiment successful."

Baher describes the TEV-DEM approach as pursuing "a bottom-up, Athenian-style direct form of democratic governance," in which the local communities take on responsibility, contrasted to the strong central government favored by many states. In this model, states become less relevant, and people govern through councils. TEV-DEM's intent is to be very inclusive, and people from a range of different backgrounds have become involved, including Kurds, Arabs, Assyrians, Syrian Turkmen and Yazidis. It sought to "establish a variety of groups, committees and communes on the streets in neighborhoods, villages, counties and small and big towns everywhere." The purpose of these groups was to meet "every week to talk about the problems people face where they live", and the group

Chapter 12. Opportunity in Syria

representatives meet weekly in "in the leading panel in the villages or towns, called the House of the People."

Thanks in part to the prodding from Sakine Cansiz for a proper recognition of the rights of women, Abdullah Öcalan allowed his thinking to evolve from its original Maoist rhetoric to a melding of thoughts drawn from communist and capitalists alike, concentrating instead on allowing people to pursue their own dreams and self-interest.

The PYD's Social Economy Plan, launched in 2012 and later renamed as the People's Economy Plan (PEP), also draws from Abdullah Öcalan's ongoing work on an approach he calls "Democratic Confederalism". It departs from the original hard-line Maoist Communism, seeking to derive the advantages of capitalism without its adverse consequences for those at the bottom of the heap. It protects private property and entrepreneurship under the principle of "ownership by use," although entrepreneurs remain accountable to the democratic will of locally organized councils. Dr. Dara Kurdaxi, a Rojavan economist, has said that the method in Rojava is not so much against private property, but rather has the goal of putting the private ownership in the service of all the people who live in Rojava.

The PYD continues to apply existing Syrian civil law as far as it can without contradicting the Constitution of Rojava. One notable example of change in that regard is family law. The PYD has instituted absolute equality for women under the law, banned polygamy, permitted civil marriage and allowed intermarriage between people of different religious backgrounds.

In short, despite its heavy ideological theories, it is moving towards exactly the model of an open secular society that for so many years made Turkey the darling of the Western governments, and fueled its relatively spectacular economic performance, both lost as a result of Erdoğan's heavy-handed Islamist approach.

Party leader Salih Muslim claims that the PYD desires Kurdish autonomy within a new democratic Syria rather than Kurdish independence. The party claims to be wedded to Abdullah Öcalan philosophies but not to the PKK itself. However, as Liz Sly reports, the affiliation is pervasive and obvious.

Turkey Takes Stock of the Situation

Pulling ourselves back from 2016 to the situation as it was in January 2013, the scenario that Erdoğan and the AKP had feared since 2003 appeared to be coming to reality. The land of the Medes appeared to be reforming.

Chapter 12. Opportunity in Syria

There was another complication: Erdoğan was already some years into a grander strategy featuring himself as the new strongman in Ankara. He didn't need his security forces consumed in a low-grade guerrilla war against the PKK, which was now carrying with them the might of the American war machine in support. If the disorganized and repellent ISIS could grab territory and begin running their own country so quickly, the better-organized Kurds could surely do the same. How long could it be before the Kurds in Syria and Iraq settled their differences and used the oil that they happened to sit upon to acquire international sponsors? Such a state would surely provide safe haven to any Turkish PKK guerrilla bands, and the Kurds within Turkey itself would be emboldened to demand autonomy for themselves. How long after that would it be before Turkey would be fighting a hot war within its own borders to preserve a significant section of its own territory?

A strong response would be required if the situation could not be contained rapidly. Before deploying military force against a coalition that included the fickle but still-powerful US, there appeared to be another option. The Turks seemed fairly satisfied with the status quo that had been forged with Barzani to limit incursions from the Iraqi border. The MIT had been holding discussions with the PKK for several years; perhaps it was worth one more try to see whether a solution existed that would continue giving Assad a headache while relieving Erdoğan of his.

In late 2012, the Turkish government and the PKK had reached that point of constructive dialog in which it was clear to both sides that something useful was happening. The Turks demanded that Sakine Cansiz, one of the PKK's chief leaders and the only one active in Europe, participate in these negotiations.

But in January 2013, she is dead, obviously assassinated.

We are back to the original question, but now much better informed: who killed Sakine Cansiz and her colleagues, and why?

Chapter 13. After the Murders: Kurds Ascendant

January 2013 is a busy month in the Levantine madhouse. The wheel of fate is turning. The question is where it will stop.

At the time of the murders in the Rue Lafayette, the Turkish governmental party, under President Erdoğan, is in league with the faction led by Muhammed Fethullah Gülen, and they are negotiating a peace deal with Abdullah Öcalan, the leader of the PKK.

We know this because the news media has obtained sound recordings of the secret negotiations held in Oslo, Norway, in 2011 between MIT Chief Hakan Fidan and the PKK representative. It is possible that MIT bugged the room and then leaked the information themselves, for some obscure reason. If not, the only other player in the room was the police intelligence service, which was controlled by the Gülen Movement.

Öcalan is in jail, so he is not negotiating from a position of strength. Despite the PKK's gains within Syria, it is still locked into a war for its very existence with their fellow Kurds of the very capable Iraqi peshmerga. Within Turkey, the PKK's operations are little more than pinpricks. Nonetheless, looking more broadly at the geopolitical scale, the PKK is actually winning.

In 2013, the US is reluctantly providing support to the PKK so that it can oppose the Syrian regime. If the Kurds can play their hand correctly, and if national borders are up for renegotiation after the Syrian government (at that time completely isolated from international support) collapses, then the Kurds may be able to establish their people in Syria in the same way that they are autonomous in Iraq. With a weak central government, they will be able to expand the envelope just as Barzani has done in Iraq. Looking into the long term, there could be a way to connect the Kurds in Iraq and Syria into a cohesive Kurdistan that does have oil, and then reunification with the Kurds inside Turkey becomes conceivable.

The Kurds outside Turkey may be looking at years of peace and the possibility of creating a legitimate nation of sorts. This is one of the few times in the past thousand years that their fortunes appear to be looking up.

On the other hand, as the Gülen Movement and the AKP see it, things are also going quite well within Turkey. Since the re-election of the AKP in 2005, the AKP and the Gülen Movement have maintained an alliance to eliminate secular opposition to their Islamist political parties. The Gülen Movement controls the police, judiciary, and education, and they use their influence to

Chapter 13. After the Murder: Kurds Ascendant

limit political opposition from the secular establishment in Turkey. Oddly, although Gülen is a cleric, the AKP is responsible for religious compliance matters.

Their power-sharing arrangement has been exposed via several leaked documents and tapes, but they control any group that might be able to do anything about it, so nothing is done. Their clear aim is to root out all secular parties in a drive to convert Turkey from a thriving modern secular state into yet another Islamic theocracy, even if that means the society and economy must return to a Third World level. But the power grab is not yet complete. Eliminating the remaining pockets of opposition requires the full attention of all concerned; at this moment, pinprick or otherwise, the PKK is an annoyance the AKP and Gülen can do without.

For a brief moment in 2012, all three parties are in favor of peace. Then one of the key negotiators for the PKK is crudely removed from the picture. Someone sent Güney to do this job. One of these primary actors, or one of their controlled organizations, has had her murdered in a manner that sends a message (if a rather obscure one). They may have miscalculated the consequences, or it may have worked out just as they planned.

One foreseeable result is the outpouring of Kurdish emotions, catapulting Sakine from being a genuine Kurdish heroine to becoming a deathless martyr. The exact impact is hard to assess, but the thousands of people who show up for the various memorial events every year, often at risk to their own lives, show the degree of enthusiasm that her story generates for the masses of Kurdish people.

If the intent of killing Sakine Cansiz was to stop the peace process, it fails. The peace treaty that has been discussed for four years is signed in as many weeks. It will last barely a year and will be much flouted on both sides even during that short period, but all that is still in the future. Öcalan directs the PKK to stand down in Turkey. Erdoğan can focus his attention on intra-Turk matters.

The AKP-Gülen Rift

The murders of Sakine Cansiz and her colleagues in Paris result in an international consensus that the Turks are the perpetrators, or if not then they were in on the plot ... but which Turks? In rapid and vehement denials, the Islamist allies drop their joint war against the other secular political parties in Turkey long enough to accuse each other of being the killers who

Chapter 13. After the Murder: Kurds Ascendant

want to stop the peace process between the PKK and the Turkish government. The rift never heals.

In a partnership between two such ruffians, eventual betrayals are inevitable. Recent revelations include that the AKP had been planning to eliminate Gülen since 2004. In later years, the AKP would suggest that Gülen was the one actually in league with the PKK, a highly-improbable claim considering Gülen's many years of attempting to eliminate the Kurdish language and culture completely.

The outward signs of the break had emerged in 2012 when the AKP-dominated legislature demanded that the head of MIT testify about the recent appointment of numerous Gülen politicians to senior positions. This is a farce: the AKP had colluded with the Gülen faction to do precisely that in order to drive out the other parties. They have succeeded in that , and Erdoğan appears to be signaling "mission accomplished" on that front. Now the AKP can shift its attention to devouring its main competitor. Not the PKK, but Gülen.

Later in 2013, Gülen will criticize the government's heavy-handed response to the Gezi Park pro-democracy protests in which thousands end up killed and many thousands are injured. In return, the AKP begins closing down Gülen's private schools and colleges, which are the Movement's recruiting grounds. This move pushes the rift to the point of no return.

The Gülen-controlled police and judiciary conduct a sudden and massive crackdown on "corruption"; the targets are, by definition, incumbent politicians and civil servants. That means they belong to the governing AKP. Erdoğan accuses Gülen of trying to bring down his government, or, even worse, of forcing it to operate as a figurehead while the Gülen forces control the real "government within a government". (In the West, this situation sounded absurd until it was duplicated just three years later in the US, where President Trump was treated to the same "deep state" rebellion).

Early in 2014, Erdoğan himself becomes enmeshed in the corruption probe when an audiotape captures him telling his son to dispose of a stash of ill-gotten cash. He gives the same contradictory responses used by politicians everywhere: the tape is a complete forgery, and, in any case, it was obtained through an illegal wiretap. The AKP then produces its own forgery: a technical report by a US company that has analyzed the tape and determined that it is a fake. The company will later confirm that it has never had anything to do with any such analysis.

Chapter 13. After the Murder: Kurds Ascendant

The Erdoğan government responds quickly. Within weeks, new laws place the Supreme Court and its judicial and police entities under the control of the Ministry of Justice, which the AKP does control. The Ministry reassigns thousands of police and other employees around the country, and fires the prosecutors who brought corruption charges.

More laws follow. The AKP gives sweeping powers to the MIT, and makes it illegal to post anything on the Internet that criticizes the government.

The end-point in this game is a failed coup d'état attempt on July 15, 2016. The AKP will claim that Gülen organized the coup. Gülen will deny involvement, saying that nobody could have bungled it as badly as it was unless they were doing it on purpose. He alleges that it was engineered by Erdoğan himself as a ruse to justify eliminating any military opposition to his rule in Turkey as an Islamist dictator. Gülen sees Erdoğan as seeking to revive the Ottoman Empire system, setting up his family to be the rulers for many generations to come.

The Erdoğan government demands that the US extradite Gülen back to Turkey to face punishment for leading the failed coup.

While President Obama wastes no time in condemning the coup, he does not move quickly on the extradition request. It has placed the US in a difficult position. Gülen had moved to the US when both leaders were considered allies against the repressive former government. But the US has alliances and treaties with the country of Turkey, whereas Gülen, for all his influence within Turkey, is diplomatically just another individual. US bureaucrats finesse the situation: they will be happy to extradite him in accordance with agreed processes, which require some evidence of Gülen's involvement in the coup before they can send him back to Turkey. Apparently the evidence does not exist; Gülen continues on unmolested in the US and remains there still in 2017.

Extradition won't be that critical after all. At the time of writing (2017), Gülen lives in obscurity in a small US town while Erdoğan and the AKP have successfully defeated the Gülen Movement and established a practical dictatorship. The West tolerates and subsidizes it, albeit with increasing skepticism and concern, because of Turkey's critical position in a region that has created so many problems for them over the past 50 years.

Economically, the EU wants Turkey as a member, despite the fact that it is violating every expectation of a EU member country. Meanwhile Turkey enjoys energy stability thanks to the flow of oil from Iraq, courtesy of the collaborators Barzani and Talabani who control the oil of the Kurdistan Regional Government (KRG) of Iraq. Their flexibility is, as always, astonishing. The same families had formerly been ardent disciples of the Gülen movement and served as its foreign outposts; perhaps they still do.

The AKP has managed a remarkable diplomatic feat. It has wangled support from the US, Saudi Arabia, Qatar, Iran, and Russia, and the acquiescence of the Syrian government. Every one of the internationally-recognized parties in the five-way war, while aggressively opposed to one another, find out that they are all allied with Turkey. In fact, considering that the Turks do not attack ISIS at all, the only regional player Turkey is not allied with appears to be the Syrian Kurds.

Intervention in Syria

Turkey is now emboldened to send its forces into Syria. The ostensible reason for intervention is the only one tolerable to the international community: Turkey intends to combat ISIS. But it does not do so.

In northern Syria, the de facto Kurdistan is known as the Democratic Project of Rojava. It is controlled by the Kurdish People's Protection Units (YPG), which are also a part of the US-sponsored anti-Assad rebel grouping called the Syrian Democratic Forces. The SDF is a motley crew by any standard, an alliance of Kurdish, Arab, Assyrian, Armenian, Turkmen and Circassian militias, all of whom could be described as "piratical" on their best days. Now they also have American air cover.

Most of these ethnic groups are among those that Turkey has repressed at one time or another. The last thing Turkey needs on its borders is an effective fighting force composed of people whose primary motivation is that they don't like Turkey. The Turks have already been caught trying to tempt some of these groups to turn against one another. The tampering is soon exposed, leading to further mistrust of the Turks and their role in this theater.

Once Erdoğan puts the Kurdish question on hold with the PKK ceasefire, he succeeds in putting the Gülen group out of the picture between 2014-2015. But events will move swiftly in Syria; when he returns to refocus on the Syrian situation, he finds it quite changed.

Turkey had disgraced itself in 2014-2015 in the matter of Kobane, where the Kurds were battling ISIS. Turkey had convinced Obama not to provide air support to the Kurds until the situation was very nearly out of control; it had blocked the flow of PKK fighters to the battlefield; and it had over-aggressively

Chapter 13. After the Murder: Kurds Ascendant

quelled crowds protesting both Turkish inaction against ISIS and its inaction to support the thousands of refugees flowing in from the Kobane area. Those demonstrations might have passed largely unnoticed had the Turkish authorities not launched tear-gas grenades into the broadcasting rig of the BBC. It might have been an accident or it might not; either way, it made perfect footage for the television news.

Turkey is losing ground in the propaganda war while the Kurds are succeeding beyond even their own expectations. The Kurdish mini-states are demonstrably working, attracting even non-Kurdish adherents, and they are coalescing across the map into a more credible entity that could be a viable candidate for an autonomous region like the one in Iraq. Erdoğan's ally Barzani, despite all his resources and substantial covert support from Turkey, is seen as a carpet-bagger and gets very little traction.

The Kurds are rapidly reaching a point where they could become a diplomatic *fait accompli*. If the Turks cannot find competent or reliable allies, they would just have to get the job done by intervening themselves.

Turkey's intervention in Syria would be pathetic if its real intention had been to take on ISIS, a claim made to justify sending troops into Syria at all. Until 2012, Erdoğan had seen ISIS as a convenient tool to harass the Syrians and destroy the Kurds. Since announcing its intent to participate in the conflict, as of 2017 Turkey has yet to engage with ISIS at all unless perhaps in self-defense. On the contrary, Turkey's first combat action inside Syria was to bomb PKK forces that actually were engaged with ISIS at the time. Its subsequent actions have been more of the same.

It's not as if the effort would be infeasible for Turkey. There's not a lot of actual combat power in this whole theater. Earlier, ISIS' main offensive against Kobane included only about 4000 fighters, and a few hundred YPG fought them to a standstill; then, with the injection of only 250 fresh PKK troops from Turkey, the YPG ran ISIS out of Kobani canton.

After that, it took only 10 Turkish tanks to bring the YPG's successful offensive to a halt. These are able troops, well-trained and capable of using many weapons and types of equipment when they come across them, but there are not large numbers of them.

The Turks launch attacks across the border whenever they can catch YPG units out of support range of the US. These attacks, along with assaults on known PKK strongholds within Turkey, lead the PKK to announce in July of 2015 that the ceasefire has been breached and it is resuming its insurgent

Chapter 13. After the Murder: Kurds Ascendant

campaign inside Turkey. However, it doesn't really have the strength for that. Some bombings do occur, but they are not significant enough to create any attention outside Turkey.

In 2016, Turkey demands that the Iraqi Kurds (the *peshmerga*) withdraw to the Euphrates River, leaving some 200 kilometers between the Kurdish-controlled enclaves in Syria and Iraq. For a while, both groups of Kurds resist Turkish pressure to withdraw, declaring that it would be foolish to unilaterally give up hundreds of square miles of territory with nobody to retain control of it. That is how ISIS arose in the first place.

Under Turkish pressure, US Vice-President Biden comes to Ankara to request the peshmerga to do just that. The US is the guarantor of their viability in Iraq, so they have to accede to this demand. The Turks and US should have foreseen that the territory, which is largely populated by Kurds, would simply realign with another Kurdish entity. In this case, the Syrian arm of the PKK is on hand to fill the void. The Turkish government's demands have resulted in an even stronger presence of the YPG and the PYD. That is exactly the opposite of what the Turks had intended.

Faceoff in Sinjar

Remember the Yazidi Kurds who were rescued from ISIS by the PKK women's units in 2014? In March 2017, they are back in the news.

The Yazidis who survived their occupation by ISIS live largely as refugees in tents on the mountainside above their shattered town of Sinjar, which lies at the intersection of Syria, Turkey and Iraq. Since the time that they rescued the Yazidis, the PYD has effectively been running the local government, opening schools, training self-defense forces and building its trademark billboards with pictures of Abdullah Öcalan. They maintain a lighted shrine on Mount Sinjar to commemorate the fighters who died in the battle with ISIS, fighters who are from the YPG.

If it sounds like a return to normalcy, it is ... in all too many ways. This pastoral tranquility exists only on the surface. Peaceable existence seems to be something that eludes the Kurds at every turn.

The town is about 7 miles inside Iraq, and it is in a majority-Kurdish part of Iraq. It is not, however, inside the boundaries of the Kurdistan Regional Government (the Kurdish portion of the Iraqi government) headed by Massoud Barzani, who wants to extend the KRG's control to all Kurdish areas in Iraq if not beyond. He has visited the mountain, and the mayor of the

Chapter 13. After the Murder: Kurds Ascendant

formal government in the area is a Barzani supporter. Over a thousand Yazidis have joined his forces to fight ISIS, but at present, they are not doing so.

In a long-term effort to regain control of the area from the PKK, Barzani's Yazidis are busy constructing siege trenches around their fellow Yazidis who are in the YPG forces that relieved the Sinjar siege and now control the town. The two groups conduct regular combat patrols and engage in small skirmishes while settling in for a more protracted siege. Each group complains that the other is distracting them from fighting ISIS, which is still quite visibly in place not five miles away.

The Turks have announced that they will not tolerate establishment of a PKK base in Sinjar to become a replica of their stronghold in the Qandil Mountains in Turkey. In a curious twist, the central government of Iraq is content to leave the PKK ensconced in Sinjar in order to limit the spread of the KRG beyond its official boundaries.

Perhaps the best summary of the situation - one that has played itself out on this very spot so many times over 5,000 years - is offered by Hayder Shesho, a leader of one of the groups that have joined the Iraqi peshmerga. In the Washington Post (22 March 2017), speaking of his own commanders in the Barzani government, he says: "*Yes, we have been betrayed by them. Yes, we have been abandoned by them. But we are Kurds*".

In January 2017, the Obama administration is finally removed from the scene that it had done so much to destabilize, handing President Trump a conundrum. In Syria, Obama had been intimidated by the Russians into being afraid to take drastic action against the Assad regime, which made him a laughing-stock since 2012 when he proved unable or unwilling to back up his "red-line" speeches. Trump wants to restore US relations with Russia, which is opposed to ISIS but is actively supporting the Syrian government in hopes of retaining their new Mediterranean naval base. However, Trump's priority is to take ISIS decisively off the board, which the Russians also claim as their primary intent.

As 2017 muddles its way along, the situation for the Kurds remains, as always, full of danger but full of potential. It appears at the time of writing that they have found their most steadfast ally in decades in the form of Donald Trump. He has stated as a key point of his foreign policy that he doesn't want the US to become bogged down in another nation-building quagmire in the Middle East (or anywhere else). He advocates swift, brutal action to get rid of ISIS.

Chapter 13. After the Murder: Kurds Ascendant

When coming into office he had no particular interest in the Kurdish problem. He soon came to see who exactly it was that was doing most of the fighting against ISIS: specifically, the YPG, the PKK-affiliated fighters who are both Syrian citizens and of Kurdish ethnicity. In response, Trump is not tolerating Turkish efforts to repress the YPG elements.

Uncharacteristically, the Washington Post has now taken interest in the Kurdish issue and has published a stream of news reports during 2017. It reported Turkish air attacks against Kurdish positions rather than ISIS locations on 25 April; those strikes also inflicted casualties on Turkey's unofficial allies, the Iraqi Kurdish peshmerga, and caused damage among the Yazidi civilians on Mount Sinjar. In response, on 28 April, US combat units from Iraq began extending their patrols to the Syrian-Turkish border with the objective of maintaining a separation between Turkish and Kurdish forces.

In April 2017, the Assad regime shot itself in the foot. Only a few weeks earlier, Trump had announced a shift in US policy. Obama had made regime change a non-negotiable condition, although he had also refused to do anything to back up that demand. Trump opined that it might be possible for Assad to stay in place if only he could behave himself. For no apparent reason, Assad's response was to conduct a sarin nerve gas attack on rebel-held but non-combatant communities outside Aleppo in April 2017.

A shocked Trump demanded a more aggressive US role in putting an end to this war. His military leadership was finally free to announce what many at the Pentagon had advocated for years: since only the Kurds were doing any fighting against ISIS, that is who the US would arm and support as extensively as might be needed. Trump brushes off concerns over the PKK's listing as a terrorist organization; his focus is on defeating ISIS, and the YPG is getting the job done. The Pentagon sends weapons and advisors, who in addition to providing access to air support will also serve as human shields; this more determined US leader will not tolerate its Turkish "ally" inflicting any US combat losses.

When Erdoğan visited the US only a few days later, Trump's team made it clear that this decision was not going to change. Turkey then committed an even worse faux pas when Erdoğan's Presidential security detail initiated a melee with US citizens of Kurdish origin who were peacefully demonstrating outside the Turkish embassy. The detail, caught on camera and eventually separated by the Washington DC police, sprinted into the Embassy and claimed diplomatic immunity. The Turks lost whatever high ground it might have held in the Kurdish matter.

Chapter 13. After the Murder: Kurds Ascendant

If it cannot attack the Kurds, Turkey hopes to prevent their continuing encroachment. Turkish forces begin a new tactic in 2017, interposing its forces directly in the path of Kurdish units, whether PKK or *peshmerga*, to prevent them from creating a de facto contiguous region joining the Syrian and Iraqi Kurdistans. That territory in turn would adjoin the Kurdish portion of Turkey.

Of course, if accidents and incidents happen, such as the Turks accidentally shooting up "allied" troops, well, that is war. But the US has a new tactic too; it is actively setting up no-go zones around the Kurdish troop positions. It is now shooting first and asking questions later. Iranian militias and Turkish army units are blasted by air cover as soon as they come within a few miles of Kurdish positions. The US does not apologize; it hands out more maps of the no-go zones.

So the war in Syria with its cast of thousands ambles along. As usual, the ordinary Kurdish people are the ones caught in the crossfire.

The Police Case In Paris

We haven't forgotten the French police and their 2013 investigation of the murders on the Rue Lafayette. The police have been stymied by the inability to verify - or to disprove - the suspicion that Ömer Güney was working for some Turkish entity.

By 2015, Güney finally makes an appearance in court, but even then it's not the actual trial, just the indictment. The police have enough evidence to place him at the scene of the crime, and that's enough for an indictment. Beyond that, they don't really have a solid motive, which they need to convict, and they'd like to keep the immunity door open in hopes that Güney will give up his handlers. The fact that the President of France had come to know and like Sakine Cansiz keeps things motivated. Even more importantly, from the police point of view, there's a matter of self-respect at stake here: if there is a foreign power running wet operations on their soil, the French want to know who it is. The investigation continues in France. Turkey continues to stonewall it.

Güney himself has let slip that he was acting on the directions of others. It's quite possible that even he does not really know who they are.

The problem remains that everyone in this tale is accusing everyone else, and each of them can trot out some credible evidence to support those charges.

Chapter 13. After the Murder: Kurds Ascendant

As early as 2013, the Erdoğan government is already accusing the Gülen Movement of committing the crime with the intention of undermining the AKP-PKK peace process and trying to make the government look bad for having those discussions in the first place. In a few months, once the corruption indictments begin to be handed down, President Erdoğan will "discover" that the Gülen Movement has infiltrated the police and judiciary of Turkey. The PKK has been saying that for many years. It also has possession of a 2011 Gülen Movement circular indicating that they have planned for the elimination of PKK leadership. It authorizes all the Turkish Armed Forces (TSK) and police to detain and eliminate members of the Kurdistan Communities Union anywhere in the world, openly if need be. This is one of the reasons that Sakine had been advised to maintain a low profile.

Other entities might have had the same general idea. At Güney's arraignment, French prosecutors present sound recordings obtained through wiretaps. Those tapes confirm that MIT was actively planning to assassinate high-ranking members of the Kurdistan Workers Party (PKK) in Europe while the peace talks were going on between the Turkish government and the PKK.

PKK press releases over the 2015-2016 period insist that the Turkish state is involved in some way in the Paris murders, and neither side disagrees that the government is behind recent attacks on PKK cells. So, as of 2015, the PKK resumes its guerrilla activities as well as its political efforts.

At the end of 2016, a trial date has still not been set when Güney dies in prison. There is no suspicion of foul play; Güney had a medical condition when he was arrested. So he will take his secrets to the grave, since the Turkish government continues to refuse to cooperate. The case is officially closed.

The families of the slain Kurdish women take to the airwaves and the streets to demand justice from the French prosecutors. The fact that the prime suspect has died does not matter much to the investigation; he would not have testified against himself anyway. Although the outcome is somewhat moot since Güney has died, the French are newly disposed to reconsider. On the battlefields and in the liberated territories of Syria, the PKK is proving itself to be the bravest and the most democratically-inclined group in the whole region. Erdoğan, on the other hand, has become increasingly autocratic and in many venues he has worn out his welcome,

The prosecutors announce that they have re-opened the investigation. The French government is willing to start looking past the Turkish smokescreen. Presumably they have some means of doing so, otherwise this is a colossal

Chapter 13. After the Murder: Kurds Ascendant

waste of time and effort. Perhaps they already have some evidence collected via their intelligence functions.

Stay tuned!

Chapter 14. The Sakine Legacy

Kurdish veneration of the heroics of their past may be vital for the culture's survival, when so many different rulers have tried to suppress the Kurds' very identity.

An unfortunate consequence of that otherwise praiseworthy habit is that the dead receive more attention than the living. Sakine Cansiz was well-known in the community because of her bravery under torture and in combat, but it took her death for her to be seen as a true reformer. Now she is an inspiration to millions of women suffering under repressive regimes and religions around the world.

3-year Memorial ceremony, 2016

Sebahat Tuncel, an MP for Turkey's pro-Kurdish Peace and Democracy Party (BDP), told Reuters. "She was a very famous name for Kurdish women. She was a feminist, and her struggle was always double-edged: against male dominance and for Kurdish rights," she said.

Chapter 14. The Sakine Legacy

Cansiz was the key figure in the PKK, whose armed struggle for greater Kurdish autonomy has burned at the heart of the Turkish nation for three decades, right up to her death.

The status of Sakine Cansiz in death is now equivalent to the status of Abdullah Öcalan among Kurdish people. She is the symbol of women and Kurdish people in general. Her struggle for peace and freedom for Kurds and women worldwide will be remembered for generations to come.

Four years after her death, Kurds are still paying her their respects.

From the ANF, on Friday, 6 January 2017:

http://anfenglish.com/women/paris-massacre-protests-in-front-of-french-consulates-across-europe

Demonstrations were held throughout Europe on the fourth anniversary of the Paris Massacre. Protesters placed black wreaths in front of French consulates in several cities and demanded justice for Sakine Cansız, Fidan Doğan and Leyla Şaylemez.

BERLIN

A demonstration was held in front of the French consulate in the German capital, Berlin, and protesters placed a black wreath saying "France sacrificed law to Erdoğan" in front of the consulate, where a woman representing justice stood watch.

In speeches during the demonstration, activists said dragging this case on, when the evidence was out in the open for the massacre in Paris, confirmed the complicity of France. Protesters also issued a call for a strong attendance to the demonstration to be held in Kleitspark on January 9 at 16:00.

Representatives from Berlin Êzidî Women's Assembly and CİK Women's Commission spoke in the demonstration. The group chanted slogans of "Sara, Rojbîn, Ronahî, Women, Life, Freedom" and "We demand justice" in 3 languages and flyers were passed out.

FRANKFURT

Amara Women's Assembly gathered in front of the French consulate in Frankfurt, Germany to protest the 4th anniversary of the Paris massacre and placed a black wreath. The protesters also submitted a file to the French consulate and pointed out that the French state should abandon this dirty game and the massacre could not be covered up this way.

Chapter 14. The Sakine Legacy

The group also called for attendance to the demonstration to be held in front of the Frankfurt Hauptwache on the anniversary of the Paris massacre, January 9, at 16:00. The demonstration concluded with chants of "Women, Life, Freedom."

HANAU

An information stand on the Paris massacre was set up in Hanau, Germany. The protesters passed out flyers and gave the message that the massacre can't be covered up. They also called for attendance to the demonstration in Frankfurt on January 9. The demonstration concluded with chants of "Jin Jiyan Azadi".

BRUSSELS

A demonstration led by TJK-E and SKB was held in front of the French consulate in Belgian capital Brussels. The protesters carried photos of Cansız, Doğan and Şaylemez and chanted "We are all Sakine, Leyla and Fidan", "Murderer Turkey", "Murderer Erdoğan".

ZURICH

A black wreath was placed in front of the French consulate in Zurich, Switzerland. The demonstration was held by the Beritan Women's Assembly and the women carried a black wreath with a sash that read "Your silence is due to complicity."

A short statement was read and women said that it is not acceptable that the case to shed light onto the Paris massacre has not yet started. The statement also included that the death of hitman Ömer Güney so shortly before the start of the case created suspicions for Kurdish women, and that France must act immediately in order to shed light onto the massacre. The black wreath was placed in front of the consulate after the statement and the demonstration concluded with chants.

COPENHAGEN

The Paris massacre was also protested in the Danish capital Copenhagen. The demonstration was led by the Sevê Women's Assembly, and the women submitted a file to the French consulate. The file mentions the 3 years that have passed since the massacre and says: "With the only suspect in the case, Ömer Güney, dying before the trial started on January 23, the evidence that MİT and French intelligence committed the murders together has been removed. The French and Turkish governments have showed that they are taking an approach of denial in a joint decision against the Kurdish people

Chapter 14. The Sakine Legacy

with the suspicious death of the perpetrator." The Sevê Women's Assembly called on women and all patriotic Kurds in Copenhagen to attend the rally to be held in Axeltorv on January 7 at 12:30.

MARSEILLE

Led by the Arin Mirkan Women's Assembly and the Democratic Society Center, hundreds of people gathered in front of the Governorate building in Marseille, France to demand the disclosure of the murderers of Cansız, Doğan and Şaylemez. Protestors carried signs that said "Is your silence due to your complicity?" and "No to political assassinations" and distributed pamphlets on the assassination of the 3 Kurdish woman politicians.

Arin Mirkan Women's Assembly spokesperson Suzan Aydemir addressed the protestors and said that the assassination was carried out by a coalition that included the Turkish Intelligence Agency, and emphasized that they would continue to struggle for justice. Kurdish politician Cuma Tak also spoke during the protest, and said that the targeting of Cansız, Doğan and Şaylemez aimed to destroy Kurdish people's desire for freedom.

RENNES

Led by the Zin Women's Assembly, protestors organized a sit-in in front of the municipal building in Rennes, France, and said that they would continue to protest until the disclosure of the people responsible for the assassination of the three Kurdish revolutionary women.

http://anfenglish.com/women/paris-massacre-protests-in-front-of-french-consulates-across-europe

****

Perhaps one of the best summations of Sakine's legacy was provided by KONGA-GEL in urging people to attend those Sakine memorials:

KONGRA-GEL Co-presidency issued a written statement for the anniversary of the January 9 massacre.

"On the fourth anniversary of the Paris massacre, we remember the three martyred Kurdish revolutionary women, our comrades Sakine Cansız, Fidan Doğan and Leyla Şaylemez. We will pursue this case until the true murderers are found and put on trial, and we will never let this case fall victim to inter-governmental interests."

Chapter 14. The Sakine Legacy

KONGRA-GEL stated that although 4 years have passed since the massacre, the hitman still hadn't given a statement, the case seemed to drag on as if to wait for him to die, and now there is a search for grounds to bury the case, and protested the French authorities.

The KONGRA-GEL statement continues:

"Although there is information and evidence that this massacre was planned by the Turkish National Intelligence Agency (MİT) and executed by MİT agents, the Paris court handling the case hasn't achieved any concrete results to shed light to the truth.

THOSE WHO THINK THEY CAN OBSCURE THE MASSACRE ARE WRONG

What can clearly be seen is that the truth about the murders of three Kurdish revolutionary women are attempted to be covered up in line with dark interrelations between governments. Similar political murders in France in the past have all been covered up. The Turkish state has committed many murders in European countries over gangs allied to them, and these were all covered up. In line with the dark relations between states, these murders were obscured.

Those who think they can obscure the January 9, 2013 Paris Massacre are wrong. Because there is a great Women's Freedom Movement who follow up on the case of the three Kurdish revolutionary women. And there is a widespread solidarity movement from free women's movements around the world for the three revolutionary women, Sakine, Rojbîn and Ronahî. And there is the struggle the brave people of Kurdistan are waging together with their allies around the world.

WE WON'T LET THE PARIS MASSACRE CASE BE SHELVED

Sakine, Rojbîn and Ronahî's case isn't just about the murder of three women. The dark relations formed among states around the century-long Kurdish issue continue in the Paris case. But we won't allow this darkness to continue.

The level the women-led Freedom Struggle that marked the 21st century has reached and the new balance of power it has created will remove these dark relations that have become the fate of the Kurdish people. For this, it is very important to shed light onto the darkness in the Paris case. This isn't just confined to the Paris case, but will also shed light onto the Kurdish reality that is attempted to be obscured as well.

EVERYONE SHOULD JOIN THE PARIS MARCH

Chapter 14. The Sakine Legacy

For these reasons, we are calling on all our people, most of all our women and our youth, to have a strong attendance in the march and rally to be held in Paris for our comrades Sakine, Rojbîn and Ronahî on January 7. A strong attendance will first and foremost be a message that we won't let this case be shelved. To achieve the desired result, everybody must see responsibility in themselves and attend the Paris march and rally with their extended circles."

http://anfenglish.com/news/kongra-gel-we-won-t-let-the-paris-massacre-to-be-left-in-the-dark

****

Sakine Cansiz' heroic story puts a personal touch on the Kurdish story. Her life mirrors the personal suffering, the braveness in combat and the sheer will to survive that characterize the Kurdish people. If it were not real life, it would be a script for a movie. Some are already under way.

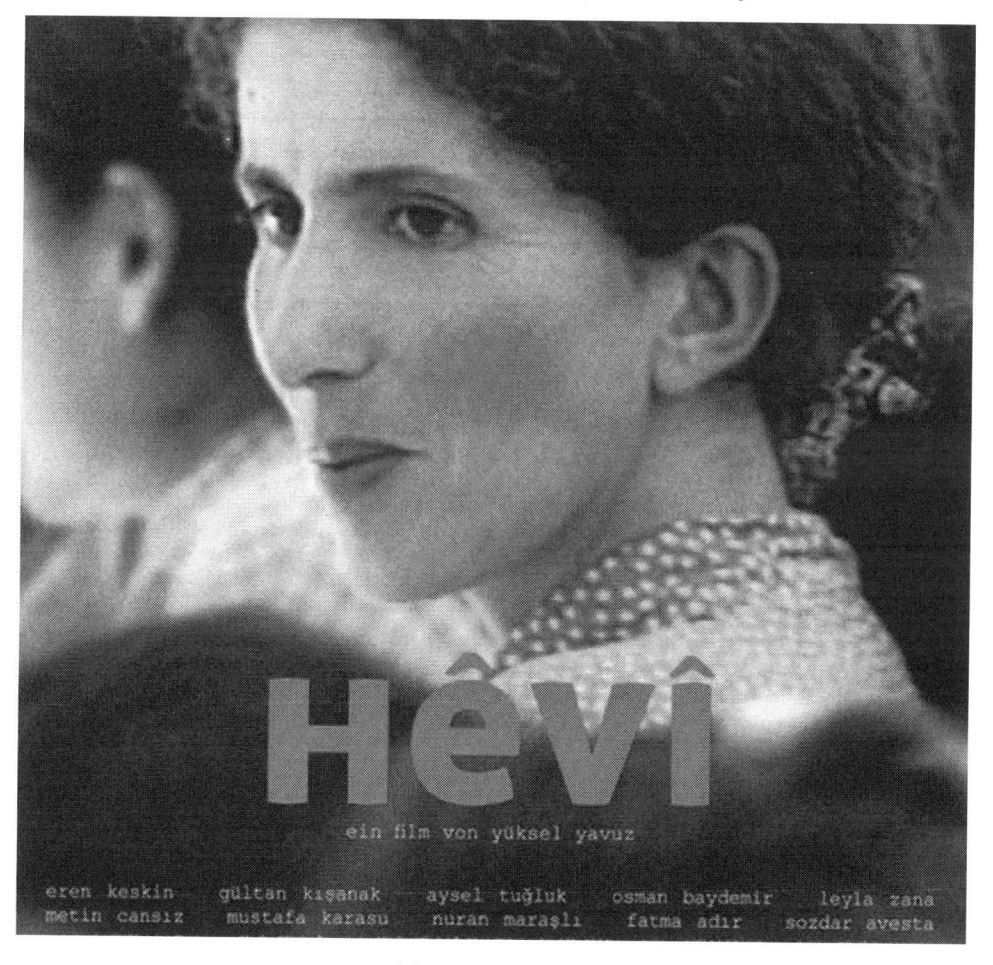

Sakine Movie poster

[183]

Chapter 14. The Sakine Legacy

Through this book, you've come to learn about Sakine Kansiz and about the Kurds. You may disagree with many of the things that they believe, have done or are doing. They're not asking for unquestioning loyalty. All the Kurds really want is to be recognized as people who have a right to exist.

As the Kurds show themselves as the most effective fighting force in the Levant, public awareness increases. More and more people wonder who these people are, so newly arrived on the scene? They're not new. They have been right where they are for thousands of years, and there they intend to remain.

Chapter 14. The Sakine Legacy

Appendix A: The Cable

[Editor's note: this cable is in the possession of Kurdish information organizations who provided it to Mr. Mirwaisi. Whether it is authentic or not, or how Wikileaks came by it, we have no way of knowing.]

SUBJECT: Blocking money flow to the PKK

1. Summary: As the United States works together with Turkey to implement the President's directive for effective action against PKK terror, we must also redouble our efforts to shut down the financial support that flows from Europe into PKK headquarters located in northern Iraq. While previous work, primarily in the form of demarches to European governments, has shown some limited progress, the overall credibility of this effort was badly undermined by the recent release in Vienna of PKK financier Riza Altun by Austrian authorities. To overcome these setbacks and register tangible progress in the near and medium term, the USG will need to work intensively on three simultaneous efforts:

-- First, we need to identify and interdict PKK money that is flowing into northern Iraq. This will require U.S., Iraqi, and European authorities to collaborate in a targeted effort that includes enhanced airport screening, more extensive customs procedures, and aggressive disruption of illicit cash transfers into northern Iraq and between northern Iraqi entities and PKK terrorists.

-- Second, we will push the Turks to work more effectively to identify and interdict financial flows. MASAK, Turkey's Financial Crimes Investigation Board, is the GOT's sole money laundering and terrorist financing investigative body. It needs to streamline its investigations and work more effectively with financial police, prosecutors, and judges to effectuate successful prosecutions.

-- Third, we should more sharply focus our work with the Europeans. Previous demarches sensitized the EU to PKK criminal activities. Now we need to narrow our focus by identifying and going after the two top targets of Riza Altun and Sakine Cansiz. Given their previous arrests, cases against them have been started. We can help by providing the most extensive dossiers possible and coordinating with law enforcement and intelligence counterparts in Europe to ensure these two terrorists are incarcerated. End Summary.

Background

2. The PKK raises upwards of USD 50-100 million annually through fundraising activities to sustain operations in Turkey and northern Iraq. Sensitive reporting shows the top four countries for fundraising are Germany, France, Switzerland, and the United Kingdom. Other regions important to PKK/KGK fundraising include Austria, the Balkans, Belgium, and the Netherlands. Sensitive reporting has identified PKK fundraising leaders in Europe, but we have limited actionable intelligence on how the money flows to the PKK. Available reporting indicates the use of hawala networks (informal multi-country remittance system), cash couriers, narcotics, and gold to move money.

3. Funding of PKK activities is done through a wide variety of methods. These include fundraising, cultural, social, and sporting event sponsorship, membership fees, and commercial business ventures. PKK financiers also traffic in narcotics, smuggle both people and goods and charge extortion and protection fees. While the latter activities can be prosecuted as criminal offenses, the former activities can only be prosecuted under terror finance laws when clear ties to PKK activities can be proven.

Legwork is Already Underway

4. Over the last year, S/CT has been active in driving political-level demarches to all European capitals on terrorist financing. S/CT Deputy Counterterrorism Coordinator Frank Urbancic has traveled widely in Europe to raise awareness and to bring together prosecutors, judges, financial police, financial intelligence unit personnel, and Justice and Interior Ministry officials to discuss ways to investigate and prosecute money laundering and terrorist finance cases related to the PKK. The Regional Legal Advisor has hosted workshops for relevant officials in Turkey and arranged meetings and seminars for European and Turkish counterparts.

End Materials

The counterparts are to facilitate a task-force mentality to work together to fight the PKK. At the November U.S./EU Troika on Terrorist Financing, the new EU Terrorism Czar appeared committed to ensuring EU cooperation. Turkey has recently finalized a terrorist extradition with Switzerland (on hold pending an administrative hearing) and last week two PKK members were successfully extradited to Turkey from Germany. Pressure should be maintained in all EU countries to prosecute or extradite.

Three-Part Strategy

Working with Europe

5. As we have learned from efforts to shut down al-Qaeda financing since September 11, joint law enforcement and intelligence sharing are essential. Numerous European countries have asked for our assistance in providing actionable intelligence, and S/CT continues to work on this issue. Continued networking with prosecutors and investigative judges is paramount. Investigative judges carry out the investigations and direct law enforcement in Europe.

6. Our immediate goal is to deny the PKK use of the European financial and air transport systems to move money from Europe into northern Iraq for their operations. We can accomplish this via enhanced intelligence sharing, more careful airport screening and strict enforcement of cash declaration requirements. We also should press the Europeans to take action against the two most notorious PKK/KGK financiers in Europe, Riza Altun and Sakine Cansiz. Riza Altun is known to be a top PKK financier. He fled judicial arrest in France in July and Austrian authorities allowed him to fly to Iraq on July 13, but he recently has been seen traveling again in Europe. Sakine Cansiz is a PKK/KGK financier and weapons and tactical strategist. She was arrested in Germany but released by a Hamburg court on April 27 after 40 days of detention and remains in Europe. Their re-arrest and prosecution would limit PKK/KGK activities and signal that Europe is not a free zone for PKK/KGK fundraising.

Working with Iraq

End Materials

7. Inside Iraq, as reported ref B, we face a cash economy that will make disrupting money flows inside Iraq difficult. The upcoming S/CT-led assessment team to Erbil should provide recommendations on the most efficient ways to stop money flowing to the PKK once it reaches Iraq. The apparent lack of legal authority for the government to seize assets before conviction might be a major roadblock. Sensitive reporting indicates that the KRG has infiltrated the PKK in northern Iraq. If so, we should press the KRG to help identify illicit money flows so we can interdict them before they reach the PKK.

Working with Turkey

8. The PKK also raises money in Turkey. The Turkish financial intelligence unit (MASAK) lacks the technical and analytical capability to identify or interdict terrorist finance activity. The post will continue its efforts to get Turkish law enforcement and intelligence agencies to share information and cooperate to make interdiction possible. We also need to ensure that if we get Europeans to clamp down on cash couriers and transfers, Turkey similarly needs to make undeclared bulk cash transfers illegal, seize bulk cash assets, and identify money transfers through the banking system that are headed to the PKK.

Appendix B: References

A Kurdish-centered organization in the US: Washington Kurdish Institute 2001 L Street NW, Suite 500 Washington, DC 20036

- Tel: 202.484.0140
- Email: info@dckurd.org.
- Website: http://dckurd.org/about-us/.

There are numerous video clips about, or including, Sakine Cansiz. Unfortunately most are in Kurdish, but they will give you a sense of the person, especially the interviews:

- Sakine Cansiz' life was memorialized in the documentary "Sara". Links about the movie include:
- https://twitter.com/SARA_Belgefilm/status/791352225780162560
- She was also one of four women profiled in the movie "Hevi", which also features her colleague Gülten Kışanak.
- The trailer is at https://www.youtube.com/watch?v=vj4vKpyPxdI.
- The main movie (99 minutes) is apparently still seeking production funds. The landing page is at http://www.newafilm.net/projekte/hevi.html.
- YouTube videos:
- https://www.youtube.com/watch?v=o2yEZwsC254 (15 mins)
- https://www.youtube.com/watch?v=1oCh5ZFoTA0 (57 mins)

One of the most sustained writers about Kurdish affairs is Chris Kutschera. He has published a compendium of his articles in his book, The Long March of the Kurds (actually "La longue marche des Kurdes: 40 ans de reportage au Kurdistan"). Download the PDF at

- https://www.numilog.com/Pages/Livres/Fiche.aspx?LIVRE_ID=140284.
- It is currently priced at E15.00, but it is unfortunately available only in French.

End Materials

Other key internet-based news outlets that cover Kurdish issues include the ANF (cited in Chapter 1) and AL Monitor. Here are links to key articles on their sites:

- ANF: https://anfenglish.com/news/culprit-of-the-murder-in-paris-of-sakine-fidan-and-leyla-dies-update

- AL Monitor: Mustafa Akyol, "How Turkey's AKP undid its legacy on 'Kurdish question'", AL Monitor, 31 October 2016, http://www.al-monitor.com/pulse/en/originals/2016/10/turkey-kurds-jailed-mayors-akp-undid-legacy.html

- PKK tactics, 1990s to 2007: https://jamestown.org/program/pkk-changes-battlefield-tactics-to-force-turkey-into-negotiations/

One of the few sources that is generally objective on the affairs of the region is the Jamestown Foundation, which seeks to keep a light on areas that restrict conventional news.

- For instance, https://jamestown.org/program/pkk-changes-battlefield-tactics-to-force-turkey-into-negotiations/

For a banned organization, the PKK website is remarkably well documented: http://www.pkkonline.com/en

Finally, for heavier academic reading on this topic, consider Hamid Akin Unver, "Turkey's Kurdish Question: Discourse & Politics Since 1990", Routledge Press, 2015.

End Materials

About the Author

Hamma Mirwaisi was exposed to the oppression of Kurds while still a youth, as his education was frequently interrupted by Iraqi government harassment. Forbidden from entering university in 1968, he had little choice but to join the *peshmerga* (freedom fighter) forces of Mustafa Barzani from 1968 to 1975 in their battles against the Iraqi Government forces.

Although the conflict was resolved by treaty in 1975, he foresaw reprisals by Saddam Hussein's secret service against his extended family. He took his wife and two children to Iran, and in 1976 they entered the US as legal refugees, settling in Valley City, North Dakota.

Mirwaisi completed BS and MS degrees in Electrical Engineering at the University of North Dakota. That led to a technical career, beginning in 1982 at the Sperry Corporation in Minneapolis. Sperry's merger with Unisys Corporation caused the end of his program, and he took up Ph.D. studies in Radio-Frequency (RF) Engineering at the University of Colorado at Colorado Springs. Eventually he returned to work at Honeywell, where he completed his career, becoming the Senior RF Engineer on the Air Force Satellite Communication program.

End Materials

The tragedy of the Kurds intervened again in 1995. His sister and her two-year-old daughter were drowned while escaping Saddam Hussein's reprisals against the Kurds for their rebellion during the first Gulf War.

He returned to Kurdish affairs in 2004, when the US Army called on him to serve as an interpreter in the second Gulf War. At the end of that assignment, he began seeking American corporate sponsors for the rebuilding of Kurdistan. However, the Barzanis, who controlled the Kurdistan Regional Government, saw the initiative as a scheme to undermine their own influence and expelled Mirwaisi from Iraq. The doors to government and corporate sponsorship of works in Kurdistan (at least those that did not include a Barzani rake-off) slammed shut.

Since then, Mirwaisi has devoted his efforts to spreading the word about Kurdish history and culture through writing and speaking. After his first book, Return of the Medes, he was invited to serve for a year as an honorary member of the Kurdistan National Congress (KNK), a Kurdish parliament in exile that sits in Brussels. He is the author of many other books on Kurdish affairs (see the Caltrop Press webpage: https://www.caltrop-press.co.business).

End Materials

One Last Thing...

If you enjoyed this book and found it useful, please consider posting a short review on the site where you purchased it. If you don't know or don't recall, you'll find links at http://www.Caltrop-Press.co.business.

Two or three sentences is all it takes. Your support and input really does make a difference, and both Caltrop Press and the author will be reading all the reviews so we can get your feedback and make this book even better. The great thing about an e-book is that we can always update it!

Thanks again for taking the time to read about the Kurds. If you found it interesting, please tell others!

Made in the USA
San Bernardino, CA
21 May 2019